Napoleon's Children

Susan Normington

TABLE OF CONTENTS

TABLE OF CONTENTS	3
Chapter One	5
Chapter Two	62
Chapter Three	104
Chapter Four	153
Chapter Five	205
Chapter Six	251
Chapter Seven	293
Bibliography	327

Chapter One:

The Search for an Heir

All along the cliffs, in every inlet and haven the indolent waves washed against the flat-bottomed invasion boats. Beyond the blue water, clearly distinguishable in the bright summer sunshine, lay the white coast of England; on the water itself the British men-of-war maintained their guard. The world's greatest army confronted the world's greatest navy. It was a sight that set the eyes of Hortense Bonaparte prickling with a desire to weep at so much beauty and romance. The soldiers gathered round her carriage waving their shakos, bearskins and képis, with deep rumbling shouts of *Vive l'Empereur!*, or held out bouquets of flowers, and her heart swelled with pride, anticipation and alarm. 'Our troops, proud of never having known defeat, impatient after two years' idleness, vibrant with energy and courage, could already picture themselves on the opposing coast.... But at the sight of so many obstacles an involuntary terror gripped my heart.'[1]

It was frightening, but deliciously so: 'a grandeur never known before'. Each day she drove out among the troops; each afternoon she dined with Napoleon, who was both her step-father and brother-in-law; each evening she returned to the house nearby which she shared with Caroline Murat, her sister-in-law. There the day's tensions were protracted and heightened in the nervous opening advances of illicit love. She took her seat at the piano;

Charles de Flahaut, so very handsome in his aide-de-camp uniform, came across to stand beside her and sing ballads to her accompaniment; and never for a moment did either of them dare to exchange a glance or utter a word that might reveal to the watchful eyes of the others how far and how fast their affair was progressing. It was a dangerous game, and the more enticing for that. It was a game in which she could expect no mercy if she were discovered; neither Caroline nor her husband, Joachim Murat, would miss using such a discovery in the endless feud between Bonaparte and Beauharnais.

The envy that good-hearted, quick-tempered Caroline bore for Hortense has been exaggerated, due principally to the portrait drawn of her in Hortense's memoirs. But there is no denying that the whole Bonaparte clan set out on a relentless vendetta against the Beauharnais' from the day that Napoleon married the widowed Josephine. The Bonapartes were led by their mother, who suspected, quite wrongly, that Josephine would sneer at her Corsican rusticities, and spurred on by their own dismay at the prospect of their soldier brother's spoils being shared outside the family. Napoleon heightened the bad feeling by adopting Josephine's two children as his own, and, infuriatingly, held them up as models: Eugene for his honesty and loyalty, Hortense for her intelligence and obedience. He married Hortense to his brother, Louis and, when he appointed himself Emperor and made his brothers, Joseph and Louis, princes, Hortense was entitled to be addressed as 'Your Highness', while Caroline remained merely 'Madame Murat'.[2] He declared the Imperial title to be hereditary to his own male children, whether legitimate or adopted, and, if he had none, to Joseph and his sons (he had only daughters) and then to

Louis and Louis' sons. When his sisters protested he replied: 'I love Hortense!'[3]

It was an unfortunate remark, for some of the Bonapartes had already tried to convince Louis that Hortense had been unfaithful to him and that Napoleon was the father of her son Napoleon-Charles. Louis set spies to watch her every movement. This gave him some assurance that her next child, Napoleon-Louis, was his own. But his suspicions remained.[4]

It had been an unpromising marriage from the beginning. Hortense claimed that her mother had persuaded her into it against her will; certainly, Louis had been bullied to the altar by his brother despite his protests that he wanted to marry Hortense's cousin, Emilie. Hortense, a child of the Revolution and the Terror, had grown up to be profoundly secretive, with a deep need to be loved and admired. She revelled in the brassy Imperial trappings which Napoleon affected, and her head was turned by them. Apart from her Bonaparte relations, she had from her school days been surrounded by devoted friends; yet she was unhappy and, while constantly accusing others of envy, was consumed by it herself.

She envied Caroline her marriage to the handsome, brave yet wayward Murat. Her own husband, Louis, was the only one of the five Bonaparte brothers ever tempted to put conscience before self-interest, and was consequently despised by the others as a fool or a traitor to the clan. He had served with honour in the Italian campaign of 1796 and 1797, but returned with a mysterious disease. Napoleon said syphilis, but it was probably a rheumatic ailment aggravated by psychological disorders, which made him a burden to himself and others. At the age of twenty-three, when he married the eighteen-year-old

Hortense, he was a querulous, suspicious invalid, sick beyond recovery.

While Louis was in command of the 5th Dragoons a volunteer joined the regiment; an aristocrat, the illegitimate son of Talleyrand and the Countess de Flahaut. Charles de Flahaut de la Billarderie was a tall, slender young man with a bold nose and impudent blue eyes. Bravery won him promotion, and Talleyrand's influence brought him appointment as an aide-de-camp to Joachim Murat, Marshal of the Empire and Military Governor of Paris. Charles, paying a duty call on his former dragoon colonel at his house in the Rue de la Victoire, met Hortense for the first time. As they shared the same singing teacher, and since Hortense had a talent for composing little sentimental songs and Charles had a voice that perfectly suited them, what could be more natural than that they should practise together? When Louis found out the servants were forbidden to allow Lieutenant Flahaut admittance. However, the couple continued to meet at the Murats' estate at Neuilly just outside Paris.

Why Hortense allowed herself to be captivated by Flahaut rather than any other of the eager young men who admired her is not clear. She was certainly looking for love, but beneath her demure, wistful exterior there was a strong, calculating mind that would not have permitted her to be swept off her feet by a mere sentimental fancy. Perhaps she saw an opportunity to annoy Caroline, who kept a tender, and not entirely motherly, eye on Joachim's young aides-de-camp and would be expected to feel piqued if Hortense poached on her territory. She complained to Hortense one evening that Flahaut was in a bad temper and refused to dance with her. Hortense pleaded with the young man and he at once moved off with the furious Caroline.[5] The indignity was not forgiven. Some time later, in the autumn of 1804, Hortense called at Neuilly, when she was told that Caroline had gone for a trip to the island in the middle of the Seine on which she had made a little sanctuary with a Temple of Love. Hortense waited. Afternoon grew into dusk. The moon came out. In its romantic light Caroline returned. As she came up from the landing stage she was leaning languorously on Flahaut's arm. At the sight of Hortense she pretended both surprise and embarrassment. Hortense nearly fainted with annoyance and jealousy.[6]

Despite their rivalry, there was a genuine bond of friendship and affection between the two young sisters-in-law, at least on Caroline's part, though this was frequently strained by the Emperor's mischievous determination to keep his relations in a state of continual feuding. There was, for instance, a serious tiff in March 1805 when Napoleon arranged for the Pope to christen Hortense's son, five-month-old Napoleon-Louis. Murat asked that Caroline's latest child should be christened at the same time, but Napoleon refused permission on the ground that the Pope would have to perform two entirely different ceremonies: one for Hortense's potential heir to the throne, and another for Caroline's ineligible infant. When Caroline had recovered her good humour, she invited Hortense out to Neuilly and watched the burgeoning of her affair with Flahaut (though she does not seem to have discovered, any more than Louis did, that they were also meeting secretly in the Bois de Boulogne). She also kept Hortense informed on the progress of Napoleon's occasional adulteries with Madame Duchatel, one of Josephine's dames du palais, which were conducted behind the discreet walls of the park at Neuilly.[7] Hortense took a lively interest in such affairs, for if Napoleon could be kept amused with ineligible married women there was less likelihood of his divorcing Josephine, whom the Bonapartes accused of being too old to bear him children. Napoleon could pretend to be capable of a normal liaison and thus conceal the fact, proclaimed by the Beauharnais and denied by the Bonapartes, that he was incapable of fathering children, no matter how young the woman he married.

The truth was that, though virtually impotent, he was potentially fertile. Sexual inadequacy made him timid with women, and timidity resulted in his uncouth and caddish attitude to them; he indulged in open extra-marital affairs in order to keep up a pretence of masculinity. There were also occasions when he could be roused to normal lust and performance, often a month or two after he had enjoyed the butchery of battle.

*

Thus it was that as the summer of 1805 drew towards autumn at the camp above Boulogne, Caroline planned to conduct a little experiment aimed at restoring her brother's confidence and discomforting Hortense. She pondered on it while Hortense allowed herself to be persuaded to play one more song, which Charles de Flahaut, with not too much diffidence, sang. Next morning, as usual, they drove out for more parades and reviews of the 170,000 infantrymen, 9,000 cavalrymen and 2,500 vessels that would carry them all across the Channel.

But Napoleon distrusted the sea. As he gazed out over the Channel, the prospect grew less inviting each day and soon he decided to seek more blood and glory on dry land. Later he would attribute his change of heart to the defeat of the French fleet at Trafalgar in October; nearly two months after he had ordered Joachim Murat off incognito into Germany, reconnoitring a route along which he might best march against Austria. Joachim's post as Governor of Paris was given to Louis, the camp at Boulogne was struck and the vast army began to march eastward. Hortense and Caroline returned to Paris where, throughout October and November, reports arrived of victory after victory, as the French surged into Austria behind Joachim's cavalry, driving back the Austrians and their Russian allies to the final defeat at Austerlitz on 2 December 1805.

Napoleon rested on his laurels at Schönbrunn until the end of the year, when he moved back to Munich, where he promoted the Elector of Bavaria to king and married his daughter to Hortense's brother, Eugene, to the renewed annoyance of Caroline and the rest of the Bonapartes. However, Caroline continued to write to Hortense in the friendliest fashion – even when Napoleon married another of Hortense's cousins, Stephanie de Beauharnais, to the heir-apparent of Baden in March 1806, and, heaviest blow of all, appointed Louis as King of Holland in July, thus making Hortense a queen. But Caroline was comforted by the one secret piece of knowledge: the little experiment that she had planned during her stay with Hortense at Boulogne Camp was proving successful.

*

Caroline, like Hortense, had attended Madame Campan's Academy in St Germain-en-Laye and had kept in close touch with her old school. Two of her Murat nieces, Marie-Antoinette and Clothilde-Jeanne, were boarders there, as were several of Hortense's relations. These included Stephanie de la Pagerie and Stephanie de

Beauharnais, who in January 1805 had acted as witnesses at the marriage, directly from school, of their seventeen-year-old friend, Eleonore Denuelle to Captain Jean Revel of the 11th Dragoons. Eleonore's parents were a rather dubious couple, suspected of running illicit gambling parties at their apartment in the Boulevard des Italiens. Of Revel's character there was soon no doubt at all – three days after the wedding he disappeared, taking all the bride's movable property with him, and two months later he was arrested on a charge of forging a brother officer's backing to one of his own notes of hand.[8]

At Madame Campan's request, Caroline took Eleonore into her protection. In May, Revel was transferred from the Paris Conciergerie to Versailles to stand trial. 'I am informed that the case looks bad against him,' Joachim wrote to Fouché, the Minister of Police, 'I have told you how much we wish to protect him from a sentence whose infamy will inevitably affect his unfortunate wife.' He asked Fouché to let him know what steps he should take to achieve this – or perhaps 'you would take the trouble to put an end to this business yourself'[9]. But Fouché, who was not always in the habit of obeying instructions even from Napoleon, was not in the mood to accept them from the rest of the family. Justice took its course and on 12 August 1805, a few days after Caroline had left Paris for the camp at Boulogne, Revel was sent to prison for two years – a comparatively light sentence in view of the seriousness of the crime and perhaps an indication that Fouché had relented and had a word with the judge.

Eleonore was an attractive young woman – 'very pretty but without much sense', wrote Hortense – grateful for Caroline's kindness in rescuing her from a horrifying situation, and quite overwhelmed when Caroline, returning to Paris in the autumn, gave her a position in her household as Dame d'Annonce. With the post, very unusually, went a small pavilion in the grounds at Neuilly for Eleonore's sole occupation. Eleonore was left in no doubt as to the purpose of this secluded bower when Napoleon returned from the Austerlitz campaign and Eugene's wedding at the end of January 1806. Caroline presented her new Dame d'Annonce to him at lunch one day; the introduction coincided with one of the Emperor's rare periods of sexual potency, and by March Eleonore was pregnant and established in a house in the Rue de la Victoire, the street where Napoleon had begun his married life with Josephine.

He was unusually sexually active during this first quarter of 1806. Josephine surprised him one day in the arms of his sister, Pauline,[10] and he was visited on several occasions at the Tuileries by Françoise Pellapra, whom he had first met a year before in Lyons. By April the spasm was past and he settled down to prepare once again for war, this time against Prussia. But first he marked Stephanie de Beauharnais' marriage to Prince Karl of Baden with a ball held in the Tuileries, the first of many in which he encouraged the young women of his family to put on great shows of conspicuous expenditure in honour of his Imperial presence. Hortense organized and led one quadrille, in which the four sets of four dancers were dressed in white satin and garlanded with flowers, while Caroline's team were clothed in velvet in the Spanish style. 'My quadrille was more successful than Caroline's,' Hortense noted modestly. 'This small advantage drew down on me a little more jealousy on her part.'[11]

Bad feeling over Louis' promotion to the throne of the newly-formed Kingdom of Holland followed, though in this instance Caroline was scarcely more dissatisfied than Louis and Hortense themselves. Not that Louis was loth to be a king, but he preferred a realm with a sunnier climate – Piedmont, for example – instead of the damp, flat Netherlands, which were certain to play havoc with his rheumatism. As for Hortense, she shuddered at the thought of being cooped up with Louis, far from the gaiety of Paris, surrounded by thick-skulled Dutchmen stinking of beer and gin. Besides, it would bring to an end all opportunities to see Flahaut. He could always go to Paris on the pretext of seeing his mother, whose name he used when corresponding secretly with Hortense, but finding an acceptable excuse for visiting Amsterdam or the Hague would be difficult.

In mid-June Hortense was at her house in the Rue Cerutti, Paris. The courtyard was full of wagons and coaches. The house was largely stripped of pictures, furniture and linen, though it still held the lingering aroma of boiled tripe in which Louis bathed for medical reasons. Louis had already left for St-Leu, their estate near the Forest of Montmorency, which was to be their point of departure for Holland. Hortense supervised the loading of the last convoy and sent it on its way. Nobody was left in the house with her except her lady-in-waiting and one servant, who entered with the news that a person desired to speak with her alone.

The lady-in-waiting retired. The servant ushered in the 'person' – immediately recognizable, despite an attempt at disguise, as Charles de Flahaut. Hortense stood motionless – transfixed, she said, by surprise and fear. 'It was the first time I had found myself alone with him since I had fallen in love with him.' As he took a pace forward she uttered a cry. He begged her to be quiet lest they should be discovered. 'Let them think as ill of me as they like,' she replied, 'provided I am guiltless'. She then confessed that she loved him deeply, but loved her virtue even more. 'I wished him happiness; I promised him my friendship; and I left him in a state difficult to describe.'[12] She departed in tears to St-Leu and from there to the Hague. Within a month Louis set off to Wiesbaden, taking her with him. When he found no cure at Wiesbaden and decided to try Aachen. Hortense persuaded him to go on ahead while she made part of the journey by water, sailing down the beautiful stretch of the Rhine from Mainz to Koblenz.

They were three days of bliss; her little Napoleon-Charles, not quite four years old, playing beside her on the deck of the yacht provided for her by the Prince of Nassau, the romantic landscape rising on either hand, here vineyards and there forests, chapels in the shade of the steep narrow valleys, castles projecting from rugged cliffs – Louis so far away with his rheumaticky leg, his headaches and his filthy baths. She picked up her guitar and sang sad songs of love and war, and, for the first time for many months, composed some songs of her own. Her good fortune did not end here; soon after her arrival at Aachen, Louis received orders from the Emperor to return to Holland in readiness for the next war. Hortense stayed behind for ten days, during which Flahaut appeared, now a captain and as eager as ever for love and war. Hortense, knowing that he would shortly be in battle, was cruelly tortured by the necessity to keep silent about both her desires and her fears. For she had no opportunity to be alone with him – at least, that is what she said afterwards, reflecting on the harshness of fate which denied her even the solace of bidding him goodbye, 'my hopes and fears imprisoned in my heart.'[13]

Louis had been given command of a reserve army stationed on the Rhine. When he went to his headquarters at Wesel in the autumn, Hortense happily joined her mother, Josephine, in Mainz, spending the winter of 1806–7 fêting the news of victories and entertaining the young officers making their way to and from the battlefront. She recorded that several of them became infatuated with her, but this did not surprise her since she was aware that she had this effect on most men.

When Hortense left Paris for St-Leu and Holland in June 1806, she was so affected by her tearful farewell to Flahaut that she failed to say goodbye to Caroline. She atoned for this by writing two letters during the following month, and Caroline, by now created Grand Duchess of Berg and Cleves, replied by inviting her to 'come and be bored with me at Düsseldorf.... I expected to leave the day after the Emperor's birthday [he would be thirty-seven on 15 August].' But Caroline did not leave. Hortense claimed to believe that she stayed in Paris because she was ashamed of the insignificance of her Grand-Ducal capital, Düsseldorf, compared with Hortense's royal splendours at the Hague. But the truth was probably that Caroline was engrossed in the progress of her experiment with Eleonore Revel, now calling herself Madame Saint-Laurant, and, in fact, no longer married to Revel, having divorced him at the end of April.

Eleonore's pregnancy – the proof, long hoped for by the Bonapartes, that Napoleon was capable of fathering a child – was progressing perfectly. Far beyond the Rhine the French army drove forward – Murat as always at their head. On 7 November he received the surrender of Blücher after conducting one of the most brilliant cavalry campaigns in history. 'Sire,' he wrote to the Emperor, 'the combat is over for lack of combatants.'[14] Napoleon sent him off to lead the troops now advancing against the Russians. By the end of November Joachim was caracoling into Warsaw in his white plumed hat and silk breeches, gold spurs and jewelled scabbard, and tiger-skin saddle-cloth. He was joined in Warsaw on 19 December by Napoleon who, though he did not yet know it, had become a father twice in the past two months.

At two o'clock in the morning of Saturday, 13 December 1806, Eleonore Denuelle gave birth to a son, attended by Pierre Marchais (the accoucheur) and Guillaume Andral, who had been a student with Joachim Murat at Cahors, had joined his staff as a doctor in 1800 and was to remain with him throughout his career. When these two registered the birth at the Second Arrondissement Town Hall on the following Monday, they were accompanied by Jacques-Aymé, Chief Administrator for the Grand Duchy of Berg and Cleves, though neither he nor the doctor mentioned their Murat connections. The child was described as 'Charles, son of Eleonore Denuelle, of independent means', and of '*un père absent*'.[15]

Caroline immediately sent the news to Napoleon by courier. Nobody, however, seems to have informed him of the birth of his other child, which had occurred in Lyons on 11 November. The mother was Françoise-Marie-Emilie Pellapra, the pretty scatterbrain whom he had met in Lyons in the spring of 1805 and who had eagerly followed him to Paris to be seduced in an alcove adjoining his map-room in the Tuileries. She was slim and attractive, dark-haired and blue-eyed, married to a dour minor government official who was far from appreciating the honour conferred on his wife by the Emperor. Later, when Napoleon heard of the birth and rewarded the cuckolded husband with a post as

17

tax collector, Alain Pellapra relented a little, but his first instinct was to deny paternity of the child. After sending Françoise back to her native Lyons for the birth, he insisted on the child being left there with his mother-in-law, Madame Louise Leroy. The baby girl was given a mixture of her mother's names, her grandmother's and that of Napoleon's deceived wife, for it was still popular to name children after Our Lady of Victories, the gracious Josephine, and Madame Pellapra was giddy-minded enough not to see anything odd in it. For most of the next four years little Emilie-Louise-Marie-Françoise-Josephine stayed in the Leroy apartment in the centre of Lyons. From the balcony she could peep across to the plain of Les Brotteaux, the scene of some of the most hideous atrocities of the Revolution. Day by day her cheeks plumped into an Italian chubbiness, her small nose gently curved into a budgerigar beak. There could be no doubt that she was a Bonaparte.

Although the existence of little Emilie remained unknown to him for a long time, Napoleon received Caroline's letter telling him of Eleonore's son on the last day of 1806. He ordered that the name of the infant Charles' 'absent father' should be recorded as General Macon, the French Military Governor of Leipzig, who had conveniently died of fever in October. Next morning, while his army splashed through torrential rain in pursuit of the Russians, Napoleon halted at the posting house at Bronie, a Polish village between Warsaw and Pultusk. There he caught sight of a young woman with fair hair, blue eyes, a radiant complexion and an expression that was at once eager and virginal. She was, in fact, a married woman, twenty-one years old, the mother of a young son, Antoine, and wife of a septuagenarian husband, Count

Anastasius Colonna-Walewski.[16] His blood still heated from the slaughter at Jena and his confidence bolstered by the successful Denuelle experiment, Napoleon decided to possess this strangely exciting young woman. It was not a difficult conquest. The Polish nobility were enthusiastically offering their most beautiful women at the altar-couch of the minotaur in the hope of winning his support for the restoration of their national independence. The Countess Marya Walewska did not volunteer, but she was a fervent patriot ready to answer to the call of duty – and it appears that the count was more than ready to sacrifice his wife's honour as well as his own.

Napoleon, a stickler for Imperial etiquette, appointed General Duroc, the Grand Marshal of the Palace, as his pander. 'Duroc will make all easy for you', he wrote to her. 'Oh, come, come, your every wish will be gratified. Your country will be dearer to me when you take pity on my poor heart.' Egged on by her friends, encouraged by the tacit consent of her husband who suddenly discovered – in mid-winter and at his time of life – that he had urgent business in Rome, Marya allowed Duroc to lead her to the Emperor's private apartments. There she was overtaken by a sudden fit of revulsion and refused to submit. Swiftly switching from bribe to blackmail, Napoleon picked up his watch and shouted 'You shall – I repeat, you shall – love me! You see this watch in my hand: just as I dash it to fragments before you so will I shatter Poland and all your hopes if you drive me to desperation by rejecting my heart and refusing me yours.'[17] The threat worked. She yielded. But his brief spasm of lust was fruitless. He set off in pursuit of the Russians and Prussians once more.

*

In January 1807, having heard of the interest Hortense was showing in the gallant young officers of the Grande Armée, Louis ordered her to return to the Hague. On her arrival she riposted by dismissing one of her four dames du palais, whom she accused of being on too intimate terms with Louis. 'The relentlessness shown by the Queen in that affair lost her the respect in which she had previously been held,' said one of the members of the household.[18] But there was much to explain, if not to excuse, her spitefulness. Louis was keeping her under closer and more humiliating surveillance than ever; and from Paris there was constant, tantalizing news of the delights she was missing:

My life has been all excitement for the past month' Caroline wrote to her on the last day of February. 'I dance at night, sleep part of the day and spend the remainder attending to my correspondence and receiving visits.... Why are you not here, my dear Hortense? You would have enjoyed our dances so much.... I go to the Empress's almost every evening, we talk about you, always with renewed pleasure. She misses you, and that gives us another thing in common. She also talks about little Napoleon a great deal – how she does love him![19]

The little Napoleon whom Josephine loved was not, in this instance, her husband but Hortense's elder son. He was also a favourite with the Emperor, who complained that other children in the family had no respect for him: 'Joseph's daughters still call me Consul, whereas little Napoleon, when he passes the Grenadiers in the garden, shouts to them 'Long Live Nonon the Soldier!'[20] Hortense was indeed bringing her boys up to have great admiration for Uncle Nonon the Soldier, though not their father. Except for the children, her marriage had brought her no happiness at all.

It was all the more irritating, therefore, to receive Caroline's chatty accounts of presents from her four children on her birthday, of the concert she had given for Josephine on her saint's day, of the regularity with which she received letters from Joachim, whom she genuinely loved despite his illicit love-affairs – and her own. There is no doubt, either, of Caroline's affection for Hortense – when her interests and those of her children were not at stake. 'I kiss you very tenderly', she ended one letter. And another: 'My dear Hortense, believe in my tender constant friendship, and accept many caresses from your affectionate Caroline.'[21]

But it was not Caroline's affection that Hortense craved, and certainly not Louis'; her heart was committed to Charles de Flahaut, more than six hundred miles away in Poland, and now a squadron commander in the 13th Regiment of Chasseurs à Cheval. The Polish Countess Potocka had been his mistress almost since the day he arrived in Warsaw in November 1806. Gossip about their affair reached Hortense's ears and she wrote begging him to tell her if he had fallen in love with somebody else, assuring him that she would not reproach him if he told her the truth. Young Flahaut was too old a campaigner to be caught that way. He swore there was no other woman in his life. Hortense did not believe him, although she wanted to.

The war in the east was suspended in February 1807 after the battle of Preussisch-Eylau, where Napoleon killed 20,000 Russian and Prussian soldiers and as many of his own. The slaughter could not begin again until the ground had dried out. He went into winter quarters at Osterode and in March moved to Finkelstein, where he was joined by Marya Walewska.

At the end of April 1807 Hortense's little Napoleon became unwell. A soreness of the throat developed into a brittle cough; the doctors diagnosed croup and did their inadequate best, but at midnight on 4/5 May the small boy, four-and-a-half years old, died in the palace at the Hague. Hortense collapsed, numb with grief. Caroline hurried from Paris to comfort her and, after a day or two, took her to Laeken, where Josephine was waiting for her. On 19 May all three returned to Paris and there parted: Josephine taking the surviving son, Napoleon-Louis, to Malmaison with her, while Hortense sought solace for her sorrow in a trip to the Pyrenees.

Hortense was at Bordeaux before the end of the month and at Cauterets, nearly 3,000 feet up in the High Pyrenees by 18 June. She was accompanied by a small suite of ladies, an equerry, and a reader, Louise Cochelet, who had been at Madame Campan's with her. Louis, who had left Holland a few days after her, was fifteen miles away to the west at Les Eaux-Bonnes, taking the waters for his rheumatism. Restless as always, he came over the mountain passes, moving east and south, until he was on the other side of her, at St-Saveur. Finally, on 23 June, he arrived at Cauterets, where he remained for nearly a fortnight before going off to yet another spa at Usset, near Tarascon. During his stay at Cauterets, Hortense continued to be listless and sad, but as soon as he left she appeared full of energy, walking and climbing in the mountains, making a long tour on horseback, down to Lourdes and Pau and Biarritz and across the Spanish frontier to San

Sebastian. She had agreed to meet Louis at Toulouse after he finished his cure at Ussdat, but on her return to Cauterets from Spain she wrote to tell him that she was so happy in the mountains that she intended to stay there for a while and suggested he should return to Paris without her. He refused, insisting she should join him at once. She left Cauterets on 10 August and reached Toulouse on the 12th.

There, in her own words, 'I was not able to conceal from my husband the repugnance and even fear that our reunion aroused in me. He wished it so eagerly and it seemed it would make him so happy, that a reconciliation took place in Toulouse.'[22] Eight months and eight days later she gave birth to her third son, Charles-Louis-Napoleon, of whom, in private, Louis obstinately denied the paternity.

If Louis was not the father, then who was? All the possible candidates who are known to have been in the Pyrenees at the time have been dismissed for a variety of reasons. The handsome Elie Decazes, a future minister under Louis XVIII, was an acquaintance of Louise Cochelet, and he certainly met Hortense during her stay at Cauterets; but shortly afterwards he became Louis' secretary – and it is impossible to believe that Louis would have appointed him if he had had an inkling of suspicion against him. For a similar reason, Louis' later kindly conduct to him, Hortense's Dutch equerry, Charles Bylandt-Palstercamp, may be excluded. And because they were physically unattractive, so may be Ver Huell, the Dutch ambassador to Spain who was on his way to Madrid, and the Marquis de Castellane, Prefect of Pau, who squired Hortense on the trip to Biarritz and after. Unless she had a brief affair with a stranger, can there have been any likely father for her child except Louis?

The obvious name that springs to mind is that of Charles de Flahaut, but the 13th Chasseurs, it is always pointed out, remained in Germany or Swedish Pomerania until 1808, and it was not until July of that year that Charles was promoted to colonel and posted as aide-de-camp to Bertier, Napoleon's chief-of-staff. On the other hand, there is no reason to suppose that after peace negotiations began in June 1807 Flahaut did not get leave to return to France. He had kept in close touch with Hortense through letters to his mother (who had become the Marquise de Souza by her marriage to the Portugese ambassador). He referred to Hortense as 'Sophie' or 'Henriette' or 'my cousin' or even 'my aunt': to a less practised conspirator this could have been confusing, since Josephine was also sometimes 'my aunt', and so even was Napoleon, although he was more often 'your uncle', while Louis was 'Sophie's father'; but Madame de Souza seems to have disentangled it all with little trouble.[23] Certainly it must have baffled the clerks of the Imperial Cabinet Noir, for otherwise Napoleon, jealous of all his womenfolk's lovers and doubly so of Hortense's, would never have agreed to Charles' promotion.

Indeed, perhaps there was nothing in it. No document has been found to prove that Charles was in the High Pyrenees at this time. On the other hand, there is a strong indication that Hortense was preparing to meet somebody without her husband's knowledge. About 14 June she sent her equerry, Bylandt-Palstercamp, back to Holland leaving only Louise Cochelet and three of her closest friends as the discreet and loyal witnesses of whatever she was planning. The excuse she gave for sending Bylandt-Palstercamp home was that 'he had several dangerous falls in the mountains, because of his insistence on following me over paths too difficult for his age.' But at the time she dismissed him she was still making her excursions on horseback into Spain and back; and the age of this accident-prone old dodderer was thirty-three! The day after she got back to Cauterets, with Bylandt out of the way, she wrote to Louis saying that she would not meet him as arranged and asking him to return to Paris without her. That was on 20 July 1807 – precisely nine months before her baby was born.

Whatever reason Hortense may have had for agreeing to the resumption of marital relations with Louis, the reconciliation was brief. They rejoined the Emperor, Josephine and little Napoleon-Louis at St-Cloud on 27 August; and a few days later Hortense told Louis she was pregnant. He was suspicious, and the cat-and-dog life resumed worse than before. When he returned to his kingdom on 20 September Hortense persuaded her doctors to certify that the Dutch climate was bad for pregnancies, and Napoleon stepped in to say that she must remain in France.

*

Napoleon had returned from the triumphant conclusion of his campaign against the Prussians and Russians on 27 July 1807; his postilions crowned with laurels, and Joachim Murat, to whose dashing courage he owed so many of his victories, sharing his carriage. Two days later he sent for Caroline and upbraided her for having carried on a too-public affair with General Junot, whom he had appointed to Joachim's former post as Military Governor of Paris. The scolding upset her less than the news that he had created a new Kingdom of Westphalia and given it to his youngest brother, Jerome. He had made Joseph King of Naples in the spring of 1806, and Pauline Princess of

Guastalla at the same time; while Elisa had been reigning as Princess of Piombino for a year before that. It seemed as if honours were going to everybody in the family except herself and Joachim.

She fumed with indignation and directed her energies towards making the most of the successful little experiement she had carried out with the aid of Eleonore Denuelle. Now that Napoleon was home again there would be many opportunities to urge him towards divorce, and many allies to join in the work: Fouché for one, who had no interest in the Bonaparte-Beauharnais feud, but believed the stability of France was threatened so long as the Emperor was without a son to ensure the succession.[24]

There had been some minor problems earlier in the year. Revel, released from prison after completing his comparatively brief sentence, had returned to Paris and begun pestering Eleonore for money. Her lawyer refused to help but suggested that he should approach Caroline. Revel failed to get an interview with her. Instead her secretary told him to go away and stop bothering people. Revel was an awkward customer, and he made himself so unpleasant that within a week he was hauled off to the Prefecture of Police where he was interrogated by the Inspector-General, while the police made a close examination of his lodgings. Some papers were found, which they said looked like an attempt to blackmail Caroline and Joachim, and Revel was taken off to the prison of La Force. There he was left for a couple of months to meditate on the inadvisability of becoming a nuisance to members of the Bonaparte family, and was eventually released on condition that he left for Tours within twenty-four hours.[25]

By this time the direct campaign by the Bonapartes to persuade Napoleon to divorce Josephine was under way. When Fouché proposed to her that she should make the first move, sacrificing her own happiness to the welfare of France by asking for the dissolution of her marriage, she suspected that the suggestion originated with Napoleon, who did not have the moral courage to face her himself. Hortense advised her to confront Napoleon.[26] She did, and he denied all knowledge of Fouché's approach. His mind was not, in any case, fully made up. The Beauharnais faction, who by now knew all about the birth of Eleonore's son, put the word about that the child was just as likely to be Joachim Murat's. Napoleon, knowing his own inadequacy and Joachim's proved capability in such matters, was more than inclined to agree. Doubts crept back. Was he about to discard the devoted Josephine only to demonstrate his impotence with another woman? When Eleonore turned up, unannounced, at Fontainebleau and asked the Emperor's premier valet de chambre to admit her to the presence, Napoleon flew into a temper and forbade her ever to come near him again without permission.

There was general agreement that Caroline's little experiment had failed. The loose ends were soon tidied up: the year-old child, Charles Macon, was handed over to the nurse who had brought up Caroline's elder son, Achille, now almost seven; Eleonore was found a new husband, a 27-year-old infantry officer named Pierre-Philippe Augier de la Sauzaie; an attorney, who handled confidential matters for the Murats, arranged for the sale of her house and for the payment from an undisclosed source of an annuity of 22,000 francs. When her parents were invited to sign the marriage contract in mid-January 1808 they refused, presumably hoping to get something for themselves. In doing so they made the same mistake as Revel. They were invited round to the Police Commissioner's office and from there whisked off to prison. By the time they emerged three weeks later, their daughter was already married and they were told to move at least 300 miles from Paris under pain of being put back into prison again. The following month Eleonore's first husband, Revel, was quietened, at least temporarily, with a lieutenancy in the 64th Infantry Regiment, garrisoned far away at Besançon.

*

On the night of Eleonore's wedding Caroline gave a great nuptial ball at the Elysée Palace; in honour not of Eleonore but of Joachim's niece Antoinette Murat. Antoinette, created a Princess of the Empire by Napoleon in honour of the occasion, had been married that same day to Prince Karl of Hohenzollern-Sigmaringen, whose mother, Princess Amelia, had protected Hortense in the dark days of the Revolution when Josephine was in prison awaiting death. According to Hortense, the princess regarded the alliance as rather a come-down for so ancient and highborn a German family and, 'would have preferred a young person of our family [meaning Hortense herself] to a relation of Murat, whose illustriousness seemed to her to be extremely recent'[27]. This was a favourite topic with Hortense, and one that did nothing to endear her to Caroline. Her father was a *de* Beauharnais, her mother a *de la Pagerie*, and, although there is no record of either family having been accorded the Honours of the Court under the Bourbons, they were certainly a great many cuts above the unparticled, uncouth and indeed unFrench Bonapartes, and the peasant-born Murat.

The ball was graced by the presence of Napoleon and the Empress and enlivened by several quadrilles, one directed and led by Caroline, another by Hortense. Caroline's dancers were dressed as Tyrolean maidens in short red skirts with red braces worn over white blouses, and everything was embroidered with multi-coloured flowers. Hortense, determined to display her more classical, fashionable and artistic taste, chose for her theme the Vestal Virgins, the subject of a contemporary successful opera by Spontini which told the tragic fate of a virgin condemned to death for having taken a lover. Hortense was now well advanced in the pregnancy that had begun in the Pyrenees and, as General Junot's wife commented, 'completely cylindrical, which made the punishment to which she was being taken less unjust'. Both she and Caroline had enlisted some of the prettiest women at court, and Hortense had picked a charming young eighteen-year-old named Mademoiselle Guillebeau to usher in her quadrille as the spirit of Folly. Caroline recognized Mademoiselle Guillebeau as one of Joachim's recent mistresses and indignantly ordered the young woman out of the ballroom. Hortense could have claimed that it was only playful family tit-for-tat, since Caroline had included in her own quadrille that same Madame Duchatel who had briefly lured Napoleon away from Josephine, but she preferred to claim complete ignorance of Mademoiselle Guillebeau's reputation, though nobody believed her.[28]

It created a little rift in the friendship for a while, but all was outwardly forgotten in six or seven weeks' time when Caroline gave a children's party and invited Hortense to bring her son, Napoleon-Louis to it. The entertainment included tight-rope walkers and dancers whose acrobatics made Hortense fear that they would fall on the children. At 1 a.m. the following morning, 20 April 1808, she gave birth to her third child in her house in the Rue Cerutti.[29] On 2 June he was christened Charles-Louis-Napoleon by order of the Emperor. He was a great disappointment to Hortense, who, throughout her pregnancy had been longing for a daughter. However, he was 'so pallid, so peaky, so delicate, so feminine that for a long time she dressed him as a girl'.[30]

*

When Charles de Flahaut first heard that Hortense was pregnant he wrote to his mother that 'the news ... hurts me more than I can say.... Please write often to me about her. I feel very anxious.' Now that the child was born he wrote: 'Tell my cousin that I love her with all my heart, and that the note she has sent me has made me very happy.'[31] She was in need of all the comfort he could give her, for Louis was now insisting that she should send the older boy, Napoleon-Louis to live with him in Holland. Typically, it was the warm-hearted Caroline who pleaded Hortense's case with Napoleon and got from him the ruling that a mother was entitled to keep her child with her until it reached the age of seven.[32] Equally typically, Caroline teased her with a long story about having fallen in love with Charles, who was now stationed in Paris. She said she had received Charles' assurance that he loved her in return; she knew that Hortense was the only woman who could entice him away, and she begged her not to do so. Having stirred up that little cauldron, Caroline went merrily off to Naples, where she and Joachim had been allotted the throne previously occupied by Joseph, who had been transferred to Spain.

Joseph was chased out of Madrid in August 1808, and Napoleon had to spend the first part of the winter putting him back. In January 1809, however, he returned to Paris and in April was off to fight the Austrians again. By May he was in Vienna; a week later he teetered on the edge of a disastrous defeat at Aspern-Essling, but the Austrians let their chances slip; by high summer he had crushed them at Wagram. During this brief campaign more than 100,000 men from both sides had been killed. In great elation he summoned Marya Walewska to Vienna where, in the autumn, she was able to tell him she was pregnant.

This was the positive proof for which he had been waiting. Marya Walewska, pent up with him within the jaundice-yellow walls of Schönbrunn, could not have deceived him. He could risk the challenge of a new marriage and the attempt to father an Imperial heir. Late in October 1809 he arrived at Fontainebleau determined to divorce Josephine, and the delighted Bonapartes swarmed in for the long-awaited moment of triumph. Louis introduced a sour note into the rejoicing by demanding that he too should be granted a separation from Hortense.[33] But sauce for the Imperial gander was not sauce for the attendant geese and, although Hortense was equally eager to end the marriage she found herself in a worse position than before – ordered to return to Holland with Louis and her elder son. Charles de Flahaut, recovering in Paris from wounds received in Austria, pleaded with her not to leave. With tears in his eyes he protested eternal devotion. Hortense had to obey Napoleon's command, but after a few weeks she slipped away to Plombières, the pretty little spa in a valley of the Vosges that Josephine had favoured in happier days. She had scarcely arrived when she decided to go down to Aix-les-Bains, where Josephine was resting after the shock of the divorce. Late in July, as her carriage came down the Geneva road on the outskirts of Aix, Charles rode up to greet her.

She burst into tears of joy. He escorted her to the secluded house that Josephine had rented for her, and there was little doubt among those close to her that she was on a second honeymoon.[34] By this time she was Queen of Holland in title alone for Louis had abdicated and fled to Austria from his brother's wrath. Hortense was virtually a free woman. When Charles' leave ended in September she followed him back to Paris, where she set herself up in great style in the house in the Rue Cerutti with an income from state funds of two million francs a year, in addition to all the property that Louis had owned in France.

*

Meanwhile, France had a new empress. Napoleon, despite Joachim's warnings that such a move would ensure war with Russia without guaranteeing loyalty from Austria, had persevered with his intention to marry the Grand-Duchess Marie-Louise of Austria, a royal house whose women were famed for their fertility. Her father, Franz I, had surrendered his title of Holy Roman Emperor to his future son-in-law in 1806 and never forgave him for its loss. Now he was forced to swallow the further humiliation of sacrificing his daughter and his family pride. As for the happy couple, the terrified eighteen-year-old bride, who had been in the habit of referring to Bonaparte as 'Anti-Christ', wrote to a friend, 'I pity the unfortunate woman that his choice falls on.... Say a paternoster that it shall not be me.'[35] While the gallant groom explained with soldierly simplicity: 'I am marrying a belly.'[36] Caroline went to Vienna to bring the unhappy girl to the marriage ceremony in Notre Dame, where the bride's train was carried by the resentful Queens of Holland, Naples, Spain and Westphalia, and the groom was resplendently ludicrous in white satin embroidered with golden bees and a black velvet hat drenched in diamonds.[37]

A month later, on 4 May 1810, Marya Walewska's child was born at her home in the castle of Walewice. Her obliging husband recognized the boy as his own, and he was christened Florian-Alexandre-Joseph Colonna Walewski.[38] It is possible that this news had a beneficial effect on Napoleon's confidence, for in June the 'Austrian Belly' conceived. Count Walewski made over half his fortune to his wife and in September she set off with her two sons to Paris, where she rented a house in the Rue du Houssaye. She did not mix in society, but wrote a letter to Napoleon every day declaring he was all she had to live for. The sentiments were not reciprocated. The expectant father was embarrassed by his former mistress's attentions. He met her secretly once or twice, settled on the baby Alexandre an estate in the Kingdom of Naples and the title of count, then ignored her. But she did not go away.

His other son, Eleonore Denuelle's child, Charles Macon, was still being brought up by the former nurses to the Murat children, and Caroline was still keeping an eye on him. 'The Queen of Naples commands me to ask you to come tomorrow afternoon at one o'clock with the child', her secretary wrote to Eleonore, one day in 1810, 'and to enter by the garden gate. You will be so good as to wait in the silver boudoir'[39] (so called because of the silver-embroidered curtains and silver-ornamented furniture).

Napoleon's eldest child, Emilie, continued to live obscurely in Lyons, apparently unknown to any Bonaparte. For the first four years of her life she never saw her nominal father, Alain Pellapra. She shared her grandmother's old-fashioned alcove bed in the apartment that looked out over the Brotteau. It was a pleasant, comfortable existence, loved by her grandmother, tended by a peasant girl who combined being Emilie's nursemaid with housework, entertained by an elderly maid with a gift for dancing mock stately sarabands. In later life she remembered watering the flowers on the balcony and going for Sunday walks which usually ended at the house of one or other of her aunts, whom she did not greatly care for. 'Above all, I remember distinctly that when I was only three years old I understood perfectly when I was admired for my beauty, and was flattered by this, which was the usual accompaniment of our walks.'

There is a possibility that Napoleon briefly renewed his affair with Emilie's mother in 1811. Certainly he seems to have been reminded of, or by, her and learned perhaps for the first time that he had a daughter; for in this year he had Alain Pellapra appointed to the post of Chief Tax Collector for Calvados and he himself visited Caen, the departmental capital, during May. Caen was sufficiently distant from both Paris and Lyons for Emilie to be brought to live with her parents without exciting comment when they moved there. It was a sad parting from her doting grandmother, and a miserable existence in her new home, neglected by her flighty, scatter-brained mother, slapped and scolded by her stern, resentful father. She complained at having no playmates other than the crippled and short-lived daughter of her father's principal secretary, yet was oppressed by a sense of rejection when she was sent to a day school in the town instead of being taught at home like the children of well-to-do families. She perhaps exaggerated the slights and punishments that she suffered, but in her own eyes they were real enough, and on one occasion she contemplated killing herself by jumping out of a window.[40]

In March 1811 the long-awaited heir to the Empire was born to the thunder of a one-hundred-and-one gun salute and immediately created King of Rome. The dynasty was established, the succession assured. Napoleon became daily more imperial than the emperor whose daughter he had married, increasingly obsessed with protocol, feverishly laminating vulgarity upon vulgarity. Teams of researchers combed through the records of the ancient etiquette of the Court of France, while he fussed over the doilies and fish-forks. 'There,' he said to Marie-Louise one day, pointing to a portrait of Louis XVI, 'is our uncle.'[41] He found himself confronting problems of excruciating complexity. The day, for example, when Marie-Louise officially received visitors for the first time since the birth of her son; Napoleon, checking the arrangements beforehand, was horrified to see that armchairs had been set beside the Empress's state couch for his mother and for the Queens of Spain and Holland: Joseph's wife Julie, and Hortense. Since his mother was not a queen it was unthinkable that she should sit in an armchair in the presence of the Empress; and since she was still a bit of a tartar it was improbable that she would acquiesce quietly to her daughters-in-law having armchairs while she did not. He ordered the three armchairs to be removed and taborets (the folding stools reserved for duchesses) to be set in their places. The great double doors swung open, Madame Mère, Julie and Hortense entered, took one look at the taborets, and walked straight out again.[42] Of all his family, he sometimes thought, it was Madame Mère who caused him the most grief: never properly impressed or convinced, forever muttering 'Provided it lasts!' in her thick Italian accent, remembering the days when she had been glad to take in other people's washing and Paoletta and Nunziata had delivered it to the customers, getting themselves talked about if they stayed a minute or two over their time.

Now Paoletta was a princess, and Nunziata, whose name Napoleon had changed to Caroline in his anxiety to conceal the family's Italian origin, was a queen in Naples. Caroline pleaded ill-health as an excuse for not attending the christening of the King of Rome on 9 June 1811 and asked Hortense to stand proxy for her as godmother. Assuming this relationship to the child whose mother had supplanted her own mother would perhaps have embarrassed many women, but Hortense, though she talked much of her emotional sensitivity, never in the last resort allowed her heart to rule her head. She leaped at the opportunity to get a Beauharnais hand on the new little Bonaparte's cradle.

It was to be her last ceremonial appearance for several months. Charles continued to be her lover, though she was aware that Countess Potocka had followed him to Paris. Despite Hortense's constant vows that if he loved another woman he had only to confess it and she would set him free, he denied any interest in the Polish woman. Their affair continued, ardently on her side, a little less than whole-heartedly on his. But now she was carrying his child.

In the first week of July she set off for Aix. There she conferred with her brother, Eugene, who was returning

36

from the christening celebrations to his capital at Milan, where he ruled over Northern Italy as Napoleon's viceroy. She was too well known in Aix to contemplate having her baby there so she arranged with Eugene to meet him at Lake Maggiore when the time came. She remained in Aix until the end of August, then crossed the Swiss border to Pregny, just outside Geneva, where Josephine had recently bought a house to assure herself of a refuge if Napoleon should exile her now that his second wife had a son. In increasing discomfort Hortense moved on to St-Maurice in the valley of the Rhône above Lake Geneva. There all trace of her is lost for several weeks.[43]

It is possible that she tried to continue up the valley to the Simplon Pass to keep her rendezvous with Eugene, but had to turn back to St-Maurice and gave birth to her child there. Alternatively, though less plausibly, she may have concealed her condition successfully even after her return to Paris on 10 October. Certainly, it was there that the baby was registered at the Town Hall of the Third Arrondissement, as Charles-Auguste-Louis-Joseph, born at a doctor's house in the Rue Montmartre on 21 October 1811, son of a St Domingan estate owner, Auguste-Jean-Hyacinthe Demorny, and his wife, Emilie-Coralie, normally resident at Villetaneuse.[44] The child himself was brought up to believe that he had been born in the palatial house in the Rue Cerutti.

Hortense settled back into the quiet routine of entertaining her close friends with cards and conversation, singing her fragile, wistful ballads. She was not really made for happiness; certainly not for joy. There was a sadness inherent in her features, the strong cheekbones and pointed chin that made her face diamond-shaped rather than oval, the full petulant lips, the long mournful nose, the loving, pleading, reproaching grey-blue eyes. There was from the beginning little hope that her romance with the handsome, dashing philandering Charles could last.

'Although he was always eager to see me, he was just as enthusiastic about all the pleasure that took him from my side.... I used to urge him to enjoy himself, ashamed of my hidden desire to keep him with me, happy when he disobeyed me....' They preserved the proprieties, partly because the Imperial displeasure would have struck them if Napoleon had discovered their secret. Charles continued to live in his mother's house in the Rue Verte, calling on Hortense most evenings, but not all. 'In spite of my constant longing to see him, I never once said: "Shall I see you tomorrow?" I always waited for the suggestion to come from him.'

But if she said nothing she let her anxiety be plainly seen:

Many ladies seemed to be interested in M. de Flahaut. I could see it myself. If he had told me so I should have trusted him. I never ceased telling him that there cannot be true affection without trust, that frankness redeems every fault, and that if none of us is perfect, we can at least be honest. He vainly assured me that he could never love another ... but in spite of all his protestations, I was forever dragging out of him the confession of some lapse.

For Charles, at least, it must have been a relief when Napoleon set the Grande Armée in motion again. For many years he had dreamed of marching eastwards and establishing his dictatorship over the whole of Europe and Asia. Now that he had a son to inherit his conquests there was no limit to his ambitions. By May 1812 all officers had rejoined their regiments. 'I watched the man I love depart,' sighed Hortense, 'and I was broken-hearted.' On 24 June, under foreboding stormy skies, Napoleon ordered his army of nearly 700,000 men to cross the Niemen en route to Moscow, winter and humiliating disaster.

*

Hortense's latest child, who was always called by his second name, Auguste, was about as illegitimate as any child could be. His maternal grandfather, Alexandre de Beauharnais, had always maintained that Hortense was not his lawful daughter; but Alexandre was an excitable and oft-deluded man, seeking a riposte to Josephine's accusations of cruelty, and there is no proof for his claim. So Hortense's was the first recorded slip of this kind in the Beauharnais line. For the Flahauts, however, the story was very different. Charles de Flahaut's mother, Adelaide de Souza, was the daughter of a Mademoiselle Irene de Buisson de Longpré who, before being married off with a dowry of 100,000 livres to a Norman wine merchant named Filleul, had been one of the occupants of the notorious brothel established by Louis XV for his private use in the Parc-aux-Cerfs, near Versailles. It is said that the king continued his association with Irene after her marriage and that Adelaide de Souza was his daughter. (Adelaide's elder sister, who married Madame de Pompadour's brother and became the mistress of Cardinal de Rohan, certainly claimed Louis XV as her father.) If that were so, then the baby, Auguste, was not only the son of a Queen of Holland but also the great-grandson of a King of France. While there is no certain proof that Adelaide de Souza was illegitimate, there is no shadow of doubt that her first husband, the Count de Flahaut, was not the father of her son, Charles. That title went to the apostate statesman Talleyrand, who never disguised his interest in his son's career.

Despite his illustrious and complicated ancestry, Auguste entirely disappears from history for the next five years. It was Charles who arranged for the Demorny's to bring him up in obscurity amid the plaster-quarries of the drab little village of Villetaneuse, a few miles north of St-Denis. Hortense settled a handsome sum of money on him but does not seem to have attempted to see him for many years. Charles was shortly to be involved in the horrors of the retreat from Moscow, where he acquitted himself so well that he was promoted to brigadier on 4 December 1812 (the same day that Napoleon deserted his ragged army and fled for Paris), and appointed aide-de-camp to the Emperor in January 1813. In the previous November, when the first news of the retreat reached Paris, Adelaide de Souza had Demorny sign a deed of guardianship in her favour, so that if Demorny died the boy would pass into the custody of Adelaide and her husband or, failing them, of Charles de Flahaut. She was a sentimental woman and would have been delighted to take the child into her home straight away had there not been the danger of compromising Hortense.

Caroline had meanwhile been making similar arrangements for the guardianship of Eleonore Denuelle's child. On 25 March 1812, the Baron de Mauvières appeared before the Justice of the Peace of the Second Arrondissement to apply for permission to adopt Charles Macon, a very young boarder (he was five years and three months old) at a Pension for Young Persons in the Rue Matignon, a short distance from Caroline's former home at the Elysée Palace. The baron made his application on the grounds that the child's mother was absent and possibly no longer still alive – a false supposition that could have been quickly disproved by application to her second husband, Lieutenant Augier, still a serving officer though fated to die in the great retreat. The Juge de Paix complied with the baron's request and appointed a Family Council to act as trustees, composed of three distinguished lawyers and the Mayor of the First Arrondissement.[45] There was no delay and no awkward questions. For the Baron de Mauvières was father-in-law to Claude-François Meneval, a friend of the Murats (his daughter later married one of Joachim's nephews) and a very influential man: he had been the Emperor's Private Secretary for the past ten years. On Napoleon's instructions, the boy was allotted ten shares in each of two canal companies, bringing in the very useful income of 12,000 francs a year.

In January 1813 Napoleon visited Marya Walewska at her house in the Rue du Houssaye one evening. Their child, Alexandre, a pretty, curly-haired boy now going on for three years old, was roused from his bed, dressed, and taken to the drawing room to be dandled on his father's knee.[46] In the spring, Marya took him to Malmaison, where he was petted and showered with sweets by the ever-gentle Josephine, still not quite fifty but a grandmother seven times over (eight times if one includes Auguste Demorny whom she may never have known about). She was always sending clothes to Eugene's children, but it was Hortense's that she saw most frequently, and of these two she had a special fondness for Louis-Napoleon (the Charles in his name was never used except in official documents), the child of the High Pyrenees,

There was no trace of the Bonapartes in his features; but he had his mother's fair hair, her smoky-blue eyes and her outwardly gentle disposition; and he was so biddable, so eager to please, that Josephine nicknamed him 'Little Oui-Oui', not apparently noticing that, though he invariably smiled and answered 'Yes-Yes', he by no means always actually did as he was told. He was rather a frail child in his early days, but as full of courage as he was of affection, a natural optimist. '*Petite Maman*,' he wrote to Hortense one day when he had fallen off his rocking-horse, '*Oui-Oui a fait pouf dans le dada; Oui-Oui n'a pas bobo; il aime maman beaucoup à coeur. Oui-Oui.*' [Little Mama: Oui-Oui tumbled off his gee-gee; Oui-Oui did not get a nasty bruise; he loves his Mama very much.] He was the sort of child that it is very difficult to dislike.

*

Late in August 1813 Marie-Louise set off for Cherbourg to open the new dock named for the Emperor. The news was bad on all fronts: to the south Wellington's troops had chased Joseph Bonaparte off the throne of Spain once more and were about to throw the French army back across the Pyrenees; to the east Napoleon was struggling to beat down Prussia and the other German states, who had risen against him in a great War of Liberation and to whom, that very month, Marie-Louise's father added the refurbished army of Austria. She had left St-Cloud in a temper, fearing what her reception might be, lacking any news from Napoleon for the past week, and disliking travel anyway. When she reached Caen in the afternoon of the second day the scowl had faded a little from her plump pink cheeks. She had been plied with good Norman cream by the peasant women in their tall double-pointed caps as she jolted through the meadows and orchards of the Pays de Caux and now she was sitting down to a substantial dinner. Like most of the Austrian princesses she was a creature of ample fleshly appetites.

She did not look forward to the prospect of receiving the local dignitaries, but the task was soon over and she enjoyed the evening festival in the Prefecture garden. The prefect's wife chanted a welcoming recitative, backed by a chorus of important local ladies in Cauchois costume who laid wreaths and baskets of flowers on the terrace at the Empress's feet. They were followed by important local gentlemen, equally spuriously disguised as farmhands, who presented a magnificent horse shod with silver and a white bull with gilded and garlanded horns. Finally, there appeared what Marie-Louise noted in her diary as 'the prettiest little girl you can imagine'.[47]

It was Emilie Pellapra. The pageant-master had originally intended that she should enter on the back of the bull, but her mother did not trust the animal, so Emilie was brought forward on a farm cart decorated to resemble a triumphal chariot. She was flanked by two small gilded barrels containing milk and cider, and held two crystal goblets in her hands. With perfect composure she poured libations to the Empress and recited:

> Fruits of
> Pomona,
> delights
> of   the
> dairy,
> Sweetest
> treasure
> of   the

Neustrian
fields:
Queen,
this
simple
tribute
would
scarce be
Worthy
of you,
Were't
not
offered to
a   tender
mother
by a little
child.

The verses were admittedly not distinguished but, as
Emilie confessed in later life, 'were well enough received
on account of my pretty face'. She curtsied and was about
to retire when an equerry told her to stay. He led her to the
Empress and told her to kneel, which Emilie declined to
do, explaining that she had already said her prayers once
that day. Nevertheless the Empress presented her with a
pale blue enamelled watch bearing her monogram – and
appeared never for a moment to notice the striking
resemblance between the little girl and her own husband
and son. She continued on her way, leaving Emilie well
satisfied. She was soon excused from the horrors of the
day school, at which she caught scarlet fever. The prefect's
charming wife came in and played with her, her mother
petted her, her father paced up and down the garden

pondering on where best to bury his valuables before the Russians arrived.

Her true father, having drained France of her young men's blood, was reduced to conscripting boys and cripples. They came unwillingly, herded by his Special Gendarmerie with orders to round up the stragglers and shoot one in every ten. Throughout the winter of 1813/14 the Allies moved forward, scenting the kill. Napoleon fought back. They offered terms to avoid further slaughter. He pretended to agree, chicaned, played for time, lost. He fell into wild rages, vowing terrible punishment on those who had turned against him, in particular the King of Bavaria whose daughter Eugene de Beauharnais had married. 'Munich must burn, Munich shall burn!' he screamed, but the threat, like Hitler's against Paris 130 years later, remained unfulfilled.

*

In the evening of 28 March 1814 the Regency Council, set up by Napoleon and presided over by Marie-Louise, met in the Emperor's study in the Tuileries to consider his letter written twelve days before, ordering the Empress, with the King of Rome and the Imperial Treasure, to be escorted towards the Loire if Paris was threatened. In the Council's opinion that moment had arrived.

As Marie-Louise came out of the study she found Hortense waiting for her, desperately anxious to persuade her to stay. 'If you leave Paris you will lose your crown,' Hortense warned her. Marie-Louise shrugged: 'That's true. It is not my fault – the Council has decided.'[48] Her packing had been done long ago. Within a hour or two the convoy set off in the darkness; great travelling coaches for the Empress, her son and her attendants, wagons for the

Treasure worth forty million francs. They were at Rambouillet before dawn, next day they reached Chartres and from there lumbered slowly across the Beauce plateau and down into the Loire valley where they halted at Blois on 2 April. Paris had surrendered the day before. Marie-Louise wrote to her father asking him to pledge Austria's support for a regency, but before she received a reply Napoleon abdicated, renouncing the thrones of France and Italy on behalf of himself and his heirs. While she hesitated at Blois, one of Tsar Alexander's aides-de-camp arrived with an escort to take her back to Rambouillet. She was not an unwilling prisoner.

When Napoleon once again deserted his troops and ran from Fontainebleau he was accompanied by Charles de Flahaut, now a lieutenant-general, a Count of the Empire and a Commander of the Legion of Honour. He was sent by Napoleon to Rambouillet to invite Marie-Louise to join him at Fontainebleau, but she refused And when Charles was invited to accompany Napoleon into exile on Elba, he too declined. 'It was his desire to keep me with him,' he wrote to his mother, 'but I told him that I owed myself to you before everyone.... If the Russians have delivered us from their odious presence, I shall return to your side, dear Mama, without shame and without regret, and ready, if Henriette will agree, to make a happy life with her.'

But Hortense had other ideas. She had an excellent head for business and a rare gift for dissembling. 'I have always tried to hide my emotions,' she confessed: 'I believe the deeper they are, the more one takes care to restrain them.' Far from sharing Charles' wish that the Russians should go away, she was eagerly hob-nobbing with the Tsar, whom she charmed so successfully that she won his warm intercession at the court of the restored Bourbons. It was thanks to Alexander that Louis XVIII softened the blow of her losing the title of Queen of Holland by raising her estate of St-Leu to the dignity of a duchy. As for Charles' proposal that she should 'make him very happy', her Bonapartist connections were now an embarrassment which would be made far worse by marriage to Napoleon's former aide-de-camp. Besides, a divorce, which Louis was still eager to obtain, would have meant losing the custody of both the boys. To Charles' surprise and confusion he found his offer ignored. At this point Auguste-Jean Demorny died, leaving the guardianship of the young Auguste to the Baron and Baroness de Souza, and the child was henceforward seen more openly at their house in the Rue Verte.

Hortense, meanwhile, was at Malmaison with her mother and the two boys. The King of Prussia brought his own two sons, the younger of whom was to become the first emperor of Germany more than half a century later. Marya Walewska came too, with her chubby, lively Alexandre, just four years old. She brought news of her visit to Fontainebleau just before the abdication. She had waited all night but Napoleon had failed to send for her, though when he learned that he was to be sent to Elba and that not many wished to go with him, he wrote: 'When you have arranged your affairs, if you would care to go and take the waters at Lucca or Pisa I should have a deep and lively interest in seeing you, and your son, for whom my feelings will never change.'

Josephine, the only woman who had really understood him, seen through him and yet still loved him, dearly wished to share his exile. When she heard of Marie-Louise's refusal she was horrified: 'If it were not for her, I would join him myself. It was only while he was happy that I could remain separated from him. I am certain that he expects me now.' He was never to see her again. Before May was out she caught a chill and died.

In Caen, Emilie Pellapra was seeing some of her nightmares come true in a very odd and quite unfrightening way. Overheard scraps of adult conversation about the prospects of invasion had put a terrifying image of 'The Enemy' in her mind. He was a horseman, fiercely moustached, brandishing a sabre, and galloping wildly across France, no doubt in search of the money her father had by now safely dug into the garden. But when 'The Enemy' descended upon this pleasant corner still untouched by war, he proved to be not terrible at all, just a bevy of handsome young officers who soon danced their way into Caen's more fashionable salons. At their coat-tails came a less enchanting figure: the new King Louis XVIII's nephew, the Duke of Berry, presenting a momentary problem to the Pellapra family, for Emilie's father was a convinced Republican, and her mother still adored the Emperor. But facts were facts and good jobs not to be put in peril, especially at such a time. So Monsieur Pellapra ordered round the open carriage, put his wife and daughter in it, and sent them off to applaud the duke's arrival.

Seven-year-old Emilie was disgusted. 'The same people who had shouted *Vive l'Impératrice!*', she recalled in later years 'now made themselves hoarse yelling *Vive le Duc de Berry!*' Instead of the line of carriages with beautiful women who had accompanied Marie-Louise, there was just one ancient and travel-stained barouche bearing 'an ugly, stout, heavy, common-looking person, not at all my idea of a prince'. Next day her parents attended the lunch at the Prefecture in the duke's honour, and her nurse took her into the gardens to see the guests leave. Her mother called her over and presented her to the duke. He smiled at her and said how pretty she was. She smiled back. Then, with a bow to her mother, he added, 'though she will never be as pretty as you, Madame'.

Emilie pursed her lips. It was not the sort of thing he should have said in front of her. It was also quite untrue, since everybody agreed she was the prettiest person anybody had ever seen. She had been right the first time: he was stupid, awkward and very, very common, quite unlike Marie-Louise who, in this very same garden, had shown a true appreciation of Emilie's charm, and had not made any silly comparisons, and was the daughter of an emperor as well as the wife of one, and not common at all. It was, perhaps, essential to be the daughter of one emperor if one was to understand all the qualities of the daughter of another.

Marie-Louise had gone home to her father, taking her son, deprived of the title of King of Rome, with her. She did not stay long in Vienna. The fears and excitements of the past months had disturbed her weak chest. She was easily prevailed upon to leave the boy with his grandfather while she went to take the waters at Aix, escorted by General Neipperg. The general, who had already acted as equerry to Marie-Louise when she spent a month with her family in 1812, was a Swabian of noble family, not quite forty years old, a hero from a playbill with crisply curling hair, a confident tilt to his head, and one dashing flashing eye: the other, its socket now concealed by a black patch, he had lost in combat twenty years before. By September she had taken him as her lover.

From Elba, Napoleon sent a letter to Meneval, who had remained with Marie-Louise, asking that she should bring their son to see him. There was no reply. But the other Marie came, Marya Walewska, sweet-tempered, eager to please, a little plumper than when they first met and accompanied by a child so pretty, with golden curls falling on to his shoulders, that the islanders believed the pair really were the Empress and the King of Rome. For the sake of secrecy Napoleon hurried them off to his summer quarters up in the mountains. While they ate supper in a tent under the chestnut trees, Alexandre sat on his father's knee and answered questions:

'What are you going to do when you grow up?'

'I shall go to war, like Napoleon.'

'Are you fond of Napoleon?'

'Oh, yes!'

'And why do you like him?'

'Because he is my father, and my mother told me to.'

Even as a child he managed to be undiplomatic.

From Marya Walewska Napoleon demanded news of Marie-Louise. She claimed to know nothing at all, shielding him from the truth, with the result that when she begged to stay with him he refused, believing that there was still a chance that his legal wife would return. After two days she had to go, back to the ship that carried her through a furious storm to the Italian mainland.

*

From the moment he arrived on the island Napoleon had been planning his return to France. His fleet of half-a-dozen ships moved busily about the Ligurian Sea carrying secret information to and from France and Italy, and, in particular, linking with the messenger service to Joseph, who, from his estate at Prangins in Switzerland, coordinated all the Bonapartist plots. Though the details of the messages remained secret it was quite clear to the Bourbon government that something was going on. They had only to listen to the veterans of the Grande Armée assuring each other that their 'Little Corporal' would return 'when the violets bloom'. Looking for centres of treason in Paris, they turned a suspicous eye on Hortense, who, scenting a change of power, returned from her estate at St-Leu in mid-November and was soon entertaining Charles de Flahaut, his handsome cousin La Bédoyère, and many other former Bonaparte aides-de-camp to elegant little soirées of music, billiards and readings.

'My Salon became so agreeable and select', she admitted, 'that this small success aroused a new sort of enmity – from women who did not restrict themselves to attacking me on political grounds.' But it was her politics that bothered the government, and on Christmas Eve a clerk at the local Town Hall warned her that her house was to be put under seal the following day in accordance with an order made the week before, confiscating all property belonging to the Bonaparte family. Fortunately, she could still count on the support of Tsar Alexander. She at once protested to the Russian Ambassador that she had no property belonging to her husband and that her own was protected by her personal agreement with the Bourbon government under which she had become Duchess of St-Leu.

She staved off this threat, but another hung over her. As soon as Napoleon lost his control over the French courts of law, Louis brought an action in Paris for the custody of his elder son. The suit dragged on. On 8 March 1815 verdict was given for Louis: Hortense must hand over the boy within three months. But the boy was nowhere to be found. Hortense had hidden him two days before.

On Monday, 6 March, as she returned from a drive in the Bois de Boulogne, Lord Kinnaird, who was in Paris in search of art treasures looted during the twenty years of war, rode up to her carriage and related the startling news he had just heard from the Duke of Orleans: Napoleon was in France. As predicted, *Père la Violette* had come back with the spring. On the first day of March he had landed at Cannes. He was now making his way north by mountain roads, avoiding the lower valley of the Rhône, the fury of whose inhabitants had scared him to tears on the way to Elba. He would eventually descend from Grenoble to Lyons, and thence, thanks to the fervour of the Bonapartist factions and the incompetence and unpopularitiy of the Bourbons, continue to the capital unopposed.

But to Hortense on this bright Monday morning in Paris the problem was what she should do until he did arrive. Not even she could imagine it would all be over so quickly and without bloodshed. 'Do you think there is anything to fear for the children?' she asked Kinnaird. 'I don't think so,' he replied, 'providing they're not held as hostages.'[49] The thought sent her hurrying home. As soon as it was dark she had Louise Cochelet take the boys to the apartment of her friend, the Baroness Riouffe, in the Rue St-Georges. The baroness was away in the country but her mother promised to look after the children and not to make any attempt to get in touch with Hortense unless they became ill.

Marya Walewska, who had been staying with Joachim and Caroline in Naples, set sail with Alexandre as soon as she heard the news. After narrowly escaping capture by an Arab corsair, they landed safely in France. While Marya pursued him from the south, Françoise Pellapra advanced upon their common lover from the north. According to family tradition, Françoise journeyed down the high road to Lyons disguised as an egg-wife on the way to market, she perched in a pannier on one side of her donkey, her eggs on the other – though the top layer of eggs concealed tricolour favours to be exchanged for the white Royalist cockades of the government troops.[50]

It sounds like one of Emilie's romantic inventions, but it is certainly true that Françoise went to Lyons and that Emilie (was she hidden under the cockades?) found herself one day gazing down again from her beloved grandmother Leroy's balcony upon hordes of people scurrying to and fro, along the streets, over the bridges, in and out of the city gates, carrying baulks of wood, dragging cannon, setting up barricades – all to keep out the great and noble Emperor whom her mother was always describing and praising to her, and whose wife, the Empress, had been so gracefully impressed by Emilie's beauty. And then the next morning (Tuesday 9 March), when she peered through the balcony railings she saw another horde of people (or was it the same one, changed overnight?) pulling down the barricades, setting up triumphal arches, decorating windows and walls with flowers and pasteboard eagles, replacing the Bourbon lilies on the flagstaffs with tricolour flags. That night the small plump man rattled down in his coach from the Dauphiné, smiling at times, pursing his lips and frowning at others, trying to look both fierce and friendly at once. Then he got on to a horse and hit it about the head to show how masterful he was, and the cry of *Vive l'Empereur!* swelled from a ripple to a roar, and everybody went mad.

On 12 March, Marchand, the Emperor's premier valet de chambre, called at the apartment to take Françoise Pellapra for an audience with his master. She did not return until late in the night. Next morning she was away again with Emilie, caught up in the motley, feverish throng that followed him to Paris. There she took rooms at an hotel and waited to be summoned again.

*

The news of Napoleon's escape from Elba reached Vienna on the same day as it was known in Paris – 6 May. Exactly a week later the representatives of the Allied Powers gathered in Congress in the city declared him an outlaw. Exactly a week after that the former King of Rome was told that his governess, the Countess de Montesquiou, had been dismissed and replaced by the Austrian Countess Mitrovsky. It was a very unwelcome present on the boy's fourth birthday, for he had grown extremely found of his 'Maman Quiou'. The previous evening Marie-Louise had brought him from Schönbrunn to the Hofburg within the city walls, as a precaution against kidnapping. Henceforward there was to be no French influence around him – he would be nurtured and fashioned as an Austrian princeling.

Hortense arrived at the palace early next morning and was shown into the Emperor's salon. He kissed the children, whom she had dressed in uniform, one as a hussar the other as a lancer, but he was very cold to her. She fell into step with him as he paced up and down; the children drifted to the window and gazed at the crowds seething in the gardens. Presently he said: 'I never thought you would desert my cause.' She protested that she had not done so, nor wished to do so. He was in an icy fury because she had persuaded the Tsar to get her promoted from countess to duchess and thus preserved her estates when all the Bonapartes had lost theirs. She should have left the country. 'Sire, you don't know the circumstances that compelled me to remain in France. My mother wanted me to. I was all that she had. And you know that my husband would not support me.' She added that it would not have been right for her to reject a settlement that benefited her children.

'You shouldn't have stayed in France. A piece of black bread would have been better,' he insisted. 'You acted like a child. When you've shared a family's good fortune you should share the bad.' She resorted to tears, which had sometimes moved him in the past. 'Oh, Sire, then I was mistaken. I hoped you would be pleased that your nephews could at least remain on French soil. And where could I find friends to whom I could take them?'

It worked. 'Well', he said gruffly, 'you can't give me any satisfactory reason but you know I am always a good father to you. I want to forgive you. Let's say no more about it.'[51]

All was as before. Caught up in the general emotion she even began to believe that his return might be permanent, especially when she watched him reviewing his troops, led by the 600 grenadiers of the Old Guard who had returned from Elba with him, each man decorated with the order of the Legion of Honour. Françoise Pellapra and Emilie were among the other guests who looked down on the parade from the windows of the Tuileries, though there is no record of their having met Hortense. The Place du Carrousel was filled with troops, the windows and roofs of all the huddled houses nearby were crammed with spectators who took up and echoed back the cry as the cavalry flourished their sabres and the infantry waved their shakos on the end of their bayonets, all roaring *Vive l'Empereur!*

Charles de Flahaut was sent to Austria to persuade Marie-Louise to return, but he got no further than Stuttgart, fifty miles across the Rhine, before being turned back. The Emperor asked Hortense to open up Malmaison, Eugene's property since Josephine's death, and act as his hostess there on occasions, thus making her the first lady in the land. In Paris, for fear of assassination, he moved from the Tuileries to the Elysée, where the garden could be more easily guarded. They were walking there one lunchtime when he told her that Louis had again asked for a divorce. Hortense asked him to decree that she should have custody of the children. He refused. A father had the right to possess his own children. 'What can you do about it? If your son was born crippled or cross-eyed, you couldn't do anything. You can't stop that sort of thing; you have to resign yourself to it.'[52]

There were other things to be resigned to. War, for instance. He feverishly dragged men to the colours, distributed new eagles, put on patriotic displays. The night before he left Paris to take command of his army he was working on his maps when Hortense's younger son, Little Oui-Oui, ran into the study and buried his face in the Emperor's lap, crying, 'Sire, my Governess says you are going to war. Don't go! Don't go!'

'Why not, child?' said Napoleon. 'This is not the first time I have been to war. What is there to cry about? I shall soon be back.'

'The wicked Allies want to kill you,' the boy sobbed. 'Please, Uncle – let me go with you.'

Napoleon picked him up, kissed him, and then called Hortense. 'Scold his Governess for upsetting him,' he said, and as she went out: 'That boy will have courage and a lofty spirit.... Perhaps he is the true hope of my dynasty.'[53]

He sent Marchand with a sealed package to Marya Walewska and another, containing a gold bracelet studded with rubies, diamonds and emeralds, to Françoise Pellapra. At five o'clock in the morning he left for Belgium. It was Monday, 12 June 1815.

*

Just nine days later, a little before dawn on Wednesday, 21 June, he was back again, his nerve entirely shattered. He had deserted his beaten army for the last time; fought and lost his last battle; sent to death the last of the million or so men whom he had sacrificed to his ambition, counting merely from his assumption of the Imperial title in 1804. Next day, despite the efforts of his brother, Lucien, to stiffen his courage as he had done during the *coup d'état* that made him First Consul, Napoleon abdicated, to the surprise and confusion of Flahaut and other aides-de-camp, who were re-assembling the scattered troops and bringing up the National Guard. On Saturday evening Napoleon told Hortense he had decided to quit Paris and take refuge at Malmaison, and she 'so as to have nobody to bother about except the Emperor', took the strange step of leaving both the boys in the city upon which the allied armies were rapidly advancing, hidden in rooms above a stocking shop in the Boulevard Montmartre.

At Malmaison, still haunted by the graceful spirit of Josephine, the Emperor said goodbye to all his children except the only legitimate one. Françoise Pellapra, bringing anxious warnings of plots against him, took lodgings in nearby Rueil and managed to see him at least once more. Silly, pretty, loyal, submissive, never causing trouble or claiming privilege, she was the only one of his mistresses of whom he spoke with a semblance of genuine affection in later years: perhaps because she came closest to his ideal of what a woman should be. 'In France,' he said, 'women are too highly regarded. They are in fact nothing more than machines for producing children. One sex must be subordinate to the other.'[54]

Baron de Mauvières brought his ward, Charles Macon, whose mother had long lost interest in him. After the death of her second husband, Pierre Augier, during the retreat from Moscow, she had married, in March 1814, a German named Karl August Emil von Luxburg (a union complicated by a suit brought by her first husband, Revel, for annulment of his divorce from her in 1803). To compensate for this maternal neglect, Napoleon settled a further 100,000 francs on the boy, whom he was now accepting to be his son.[55]

He had Hortense brought to his privy garden and, taking her to one side, pointed to Mauvières and the boy. 'You see that child', he said. 'Who does he look like?' He was untypically tall for a Bonaparte – Hortense took him to be nine or ten years old, instead of eight, but there was no doubting the likeness. 'It is your son, Sire', she replied. 'He is the image of the King of Rome.' She realized who he was at once, having heard all about him from Caroline. She also guessed what was in Napoleon's mind and said hurriedly: 'I would take care of him myself, with pleasure, but that would give evil tongues an opportunity to wag about me, don't you think?' He agreed, and then took Mauvières aside for a private talk.

Hortense asked the boy whether he was happy at school, and what he played at: he told her that for some time past he and his friends had been having mock battles between the Bourbons and the Bonapartes. 'I am on the king's side,' he said, and when she asked him why: 'because I like the king and I don't like the emperor.' It was clear that he knew nothing of his birth and had not recognized the tubby little man who had been talking to him earlier. Mauvières took him back to Paris and Napoleon went to lunch, marvelling to Hortense all through the meal at the extent to which the boy resembled him.[56]

That afternoon Hortense's banker, Gabriel Delessert, came out from Paris to warn her that enemy patrols were working their way towards St-Germain-en-Laye, thus threatening Napoleon's escape route westward. She took him into the Emperor's study to deliver this disquieting news in person. Since 1812 the Cossack leader, Platov, had been determined to capture and kill Napoleon, offering his daughter in marriage to any of his men who brought him in. Blücher had proclaimed that he would shoot him out of hand as a war criminal. There was no reason why either of them should not carry out their threats, since he had been declared an outlaw by the Congress of Vienna. Only the British could be counted on to spare his life. But he still hoped to avoid surrender by getting away to America – if only he could get a passport to sail from the port of Rochefort, where two ships were being fitted out for him.

Visitors continued to filter out from Paris; and messengers and go-betweens went in the reverse direction, including Charles de Flahaut whom Napoleon sent with a new request to the provisional French government: that he should be granted the use of two naval frigates that he knew to be at Cherbourg. This was refused, but in the early hours of 29 June the Minister of Marine came in person with permission for Napoleon to sail from Rochefort – at his own risk since he had no passport from the Allies. By the time Hortense awoke the minister had come and gone, and she learned that Marya Walewska had also been received by the Emperor. She found Marya in tears and invited her to stay for lunch, so that she could regain her composure before returning to Paris.[57]

Marya had brought her sons with her: Antoine and Alexandre. She asked permission to accompany Napoleon into exile, but he refused. It was an emotional parting – Alexandre later claimed that he had seen tears in Napoleon's eyes – but in truth the affair fell considerably short of high tragedy. This Romeo had no heart to break; and Juliet, taking the two children to Belgium, met there General Philippe d'Ornano, formerly commander of the Imperial Guard, and promptly accepted his proposal of marriage. Their son, Rodolphe-Auguste, was born on 9 June 1817.

Now that he had permission to leave, Napoleon began to wonder whether he could dupe the provisional government into letting him have a final throw at winning his throne back. He went to his room, changed into uniform, and sent off a request to be allowed to resume command of the army in order to defend Paris. The messenger returned with a very sharp 'No' and the Emperor changed back again into civilian clothes, finally resigned to departure. He had already smuggled three million francs to the banker Laffitte to be forwarded to America, but he was not now sure how much money he might need to buy his way out of France. He spoke to Hortense and she offered him her diamonds. 'He consented to take a necklace worth two hundred thousand francs – for which he absolutely insisted on giving me a promissory note, despite my obstinate refusal.'

While the necklace was being sewn into a belt for safe-keeping he ordered his carriages to be brought to the front of the house. When the belt was finished and brought to him he slipped out at the back, across the park, through a door in the wall and into an unmarked yellow barouche that carried him away as fast as its four horses could gallop. He reached Rochefort on 3 July, only to find British warships cruising on guard; on 15 July he surrendered to Captain Maitland of HMS *Bellerophon*.

Chapter Two:
Growing up and Exile

From the window of her hotel room Emilie Pellapra gazed mournfully down on 'our enemies masquerading as our allies'. Her mother taught her to hate the English in particular, not merely because they were the one nation who had consistently thwarted Napoleon's efforts to subjugate Europe, but also because they now held him prisoner. Their soldiers, riding and walking up and down outside the hotel were soon joined by civilians, insatiable travellers, embarking once more on their beloved continental tours. They were as easily identifiable by their dress as the soldiers were by their uniform. Instead of the Frenchwomen's short skirts and enormous hats, these newcomers wore long straight pelisses over dresses whose skirts and bodices blazed in a multitude of clashing colours, their heads crowned with tiny beehive bonnets, while the men, festooned with seal-encrusted watchchains, the tails of their brass-buttoned blue or brown coats dangling to the heels of their short tight pantaloons, were at once distinguishable from the baggy-trousered, black-booted French in their towering top hats. It was the first time Emilie had seen members of this detestable race 'who always lied, except when they took the tiger-cat for their emblem. False as the one, fierce as the other, they have always been treacherous.' In which Emilie was inconsistent as well as unkind, for the lions of England originated in France: in Normandy, Maine and Aquitaine.

After all the upheavals in the administration caused by Bonaparte's two abdications and the Bourbon double return, Emilie's father, Alain Pellapra, had still contrived to fall on his feet. He dug his fortune up from the garden in Caen and moved to Paris, where he soon became an influential figure in the financial world. He took a house in the Rue Joubert, in the fashionable district between the boulevards and the Rue St-Lazare, where Marya Walewska had lodged and where Eleonore Denuelle had given birth to Charles Macon and Hortense to Little Oui-Oui (and just possibly to Auguste de Morny as well). Emilie was provided with a governess, a writing master and a piano teacher, all of whom she disliked in varying degrees; but particularly the governess, whom she found stupid, ignorant and vulgar. This last quality was one that she discerned in almost all her acquaintances. Thanks, no doubt, to her mother's constant talk of Napoleon she seems to have sensed her relationship to him and from early in life regarded herself as Imperial porcelain compared with the common clay around her.

This view was not shared by her father, who rightly supposing that Napoleon would not be allowed to return a second time, no longer took any pains at all to conceal his dislike of the conceited young cuckoo in his nest. Emilie made the painful discovery that it is one thing to be the love-child of the Emperor of the French, but quite another to be the bastard of an exiled tyrant. Often banished to her room for trifling offences, she grew to dread the sound of her father's footsteps along the corridors of the mournful house and the nagging tone of his voice. 'Everything was wrong, everyone was to blame.' He frequently slapped her

63

and was always chiding her – a worse punishment for so vain a little girl. Because of her likeness to Napoleon – a striking inheritance in all four of his children – she was kept indoors as much as possible by Pellapra. Madame Boucher, who spent many months unsuccessfully trying to teach her to play the piano, made way for a sterner disciplinarian, Monsieur Bertini. But Emilie was a stubborn child and had decided that she did not want to learn. Bertini reported that she was idle and not trying. Pellapra took her to his study and beat her. Her long curly hair was shorn to the scalp. She was shut up in her room on the second floor, muttering to herself: 'Well, there's one good thing – I don't have to see my father.'

Eventually this rough handling affected her health. The family doctor, called in to treat her cough, found that she was feverish and warned that she could become seriously ill if she were not given more air and exercise. She was once again allowed to go walking with Denis, the butler, to visit his wife and daughter at Courbevoc, the riverside village on the left bank of the Seine that faced Caroline Murat's former estate at Neuilly; on other days she would walk in the Tuileries gardens, blue-coated, a round black beaver hat on the curls that had now grown into long ringlets again, noting the number of people who turned for a second glance at so beautiful a child. Presently Grandmother Leroy came up from Lyons and took a house on the Quai d'Orsay where Emilie spent long deliciously pampered hours on Sundays.[1]

*

After bidding farewell to Napoleon at Malmaison, Hortense returned to Paris that same evening. The city was seething with plots and counterplots hatched by soldiers and politicians who saw a chance of snatching power or influence. Many came to the house in the Rue Cerutti to discover what Hortense knew of Napoleon's movements and secret plans. After 3 July, the day when Emilie Pellapra watched with horror the British troops marching into Paris, Hortense found herself the object of increasingly violent Royalist demonstrations and threats. She rented a house in the Rue Taitbout facing the bottom of her garden, and moved in under an assumed name with her two boys, who had until now been hidden over the stocking shop in the Boulevard Montmartre. But Hortense was not a woman to wait upon events. Within a couple of days she had rearranged the ground floor of the house in the Rue Cerutti and offered it to the Austrian Commander-in-Chief, Prince von Schwarzenberg, an old acquaintance from the days when he had been Ambassador to Paris. When Schwarzenberg gladly accepted the use of the palatial accommodation for his military headquarters Hortense came back to the snug security of the first floor. Now all that was needed was for Tsar Alexander to gallop to her rescue as he had done a year ago.

He came to visit Schwarzenberg but, to Hortense's chagrin, did not bother to go upstairs. Marya Walewska, who did manage to see him, reported to Hortense that he blamed her 'for all the misfortunes that have befallen France'. Hortense parcelled up the letters Alexander had previously sent her and returned them to him because, she said, she could no longer believe that his expressions of respect and friendship were sincere. It was a clever move, but unsuccessful. Alexander sent a sharp reply by his ambassador, accusing her of having played a political rôle unworthy of a woman. She wrote to him again, and got much the same sort of reply. When a Paris newspaper reported that she had paid him a visit, Alexander went out of his way to have the *Moniteur* publish a denial that she 'had been granted the honour of seeing him'.

By this time she had gone. After ignoring one order to leave by the prefect of police, she received another on the morning of 17 July from the German military governor, giving her only two hours' grace. She set off with the two boys, their servants, including Little Oui-Oui's nursemaid, an equerry and one of Schwarzenberg's aides-de-camp to see them safely through the Austrian lines. It was against the French that she most needed protection. At Dijon, where she arrived three days later, Royalist officers tried to arrest her and anti-Bonaparte crowds demonstrated in the streets outside her hotel. Provided with an escort of four Austrian cavalrymen, she reached Geneva without further embarrassment, and was met there by Louise Cochelet, the boys' tutor, Abbé Bertrand, who had once taught Hortense at Madame Campan's Academy, and other members of her staff, together with the rest of her carriages and baggage. The Swiss did not want her either; she moved on to Aix-les-Bains, where Charles de Flahaut joined her.

Charles was on leave from the 9th Cavalry Division, which he still commanded thanks to the protection of Talleyrand; but though his father's influence had saved him from exile with the other leading Bonapartists he was still being kept under close supervision. The day after his arrival at Aix, the prefect of the department came up the valley from Chambéry ten miles below to warn Hortense that it would be in her best interests to persuade Charles not to stay. She took the prefect's advice. Two days later Flahaut left for Geneva, where he was not allowed to remain, on to Voltaire's village of Ferney, where he was again moved on, and finally out of the mountains down to Lyons.[2]

The Austrians were preparing to withdraw their troops, and Hortense grew fearful of what fate awaited her at the hands of the French and Piedmontese. Already one of Napoleon's marshals, Guillaume Brune, had been assassinated in the Royalist White Terror that raged in Avignon; Charles de la Bédoyère, Hortense's former admirer, venturing back to Paris to visit his pregnant wife, was discovered and shot; her brother-in-law, Caroline's husband Joachim, was captured in southern Italy making an heroic and impractical attempt to regain his Kingdom of Naples and was similarly dispatched before a firing squad. The Allied Powers, who were settling the leading Bonapartists in different districts of different countries, sufficiently distant from each other to ensure that they could not easily collaborate in plotting a second return by Napoleon, suggested Hortense should move to the St-Gallen canton in north-east Switzerland. She was ready enough to go, but the Swiss regarded her as a trouble-maker and refused to have her.

In the midst of these problems, two more blows befell her. After Charles' short visit and forced departure some letters arrived for him at Aix, forwarded from his regiment. Hortense foolishly opened them. They proved to be love letters written by a famous star of the Comédie-Française, Mademoiselle Mars, and it was clear from them that she had been Flahaut's mistress for some time. Hortense knew that Charles was disloyal and had indulged in several affairs with other women, but the recent renewal of their own attachment had raised her sentimental hopes so high that the shock of reading the actress's passionate outpourings broke her down completely. She wrote a letter of reproach to her faithless lover and then fell into a series of fainting fits.[3]

She sat in tearful grief, unable to eat or speak. She was finally shaken out of this depth of despair by the second blow of fate: two of Louis' representatives came to claim possession of his eldest son, Napoleon-Louis. They took the boy off to Italy at the beginning of October, a few days before his eleventh birthday. To make her misery worse, the younger boy, Little Oui-Oui, was suffering from jaundice – though he shortly recovered and went back to his favourite game of marching up and down the courtyard with some friends, banging drums like Uncle Nonon's soldiers (whereupon the neighbours reported that Hortense was secretly raising a regiment).

Although she had made her peace with Madame Mère (now living with her half-brother, Cardinal Fesch, in Rome), Hortense was still at odds with most of her Bonaparte relations, who had not forgiven her for successfully weathering the Royalist return in 1814. She was consequently unwilling to seek shelter in Italy, where Louis, Lucien and Pauline had taken refuge. Caroline, who continued to write to her, was at Trieste, waiting to move to Austria where she was later joined by Jerome; but Austria was too remote for Hortense who was determined not to go far from the frontiers of France. Eventually she determined to try Baden, where Stephanie de Beaharnais' husband had now succeeded as Grand Duke.

It had been a tiring, harassed, bitterly cold nine days of journeying. On the first night she halted at Pregny where, at four o'clock in the morning, she awoke to discover fifty gendarmes searching the house. Three days later, at Morat on the road to Berne, she was arrested and held prisoner in the village inn for forty-eight hours. She was not entirely a victim of pointless persecution, for the Swiss police knew that she had entertained a mysterious stranger during an overnight halt at Payerne (he was General Auguste Ameil, condemned to death in his absence by a French court) and she refused to answer their questions about him. She was finally allowed to continue 'escorted by a Colonel of the Gendarmerie and followed by every spy in the country', as she caustically remarked.

It was a great relief to rumble through the quiet twilit streets of Constance and descend at the Eagle Hotel; but she soon discovered that her problems were not at an end. A chamberlain from the Grand Duke called on her and pointed out that Bonaparte's relations – 'members of the Imperial family' as Hortense still insisted on putting it – were not allowed to reside in any territories other than those governed by the Four Great Powers, Austria (which included northern Italy), Britain, Prussia and Russia. Fortunately, she was able to counter this bleak reception with the passport permitting her to stay in Constance. A few weeks later she moved into a house by the lakeside with her sixteen companions: her chambermaid and valet de chambre, Martin Lacroix and his wife, a cook and footman, a second valet de chambre, a coachman and groom; Little Oui-Oui and his nurse, Madame Bure; Louise Cochelet, with her own chambermaid and another servant; her equerry and the Abbé Bertrand, each with his own servant. She furnished the house with pieces she had sent from Paris to Pregny, but it had none of the comfort or splendour of the palace in the Rue Cerutti. 'An ill-built shanty,' Louise Cochelet said with a shiver of disgust, 'and so many windows let into it that it's more like a lantern.' Instead of a marble staircase, this one was of wood, leading to a gallery that served the half-dozen first-floor rooms, 'draughty and whitewashed',[4] all of which were soon overcrowded since Hortense encouraged her retinue to send for their children and relations to join them.

From Chancellor Metternich, an old acquaintance who had conquered many frail hearts in Paris during his embassy there between 1806 and 1809, she received a passport and an invitation to settle on an estate near Bregenz at the Austrian-controlled eastern end of Lake Constance, but Hortense was wary of getting entangled in that net, even though, as she said, 'my children are cousins of the Austrian Emperor's grandson'. Because she could not resist meddling in political intrigue under cover of charity, she was constantly in touch with refugees banished from France under the law of 12 January 1816, most of them the 'Regicides' who had voted the death penalty for Louis XVI. Royalist spies, who had her under observation, reported during the summer that, although she had ceased to receive the exiles openly, she was still in communication with them, through Oui-Oui's tutor, Abbé Bertrand.

Though Père la Violette was far away this spring, she enjoyed walking among the violets in the woodlands that sloped up from the lakeside, sadly recalling the bouquet of Parma violets – her favourite flowers – that used to be brought to her breakfast table at St-Leu. She dreamed of building a house among the trees and clearing a garden in which to grow new violets and roses. She dreamed of having Charles by her side, for she now deeply missed him and was willing to forgive. After her discovery of his affair with Mademoiselle Mars, he had obtained a passport for Germany and quit Lyons for Besançon, where he was detained until an order for his release came from Paris. He left Besançon in November 1815, but when he reached the

Rhine, instead of turning upstream, which would have brought him to Constance, he went down to Frankfurt and from there to Rotterdam. The next that Hortense heard from him was that he had arrived in England, was well received but could think of nothing except how he might get back to her.[5]

It might have been possible to arrange. Throughout 1816 Louis begged Hortense to join him in asking the Pope for a divorce on the ground that he had been forced into the marriage. This renewed eagerness to be separated from Hortense was brought on by his own desire to remarry; but the Roman Church had no reason to love the Bonapartes and no inclination to grant Louis' request. He continued to argue until 1819 and, if Hortense had supported the application, he might have succeeded. She, however, was fearful of losing all control of her children if the marriage was annulled; and, as time went on, she realized that Charles, despite his protestations, did not intend to return to her.[6] When he arrived in London he was fêted by the pro-Bonapartist Hollands and Russells and soon met Margaret Mercer Elphinstone, the daughter of Admiral Lord Keith and granddaughter of Dr Johnson's friend, Mrs Thrale. Miss Elphinstone, a rather plain young woman in her twenty-eighth year, was a close friend of Princess Charlotte. She set her cap at Flahaut, despite her father's objections, and Charles was shortly to tell Hortense that, in accordance with his promise to have no secrets from her, he had to admit that he had attracted the favourable attention of a young person who, in addition to other desirable qualities, was richly endowed with independent means. He still, of course, wished for nothing better than to rejoin Hortense, and was waiting for his passport.... She told him he must follow the dictates of his heart. He repeated that he loved her, but his friends advised him it could be a great mistake to leave England at that moment.

She knew very well it was all over, but could not bring herself to admit it. Louise Cochelet had recently made a pilgrimage to the Shrine of the Black Virgin at Einsiedeln; Hortense journeyed up the wild mountain road to the Benedictine abbey in October 1816 and, in a highly emotional scene, made a full confession. The abbot urged her to renounce her lover.[7] In June 1817 Charles married his rich Miss Elphinstone in Edinburgh. It was stipulated in the marriage contract that any children of the marriage were to be brought up as Protestants and British subjects.

*

From the moment that the deposed Emperor, now General Bonaparte again, set foot on St Helena, three months after his surrender to Captain Maitland, he concentrated all his energy and cunning to giving the world a highly distorted picture of himself; at present a harmless prisoner tortured by inhuman gaolers, and in the past a liberal and pacific leader freely chosen by the French people to protect them and their revolutionary reforms against the spite and enmity of the autocratic rulers of the rest of Europe. He calculated that if the first lie did not result in his being allowed back to Europe, then the second might help his son to seize the throne of France at some time in the future. He wildly miscalculated the extent of the fear and loathing that he had aroused and never seems to have understood that the Austrians had taken complete control of the mind as well as the body of his son. Admittedly, there were small groups of people in England determined to demonstrate their superior intellect and finer sensibilities by protesting against the treatment of this criminal, while entirely ignoring the millions of dead and the miseries of the crippled men he had scattered across the face of Europe. It was with the help of these supporters – the Hollands and Russells prominent among them – that secret communications with St Helena were established, sending clandestine correspondence into the island, bringing propaganda pamphlets out. There was little support for them in their own country, none in the unhappy lands that had been ravaged by Bonaparte's armies. But their activities disturbed the authorities and, as so often happens, did more harm than good to their protégé's cause.

There was a continuing alarm about escape plots.[8] The smuggling of messages to Europe and America began as soon as Bonaparte arrived at St Helena, and continued despite the frequent deportation of those caught in the act of receiving or transmitting information. Plans for escape or rescue were in hand within twelve months. Hortense probably played a part in some of these. The Bonaparte clan was, with one exception, noisily ineffective. Napoleon had been an awkward brother, bossy, bad-tempered, forever ordering everybody about and, at the slightest protest, ranting about their lack of gratitude; on the other hand he was the source of all the family's undreamed-of good fortune. And there lay the difficulty, for deprived of his support they were powerless to act.

Consequently, most of the work devolved on Joseph. He was the only senior member of the family who had managed to escape to America, from where a rescue attempt could best be mounted, and he had managed to get away with a large amount of money – probably one million francs – as well as valuable paintings and jewellery, including the Spanish crown jewels. He had put his estate at Mortefontaine in the name of his sister-in-law the Queen of Sweden; buried in the park of his Swiss home were diamonds worth five million francs. Bonaparte himself had money deposited with French and British banks, and had secretly brought with him a quarter of a million francs concealed in money belts that he distributed among his companions before his surrender and collected again on arrival at the island.

This did not prevent him from selling some of his silverware during the last three months of 1816, claiming that he was forced to do so since the grant of £8,000 a year paid to him through the governor, Sir Hudson Lowe, was not enough to keep him.[9] The trick worked and his allowance was increased to £12,000; he tried a more dramatic version the following year, ordering one of the servants to take his bed outside, smash it up, and tell enquirers he had been forced to do so because they were short of firewood[10] – but this aroused more smiles than sympathy. The *Anti-Gallican*, a magazine published in London by a double-traitor named Lewis Goldsmith, carried a coded message from Bonaparte's supporters in Europe (perhaps his mother, or Hortense – they were never identified): 'The rumour of the sale of your silver had made a great sensation here. It is a great blunder on your part. You certainly cannot be pressed for money, since Joseph has promised us he will provide for all your needs.'[11] He paid no attention to the rebuke and continued his campaign against Hudson Lowe. 'Everything I say about him and his bad treatment of me,' he told General Gourgaud, 'and his intention to poison me, will be believed.'[12]

The Cabinets of the former Allies were agitated by the rumours of preparation for escape – or more usually rescue – for the first three years' of Napoleon's captivity on St

Helena. But it is doubtful whether Bonaparte ever intended to take the risk of evading the guard on the island and facing an encounter with the much-feared British navy. He kept up the war of pamphlets to the end, smuggling them out on merchant ships, or in the personal belongings of those of his companions who returned to Europe. By 1819 his interest evidently lay less in his own return to power than in the fabrication of the legend of his benign dictatorship that might, in time, establish his son on the throne of France. He was slowing down – 'as fat and round as a china pig'[13] – by the autumn of 1820. Early the following year his health began to decline; he was suffering from cancer of the stomach, a common ailment in the Bonaparte family. On 5 May 1821 he died.

*

The news arrived in Vienna on 16 July. When Bonaparte's son was told that afternoon, he burst into tears which continued throughout the following day, but the loss of a father whom he last saw when he was three years old cannot have meant a great deal to him. Though he bore a recognizable facial resemblance to his father, he was by now almost entirely Austrian. Of the vast household appointed to serve him at his birth, governors, assistant governesses, masters of the horse, physicians, first women (in purple), second women (in black) – a careful copy of the traditional establishment for a dauphin – not one remained. All had been sent home so that he should not be contaminated with French voices, French customs, French words. 'Chan-Chan' his nurse, the peasant mother of Bonaparte's premier valet de chambre, Marchand, outlasted all the others, but at the end of February 1816 she too had to say goodbye. While Marie-Louise moved into her Principality of Parma, living openly with the seductive one-eyed Neipperg, the boy remained in Vienna, tutored by two Austrians who were instructed never to allow him to speak any language other than German. He lost his first name, Napoleon, and the remainder were Germanized into Franz Josef Karl. He long ago ceased to be the King of Rome; in 1817 he was deprived of the succession to his mother's Duchies of Parma and Pianza; in 1818 his grandfather, Kaiser Franz, created him Duke of Reichstadt with the title of Most Serene Highness, giving him the right to rank immediately after the Hapsburg princes and archdukes, and estates that would bring him the equivalent of half a million francs a year.

He spent each winter in the Hofburg, the great palace complex within the city; with the coming of summer he was escorted back to the seclusion of Schönbrunn. After his father's death he was allowed to take lessons in French on alternate days, but he spoke the language with a marked German accent. In August each year he went on holiday with the Imperial family to the Castle of Persenbeug higher up the Danube. There he had the opportunity to see his mother, who bore three illegitimate children before Neipperg became a widower in 1821, thus enabling her to marry him. She had regained her plumpness and got rid of the cough that had seemed to threaten an early death from consumption.[14] The young Duke of Reichstadt showed no resentment of his half-brother and sisters, or of his adulterous stepfather, but when he asked for permission to go and live with his mother it was refused.

The tidings of Bonaparte's death almost certainly brought less grief to him than they had to Hortense. She was after all the Emperor's adopted daughter as well as his sister-in-law. She had known him all her adult life. Despite her equivocal manoeuvres during the First Restoration, she had probably loved him as loyally as she could love anybody apart from her sons. The news came at a moment when she believed that she had at last found peace in a settled home. In the summer of 1816 she had obtained permission to visit her brother Eugene in Bavaria, where Little Oui-Oui spent a joyful holiday romping with his five Beauharnais cousins, but on her return to Constance she was warned that she could not remain indefinitely: the Allies, suspicious anew of 'her mode of living and the apparent extent of her correspondence', which they evidently linked with the plots to rescue Bonaparte, were putting pressure on the Grand Duke of Baden.

Apart from the sense of continued harassment, the ban did not unduly worry her, for she was by now quite eager to leave Constance, with its memories of her plans for making a permanent home there with Charles. In January 1817 she bought the castle of Arenenberg – a corruption of Narrenberg, the Mountain of Fools, and in her own words it was 'very small, very dilapidated, but sited in a picturesque position' – overlooking the Rhine where it flows out of Lake Constance.[15] It was on the left bank of the river, in the Canton of Thurgau, so the Swiss government was once more confronted with demands from Paris that Hortense should not be allowed to settle there. While the argument went on, and the castle was refurbished, Hortense obtained permission from Eugene's father-in-law, the King of Bavaria, to buy a house in Augsburg, to which she moved in May 1817.

Later that year her husband allowed their elder son, Napoleon-Louis, to spend two months with her at Augsburg; and in the summer of 1818 she took young Louis-Napoleon (Oui-Oui) with her to Leghorn, where she had been recommended to try the sea-baths. Louis, who was also taking baths at the inland spa of Montecatini, brought Napoleon-Louis over to Leghorn for what proved to be an emotional reunion, the two boys throwing themselves at their parents' feet and begging them to end the separation which had now lasted for eight years. The plea was in vain. Hortense took Louis-Napoleon back to Augsburg with her in October.[16]

She now gave serious thought to the boy's education. He had been brought up in an environment of anxiety and persecution, with the knowledge that he and his mother were banned from ever entering their native country. His formal education, by the gentle bumbling Abbé Bertrand, who still called him Little Oui-Oui, was, as his father had pointed out, poor and patchy; he was largely undisciplined. The daughter of Hortense's valet de chambre and chambermaid, who was his constant childhood companion, remembered him as 'witty, full of repartee, but a slow learner and so mentally idle that one lost patience with him'. He was 'gentle as a lamb', though on the rare occasions when he quarrelled he did not slap or punch her as a boy would, but pinched and bit. 'He would throw himself into the arms of the first comer, showering caresses on them without rhyme or reason, which made people say he had a warm, loving heart. Nothing of the kind; as soon as you were out of sight he forgot you.'

Hortense relieved the abbé of his duties and appointed a new tutor, Philippe Le Bas. When Le Bas, a level-headed and conscientious young man, took up his post in the summer of 1820 he found that his twelve-year-old pupil had 'natural aptitude but has not made much progress – he has been taught only one thing: a distaste for study.... I have at least found more docility than I expected, a desire to please me, a fear of dissatisfying me, and an excellent nature.'[17]

Louis-Napoleon was, indeed, a kindhearted boy. One snowy winter's day when he was playing the garden he saw a poor family pass the gate and, touched by the raggedness of their clothes, gave his jacket to one child and his shoes to another. He was courageous, too. A year or two later, when he was staying at Mannheim with his Baden cousins, one of the girls lost a flower from her hair, which the wind carried into the Neckar. Without hesitating Louis-Napoleon gallantly dived fully clothed into the river and retrieved the flower.[18] It was a typically romantic gesture, inviting the affection that he always craved. He was at heart a solitary, withdrawn, rather unhappy soul – still the same Little Oui-Oui, lovable, acquiescent but persistent; eager to please everybody yet still go his own way; 'gently stubborn', as his mother said.

He owed his skill as a swimmer directly to Le Bas, who immediately introduced a strict timetable which was aimed as much at building up the child's rather delicate body as developing his mind. In summer he had him up at 6 a.m. every morning for an hour's walk, gave him physical recreation from 8.30 a.m. to 9 a.m., taught him to swim from 3 p.m. to 4 p.m., and took him out for more walking from 7 p.m. to 8 p.m. The rest of the time, except for two hours at lunch and one hour for dinner, was filled with lessons in French grammar and literature, arithmetic, geography, history, German, Latin and Greek, with a final hour of revision when he returned from his walk at 8 p.m. until he went to bed at 9 p.m. Hortense often presided at these evening revisions or readings from the classics; she also taught him to sketch and to dance. But she liked to travel and, when at home, to entertain her friends (among them two officers who fought a duel over her and set scandalous tongues wagging) so that her influence over Louis-Napoleon's education decreased during Le Bas' tutorship. When Le Bas suggested that the boy should spend some hours each week at the Augsburg High School, where he would benefit from the company and competition of other boys, she readily agreed.

She was visiting Baden when the news of Napoleon's death reached her in mid-July 1821. Bertrand, who remained as her chaplain although he had lost his post as tutor, wrote to Le Bas in Augsburg, telling him to break the news to Louis-Napoleon and give him three days' holiday to recover from the shock. Hortense had by now been granted permission by the Swiss authorities to take up residence at Arenenberg and spent several months there each year, but at Le Bas' suggestion she left Louis-Napoleon at Augsburg to continue his education uninterrupted. She had also resumed a much more regal state. At the Augsburg house 'one masked ball followed another,' remarked her friend the Countess of Kielmannsegge. At these Hortense always appeared in some form of harem costume as an odalisque. When not in fancy dress she took to wearing a crown, encouraged her visitors to address her as 'Your Majesty', and was the centre of a formal royal circle at her Thursday receptions. The plays that she delighted to present and appear in were performed on a stage flanked by a painting of the Crucifixion on one side and of Napoleon crossing the St-Bernard Pass on the other.

Meanwhile the Bourbons had once again demonstrated their unparalleled talent for doing the wrong thing in the wrong way, thus losing the support of most of the French population and of the army in particular. There had been an attempted military coup in August 1820; in 1821 several garrisons mutinied and demanded the return of the Duke of Reichstadt as Napoleon II. These uprisings were repeated in the following year; and in 1823 a whole battalion of dissidents tried to win over a French army marching into Spain with shouts of *Vive Napoléon!* Old fat Louis XVIII was teetering on the edge of the grave and his ultra-reactionary brother, Charles, could be counted on to arouse more hatred for the Royalist cause. If Napoleon II did inherit his father's throne, then Hortense was sure of obtaining a prominent place at Court; but she had reason to expect much more than the honourable status of the new Emperor's aunt. It was common knowledge that the Duke of Reichstadt's health was suspect. If he were to die, then the succession had already been established by Napoleon in his edict of 1804: Joseph was to succeed, and then his sons and, failing them, Louis and his sons. But Joseph had only daughters; his estranged overplain wife was beyond further childbearing but hale enough to prevent his remarrying. So the chances were very good indeed that the Imperial crown would one day descend upon the head of one of Hortense's two sons. No wonder she began to revive a little Imperial protocol.

She also bethought herself of making an immediate claim on the Imperial estate. She wrote to two of Napoleon's executors, Bertrand and Montholon, requesting payment of the bill for 200,000 francs that he had given her in exchange for her diamonds at Malmaison. There was an embarrassed silence for more than a year. Hortense asked the former controller of her household to press the claim. He replied in June 1823, as tactfully as he could, that the diamond necklace had been given by Napoleon a short time before his death to his third executor, Marchand. It had now been examined by two jewellers who set its value at 80,000 francs; in the circumstances, the executors felt it best to buy it back from Marchand for 80,000 francs and return it to Hortense.[19] There remained the unspoken suspicion that when Hortense had let Napoleon have the diamonds in his hour of need she had overvalued them by 250 per cent.

Her third and youngest son was growing up in Paris unseen by her and, for the first dozen years of his life, without knowingly setting eyes on his father, but the boy seemed to suffer little from this parental neglect. A pretty child, with blue eyes and blond curls, he was petted and pampered by his paternal grandmother, Baroness de Souza; he was provided with ample money through Gabriel Delessert, his mother's banker who, after the death of Demorny in April 1814, was appointed joint guardian with the de Souzas.[20] Malicious tongues said that his grandmother had no real love for him (which was certainly false) and brought him up in her home in order to get control of the money Hortense had put in trust for him (which may have a germ of truth, since she was a notorious spendthrift). If so, the boy probably got good value.[21] In an atmosphere of well-mannered immorality and literary elegance he grew into just the sort of young man he wanted to be, idle but sharp-witted, expert in nothing, graceful at everything. The particle came aristocratically adrift from his surname. As Auguste de Morny he walked, talked, behaved, acquired the interests of a man of noble birth: a delight to the romantic Adelaide de Souza.

As far as his immediate family was concerned, the fiction of his adoption, which cannot have deceived him for long, was entirely dropped when he was in his teens and Charles de Flahaut admitted his paternity; the more readily perhaps because in the six years from 1819 to 1825 Margaret Elphinstone bore him five daughters but no son. Charles continued to correspond with Hortense, and it is possible that when he met her in Aix in the summer of 1829 he took their seventeen-year-old son with him. (Four years earlier, when Adelaide de Souza was widowed for the second time, Hortense sent to her 'a thousand caresses for you and your child,'[22] which must have meant Auguste.) Certainly, Auguste accompanied Charles to Scotland in the following month, July, to spend a holiday with Margaret and the girls. In Paris the Flahauts had taken a large house in the Rue du Faubourg St-Honoré, later moving to a mansion on the corner of the Avenue des Champs Elysées in what is now the Rue La Boétie. Here Margaret presided as hostess to a great number of Bonapartist supporters. Auguste was often seen there; 'a charming spark, né Hortense, and domesticated at Flahaut's' as the British ambassador's wife, Lady Granville, noted in January 1832. Another frequent guest was Alexandre Walewski, eighteen months older than Auguste and a few steps ahead of him on the path to dandyism.

*

Marya Walewska did not long survive her marriage to Count d'Ornano. Their son Rodolphe was born in June 1817; she returned with her husband to Paris in October; and she died there on 11 December 1817.[23] Her brother, Theodore Laczynski, became the guardian of the two Walewski boys, Antoine and Alexandre, and took them off to his Polish estate where he ruled in considerable feudal splendour. After a couple of years, during which they studied under a private tutor, he sent the pair to a boarding school at Geneva. Here Antoine died leaving Alexandre as sole inheritor of a considerable fortune.[24]

The Tsar ordered that Alexandre should return to Poland, where a closer eye could be kept on him. His true parentage and the romantic legends of his mother's sacrifice in the hope of freeing Poland from Russian domination made him a potential rallying point for a new liberation movement. 'Never let young Walewski go to France,' the Tsar warned his brother and viceroy, the Grand Duke Constantine. For a time it seemed that Alexandre had no desire to leave Poland. From the age of fifteen, when his uncle, Theodore, resigned his guardianship, Alexandre enjoyed the life of a grand seigneur; but the Russian authorities soon confirmed their suspicion that the guests at his lavish parties included the most fervent Polish patriots and that he was becoming a living symbol of nationalist aspirations.

The constant supervision began to irk him. He needed to leave Poland simply because he was forbidden to do so. He bought a false passport which carried him to St Petersburg, where he was soon traced by the police. They ordered him back to Warsaw but he gave his escort the slip, fled to Kronstadt and found refuge on an English ship which took him to London, whence he crossed over to Paris to live with his stepfather, Count d'Ornano.

Through Ornano the young man was soon in touch with those of Napoleon's old generals who had managed to survive the Bourbon purge: Sébastiani, Gérard and Charles de Flahaut. It was at one of Madame Flahaut's soirées that the Count de Castellane first saw Alexandre in November 1827 and was at once struck by the fact that he had Napoleon's 'eyes and voice' but was 'taller and very well made'. Castellane was descended from the old aristocracy (his mother was a Rohan-Chabot); under his sponsorship Alexandre moved across the Seine to the ancient noble quarter of the Faubourg St-Germain, where the Duchess of Gramont introduced him to the most exclusive salons. Through the Countess de Girardin, whose husband, Stanislas, was Master of the Horse to Charles X, he gained an entrée to Court circles and became a close friend of the Duke of Chartres, the eldest son of the Duke of Orleans. In the more raffish sections of high society he fell in with the dandy Count Alfred d'Orsay; when d'Orsay and his cousin, the Count de Guiche, founded the Cercle de l'Union in the Rue Gramont, on the model of the English clubs in Mayfair, Alexandre was one of the first members to be elected. Here he learned to gamble and acquired a taste for horse-racing. Like his friend, Auguste de Morny, he became a typical young man-about-town.[25]

*

Franz, Duke of Reichstadt, Alexandre's half-brother, was growing up into a personable young man, with his mother's attractive blue eyes and tight golden curls, though the heaviness of his head, the over-plump chin and rather beaky nose betrayed his Bonaparte blood. He had a disturbing habit of breaking out into an inexplicable sweat from time to time and needing to lie down and rest, but this was attributed by his doctors to his having outgrown his strength. In the summer of 1838, when he was seventeen, Franz was gazetted captain in a light infantry regiment. That same year his cousin, Napoleone Camerata, Elisa Bonaparte's daughter, saw him walking in the street and, leaning from her carriage window, shouted: 'Aren't you ashamed to wear Austrian uniform?'

He was not. Indeed, he clearly rather liked the look of himself in his tight white jacket with the deep wing collar and black tie. He entered wholeheartedly into his military training, and in the summer of 1829 he took part in his first full-scale manoeuvre as a company commander. He passed a formal military examination in March 1830, but the Kaiser would not yet let him join his unit for regular service. The sweating and coughing seemed to be getting worse. In damp chilly weather his circulation was affected by some undiagnosed malady and he had to stay indoors – a great disappointment to him, since he delighted in riding through the streets and in being recognized by passers-by. On his grandfather's orders he was not officially launched into Imperial society when he came of age on his eighteenth birthday, 20 March 1829, but hopes for an improvement in his health were raised by the appointment of a new physician, Dr Malfatti, brought from Italy in May 1830.[26]

*

In 1823 Hortense had to repay her husband's gesture of letting Napoleon-Louis holiday with her by sending Louis-Napoleon to join him at Marienbad for a month. In the late autumn, after Louis had returned to Rome, Hortense also went to spend the winter there, enjoying greater freedom from restraint by the Allied Powers now that Napoleon was dead. She was followed by Louis-Napoleon, brought by an increasingly disgruntled Le Bas who complained that the boy 'goes to bed late, gets up late, does a little slipshod work until luncheon, goes riding at midday and returns tired at 3 p.m., yawns through his lessons till 5 p.m. and then goes off to spend the rest of the day with his father'. From now on, for several years, Le Bas continued to protest that the constant travelling was seriously interfering with Louis-Napoleon's studies: 'Always journeys and talk of journeys. Even when they are not travelling the Prince's work is held up – because they are getting ready to travel.'[27] Hortense agreed that it was all very unsatisfactory – and carried on exactly as before.

Working conditions for the unhappy Le Bas became worse. In 1824 Hortense's beloved brother Eugene died, followed next year by his father-in-law, the King of Bavaria. Deprived of royal protection, she decided to give up the Augsburg house and in future spend her time between Arenenberg and Rome, where Paulette Bonaparte, who died in June 1825, had left her beautiful Villa Paolina to Napoleon-Louis. Hortense made it a centre of brilliant entertainment, reviving even her celebrated quadrilles from the Imperial heyday. Louis-Napoleon, freed from the remnant of discipline enforced at Augsburg High School, entered with great enthusiasm into Roman social life, and Le Bas was discharged. He was succeeded by Narcisse Vieillard, a former artillery officer and frostbitten veteran of the Moscow campaign, who had tutored Napoleon-Louis and was destined to become one of Louis-Napoleon's closest friends.

Hortense's dreams of a great future for her sons glowed brighter when Joseph, the smoothest, most cautious, and most influential of the surviving Bonapartes, sent his younger daughter Charlotte to Europe to be married. He had been very annoyed a year or two before when his wife hurried their other girl, Zenaide, into marriage with one of Lucien's children, from a notoriously unreliable family. This time he had made it quite clear who was to be Charlotte's husband: Hortense's elder son. Hortense was delighted. It meant that Napoleon-Louis would get a hand on a great deal of Joseph's very large fortune. Much more significantly it meant that wise old Joseph was himself foreseeing the time when Napoleon-Louis might step into the shoes of the Duke of Reichstadt as Pretender to the Imperial throne.

Napoleon-Louis was a handsome young man, dark, carefully dressed, very devoted to his mother despite having been largely brought up by his father, and deeply influenced by his younger brother, whom he described, in a phrase that would have astounded Philippe Le Bas, as 'a profound thinker'. Observers claimed to see strong Bonaparte resemblances in Napoleon-Louis' face and build, but it was impossible to find any at all in Louis-Napoleon: a trace of Beauharnais here and there perhaps, but of Bonaparte nothing, except for a similarity in height to the Emperor.

Louis-Napoleon had his mother's fair hair and grey-blue eyes, often contemplative and distant, but capable of kindling to interest and affection; his features were impassive, betraying neither thought nor emotion; his upbringing in Switzerland and Germany had given him a guttural accent and nasal intonation which increased with the years. He was well-mannered, still the gentle Little Oui-Oui, diffident, yet capable of quite unexpected bursts of boldness. He was indolent yet evidently intelligent. He was seldom seen to lose his temper or his courage. From Napoleon, that dimly remembered Uncle Nonon whom his mother had trained him to revere, he had absorbed the doctrine that all men were corruptible; from his mother he had learned the arts of dissimulation and duplicity. By her he had been indoctrinated with the belief that a high destiny awaited him. 'Because of your name you will always be important', she told him. 'Always be on the lookout for an opportunity.… One can imagine a twist of fate anywhere that could raise the heir of a great and famous name to the heights.… After the King of Rome, you and your brother are the Heirs of Napoleon.'

He was low in stature – a little above five feet three inches and ill-proportioned, with a long body and short legs, so that he appeared normal and even imposing when riding a horse or seated behind a desk, but verging on grotesqueness when he walked. He had a high forehead and a sharp military-style moustache. The one feature of his face that was inescapably noticeable was his nose; a great dominant wedge of a nose without any recognizable ancestry on either side of the family. The Bonaparte nose was beaky and smallish; the Beauharnais nose, which Hortense had inherited, was long and mournfully curved (and Josephine's was near-retroussé); but Louis-Napoleon's was bold and aggressively triangular, a cuneiform scriber like nobody's at all: except perhaps Charles de Flahaut's, who had not been seen for years, and was scarcely a memory to those in Hortense's entourage – save for Hortense herself, who met him again at Aix in the summer of 1829.

In April of that year Louis-Napoleon came of age. He was a familiar figure in Rome, galloping through the streets when he was not practising with sword or pistol: 'A very good horseman, proficient at athletic games and, although short, very active and muscular,' said Lord Malmesbury, who encountered him at the time. He regularly won the rifle-shooting prize in Thurgau and, in 1830, he joined the Military School for Officers at Thun in the Canton of Berne, where he studied artillery and engineering, marching ten or twelve leagues a day, with his pack on his back, sleeping in a tent at the foot of a glacier.[28]

*

The decree of banishment of January 1816 on all close members of the Bonaparte family did not apply to Napoleon's illegitimate children; but young Charles Macon, Eleonore Denuelle's boy, had plenty of troubles without that, for Eleonore's first husband, the dishonest and unscrupulous Jean Revel, involved him in a series of unsavoury law-suits and disguised attempts at blackmail that dragged on for years.[29] In December 1814, Revel brought a suit for revocation of the divorce that Eleonore had been granted in 1806. He dropped it during the Hundred Days, then revived it in December 1815. Although the courts rejected his appeal, he ignored the verdict and, having obtained confirmation from the Ministry of War in December 1817 that Captain Augier's death during the 1812 retreat had never been officially certified, he accused Eleonore of having committed bigamy in marrying Augier while he, Revel, was still her husband, and trigamy in marrying Luxburg while both Revel and Augier were alive.

In the spring of 1819 Revel involved the twelve-year-old Charles Macon directly for the first time by bringing a suit in disavowal of paternity – a lengthy business because he could not take action against a minor, and he therefore had first to persuade a magistrate to order the appointment of a Family Council, which in turn appointed as guardian one of Eleonore's uncles – against whom the suit could be brought. This new manoeuvre seems to have been a put-up job between Revel and the Denuelles, since they had nothing to do with the upbringing of the boy, who was still in the care of Baron de Mauvières.

Revel skirmished on through the courts with no other result than his own impoverishment. But the publicity that he obtained – he put out a pamphlet bluntly entitled *Bonaparte and Murat, Ravishers of Young Women* – was painful for the boy and embarrassing for Mauvières. After Napoleon's death, having still failed to obtain judgement in the courts, Revel approached Mauvières with a proposal that had no doubt been in his mind all along. If the baron would pay him an annuity of 3,600 francs he would drop the suit, at any rate until the boy came of age. The baron bargained him down to 1,200 francs and agreement was reached, but only very briefly; when Revel's demand for an immediate advance of 300 francs was not met, he began litigation all over again.

It had been a fatiguing business for Mauvières, who was now in his sixty-eighth year. In October 1821 he obtained authorization to hand over his guardianship to his son-in-law, Meneval, and to the appointment of a new Family Council.[30] Like Meneval, the members of this council were all staunch Bonapartists, and included Count Lavalette, Postmaster-General of the Empire, Baron Las Cases, who spent a year in captivity with Napoleon and was at the moment preparing his best-selling *Mémorial de Ste-Hélène*, which did so much to promote the Napoleonic Legend; and Baron Denon the former Director-General of the National Museums. In the following April, when the boy was sixteen, Meneval and the Family Council decided to let him begin to take over his own affairs, providing him with an allowance of 12,000 francs a year and a tutor who lived with him in an apartment in the Rue de Crébillon by the Odeon Theatre. The tutor's name was Vieillard, and it seems possible that this was the same Narcisse Vieillard who had recently tutored Napoleon-Louis and was shortly to tutor Louis-Napoleon, for the position with Charles Macon was not destined to last long.[31]

Charles had developed a strong interest in the mother whom he could not remember ever having seen, and who was now living at Mannheim. Like so many events in Eleonore Denuelle's life, her third marriage had brought with it elements of mystery and deceit. Her new husband called himself Count Karl August Emil von Luxburg, but the only genuine Count von Luxburg known to the reference books of nobility was named Friedrich Christian Johann and, moreover, was married to a lady with the sturdily Teutonic name of Maria von Gumppenberg-Pöttmes. Karl August, however, had succeeded in getting himself a post as manager of the Court Theatre in the Grand Duchy of Baden – probably through the interest of Hortense's cousin, Stephanie de Beauharnais, who had been one of Eleonore's schoolfriend sponsors at her marriage to Revel and was, since her husband's death in 1818, the Dowager Grand Duchess. From Mannheim, Eleonore sent a confidential agent to Paris who contacted Charles Macon and agreed on a plan with him that his tutor knew nothing about – until the evening of 11 January 1823, when Vieillard took Charles to the Théâtre du Gymnase in the Boulevard de Bonne-Nouvelle.

It was a new and fashionable theatre, destined to be famous as the setting for many successes by popular playwrights including Scribe, who was the author of that night's attraction – an operetta on the Aladdin theme, *La Petite Lampe Merveilleuse*. At the interval Charles excused himself and left the auditorium. He continued out of the theatre into the street where Eleonore's man was waiting with a travelling carriage. The driver whipped up the horses; the carriage rattled off eastward. When Vieillard discovered that his pupil was missing he at once informed Meneval and Meneval called for assistance from the prefect of police. But the pair were well on their way, heading for Strasbourg and thence down the Rhine to Mannheim for the long-delayed reunion.[32]

A week after the evasion Meneval wrote to Luxburg, protesting at the deceitful way in which the young man had been spirited away, and hinting at legal action. His letter crossed one from Eleonore, asking for 10,000 francs a year to continue her son's education. Revel, living above a baker's shop in the Rue Saint-Honoré and aghast at the prospect of his only steady source of income disappearing for ever, wrote to Meneval offering to drop his suit for non-paternity if Meneval would resume the 1,200 franc annuity agreed with Mauvières. Meneval accepted, and gave him an interim payment of 350 francs, and Revel promptly approached the Family Council for more.

There could be no doubt in Eleonore's mind that Charles was her son – and Napoleon's. The boy was taller, leaner than his father, his features rather stronger, but the Bonaparte nose and swarthy skin were unmistakable, and there was a gleam of violence in his eyes that betrayed the Bonaparte passion for vendetta. He made no secret of his true parentage and adopted in public the name that he already had the habit of using in private; the two final syllables of his real father's first name, Leon, to which he presently added the title of count. He spent part of the summer in a leisurely tour to the mouth of the Rhine and back, and then enrolled as a student at Heidelberg University. Meneval accepted the inevitable and, though not abdicating his role as guardian, agreed to let Leon remain in his mother's care and to provide him with money.

When Napoleon drew up his secret will a few days before his death, he expressed a wish that Leon should take up the law as a profession. But Leon showed no great aptitude for study, though he practised earnestly with sword and pistol, and in 1825 he decided to apply for a commission in the army of Baden. Stephanie's son, the Grand Duke Ludwig, required proof that the candidate had the necessary means to support his position as an officer, so Meneval was called upon to reveal Leon's financial standing. It was good: the original twenty canal shares were bringing in an average of 12,000 francs a year; both Mauvières and Meneval had kept their ward's expenses well within his income and the surplus, invested in the Grand-Livre, the French equivalent of Consols, currently amounted to 13,000 francs at 5 per cent. But by the time that Meneval's letter reached Baden Leon had changed his mind, as he was so often to do throughout his life. His mother, not yet thirty-eight, was expecting another child; there was talk of his stepfather, Luxburg, moving from the Grand Duchy. He decided to explore the other side of his lineage.

In April 1826 he turned up in Rome bearing a letter from Meneval to Madame Mère, introducing 'the young Leon, in whom the Emperor took a fatherly interest'.[33] His reception was polite but not enthusiastic, though Hortense entertained him at the Villa Paolina and romantically presented him with a lucky button which she urged him to wear 'in times of danger'. He returned to Paris, where he settled himself in an apartment in the Rue de la Paix, a comfortably-off young bachelor, but one with a nagging feeling that he was not profiting as much as he should from his distinguished though left-handed paternity. Meneval submitted the accounts of his stewardship, Leon took charge of his own affairs and, to forestall any further skirmishing, doubled Revel's annuity to 2,400 francs.

*

As Emilie Pellapra approached her teens life became less miserable for her. She had always had the consolation of her beauty. On particularly difficult days she would prick her ears for the comments of the passers-by: 'Did you see that little girl? Such a charming face!' And when she got home she would confirm these opinions by gazing spellbound into a looking-glass at 'my big blue eyes, straight features and sweet mouth'. She made clear in her memoirs, however, that 'these little attacks of conceit did not last long; I would forget myself the moment after, for I was already beginning to reveal the most salient trait of my character, which has always been to think of others first'.[34] She was able to escape from her glowering father in spring and summer when her mother took her to the house they rented at Chatenay, only seven miles from Paris but at that time sunk in rural tranquillity, a sanctuary of donkey-rides and tomboy pranks. And her father was ceasing to be quite such an ogre, his resentment of her tempered by his own success and the increasing attention shown to his wife and daughter by the Bonapartist notabilities who were gradually re-emerging into society.

Alain Pellapra was now a confidential adviser to the Abbé Louis, Minister of Finance. The house in the Rue Joubert was too small for the amount of entertaining he wished to do; while looking for a larger permanent residence he moved into an apartment in the Rue Basse du Rempart, the north side of the Boulevard des Capucines, but this Emilie considered an unworthy setting for 'my mother's charm and my conspicuous beauty'. However, the guests made no objection and called in flattering numbers, a strange mixture of old and new, the former parvenus and the new traditionalists, sometimes one man appearing in both guises.

On Alain Pellapra's side they were bankers, politicians, government officials, a Rothschild or two, the Marquis de Chauvelin, Forbin the Director of Museums; while his wife's coterie was almost exclusively Bonapartist: the Bassanos, General Despans-Cubières, Madame Gazzani, who had been briefly Napoleon's mistress and whose husband had received the customary fee of a Collectorship of Taxes, and General Duchamp, who had married a friend of the family. Françoise Pellapra never tired of telling Emilie of the exploits of the brave Duchamp – at Waterloo for instance, where he thrust his artillery so close to the enemy line that Napoleon exclaimed 'Duchamp is deserting!' On occasions Emilie was allowed into the drawing room to chat with them, and to note without surprise, that they were all astounded by her wit.

By the time she was fourteen, 'I could go nowhere without attracting attention', she confessed. 'Young men who lived near us would stand for hours under my window, hoping to catch a glimpse of me, and those who were admitted to the house fell in love with me.' Among those who underwent this exciting experience were Emmanuel Las Cases, the son of the baron who was a member of Leon's Family Council, who sent her sentimental notes and verses, and Anselme Rothschild, who escorted her on picnics and murmured endearments to her in the Pellapra box at the Opera. Both of these, together with the Bassano's elder son and the son of

Marshal Mortier, Duke of Treviso, were suggested as possible husbands for her. Indeed, Emilie admitted, 'it would be impossible for me to draw up a list of all those who signed for my charms'.[35]

Happily for her peace of mind, the decision was taken out of her hands. Her father agreed to a proposal made by the Count de Brigode on behalf of his son Arthur. The Brigodes were rich Flanders merchants who had managed to increase both their property and their position under the *ancien régime*, the Revolution, the Empire and the Restoration. Louis-Marie-Joseph de Brigode had been appointed Mayor of Lille in 1802 and two years later, as Chamberlain to the Emperor, he was one of the notables sent to escort the Pope from Rome to Paris for the coronation. Napoleon created him a count of the Empire and, after he submitted to the Bourbons, Louis XVIII made him a Peer of France. Despite all these distinctions the count thought it as well to take Arthur off on a tour of Europe before exposing him to so brilliant a wife as Emilie. Alas, Arthur never returned; he caught a fever in Florence and was dead within three weeks.

Emilie recovered swiftly from her grief. By the following spring, when she drove with her mother in the Easter Parade to Longchamp, 'my appearance was a real triumph, a flattering murmur rose from the crowd as we passed, and the papers all spoke of the lovely and charming Mademoiselle Pellapra'. It was enough to turn the head of any ordinary girl, but fortunately 'my precocious commonsense and cleverness kept me from being vain'. The family now had a château at Noisel, rented from the Duke of Levis, and a very grand mansion on the Quai Malaquais. Between the two they hobnobbed with the great. Emilie began to notice two things: first, that the Count de Brigode was always at her side and appeared resentful of the innumerable compliments she received from her countless admirers, as if he were still protecting his dead son's interests; and secondly, that although her father now mixed much in high society, the invitations often did not include her mother. She decided, though her reasoning is not very clear, to provide her mother with protection and respectability by accepting the proposal of marriage which she shrewdly guessed the Count de Brigode was about to make. He was forty-eight, she later assessed her age as a little under sixteen, though the records show that she was, in fact, eighteen.

The count formally asked Monsieur Pellapra for his daughter's hand. Monsieur Pellapra hesitated; he and Emilie were on increasingly good terms and she had been helping him by taking down from his dictation the speeches that he ghosted for various ministers, but in the end he was persuaded by the count's promise to settle 40,000 francs a year on Emilie. The prospective father-in-law and son-in-law set out on the long traditional round of formal carriage-drives, delivering their visiting cards to as many acquaintances as they could muster. Pellapra gave a grand engagement ball at the mansion on the Quai Malaquais and strutted with pride at the presence of Prince Leopold of Saxe-Coburg-Saalfeld, widower of the Prince Regent's daughter, Charlotte, uncle of little Princess Victoria of Kent, and future King of the Belgians.

'He thought me very pretty,' recorded Emilie, 'and, frankly, I must admit he was right. When I think of the face that looked out from the wreath of roses, and the figure set off to the greatest advantage by my white dress, trimmed with the same flowers, I cannot help knowing that nothing more lovely was ever seen.'[37] On 11 April 1825, in the Chapel of the Peers at the Luxembourg Palace, she became a married woman and a member of the aristocracy.

Having married Brigode to give her mother protection, she naturally took her with her on the honeymoon and, when this continued in the Pyrenees and Switzerland, all three went rambling round the mountains together. It was not until the Christmas of the following year that Emilie realized she had entered into a pregnancy which ended with a premature confinement in July 1827. As so often happens in such matters, it was the sensitive husband who suffered most. Emilie had twins; the count had an apoplectic stroke. Two months later he was dead.

Emilie retired to the Château de Ménars, which her husband had only recently bought; a charming summer palace set in a beautiful park, once the home of Madame de Pompadour. After eighteen months of seclusion she put on half-mourning and returned to Paris. With the mourning crêpe removed from the four-horse landau and a touch of colour on the coats of the two servants mounted at the back, she reappeared in the Bois de Boulogne and turned the heads of a fresh batch of young men, some of whom made quite a nuisance of themselves, even following her back from Paris to Ménars. Among these eligible bachelors was the youngest son of Marshal Maison, a finely built man with a talent for painting, who called in for dinner and stayed for ten days. He might have remained longer had not Françoise Pellapra, anxious that history should not repeat itself, suddenly taken to dropping in to her daughter's bedroom late at night and unannounced. Emilie, though grieved at the implication, accepted the point that her mother was making. Young Maison moved on.[38]

He was succeeded by others. 'I shall not attempt to enumerate the offers I received', wrote Emilie, restricting herself to naming a specimen half-dozen. She was in demand by hostesses of the highest rank and did her share of lion-feeding in return. When she was at Ménars, she had the Duchess of Berry to lunch, widowed by the assassination of her husband, the same 'ugly, stout, common-looking person' Emilie had met in Caen in 1814. When she was in Paris, Emilie was invited to where the Duke of Orleans lived and plotted discreetly against his cousin King Charles X.

The year 1830 opened with Paris in the grip of extreme frost. The Seine was frozen so hard that carriages could be driven on the ice. The chill seeped into even the richest houses despite the fires that were kept blazing in the grates, and at night the rooms grew bitterly cold. Fernand, the younger of the twins, developed a fever one January evening and, watched by the heartbroken Emilie, was dead before morning. Emilie went into mourning again. Françoise Pellapra took her, partly in earnest partly as a light distraction, to discover what sort of future the famous Mademoiselle Lenormand would predict for her.

This noted pythoness, now verging on sixty, had been a fashionable fortuneteller for well over a quarter of a century. At one time she was said to make an annual income of 20,000 francs, some of it from casting horoscopes but most from chiromancy, an art at which she became so expert and, indeed, intrepid that she would on occasion read clients' hands without bothering to ask them to remove their gloves, rather in the manner of a ventriloquist throwing his voice while smoking a cigarette and drinking a glass of water. Josephine, racked with anxiety in the months and years before Napoleon divorced her, was one of Mademoiselle Lenormand's many prominent devotees, and the sibyl had considerable success during the Restoration with an aprocryphal set of memoirs attributed to the late Empress, as well as some highly coloured and fanciful recollections of her own. Emilie found her disappointingly unprepossessing – a rather common old woman in a hideous black velvet cap.

'You are a widow, Madame,' intoned Mademoiselle Lenormand, 'but you will marry again before the autumn. Do not waste time in trying to guess who your husband will be, for you have not even encountered him yet. The waves of the sea now break between you, and he will cross two oceans before he meets you. He is young, handsome, rich and good. You will be as happy as you deserve to be. You will also travel much and see many foreign Courts.'[39] Emilie and her mother, satisfied that they had at any rate had their money's worth in promises, left on a ripple of laughter.

It was not long afterwards that the lawyer employed by Alain Pellapra to deal with the constant flow of proposals for Emilie's desirable hand informed her father that an offer had been made on behalf of the son of the Prince de Chimay. His mother, formerly Theresa Cabarrus, had become famous during the Revolution for the influence she exerted through her husband, Tallien, in bringing down Robespierre. She befriended Hortense and Eugene while Josephine was in prison and remained a friend of the family long afterwards. The fame that she won as 'Notre Dame de Thermidor' changed to notoriety with her escapades during the wild days and nights of relief that followed the end of the Terror. One of the most repeated stories about her was that she wagered that all the flimsy clothes she was wearing at one well-attended party did not weigh as much as two six-franc pieces. The bet was accepted, scales were brought in, Theresa stripped, and won. She was a beautiful woman with the sort of aggressive femininity that terrified Bonaparte, who banned her from his Court on grounds of decency. After two divorces and a series of rich lovers she settled down in apparent respectability with her third husband, the Prince de Chimay, to whom she bore two sons and two daughters. But she did not sound at all the sort of mother-in-law Emilie could be happy with. Emilie begged to be excused.

Fate and her parents decided otherwise. One morning her mother led her into the drawing room and presented to her a tall, comely young man – Joseph de Chimay. He had recently been in England and in Toulon, so he had crossed one sea and at least been in close proximity to another. He was certainly rich and appeared to be good. Mademoiselle Lenormand's gift of prediction had not withered with the years.

It was love at first sight for Joseph and Emilie. The contract was agreed after some doughty bargaining. The groom was twenty-two; the bride admitted to the same age, though she was, in fact, two years older. The marriage was fixed for high summer at the church of Saint-Germain-des-Prés, the oldest in Paris. It was only a short distance from the Quai Malaquais up the Rue des Petits Augustins, but the wedding journey turned out to be full of incident. Paris was indulging in a Revolution. Emilie's friends at the Palais-Royal were evicting those at the Tuileries. The streets were littered with tom-up cobble-stones, the air was noisy with the raucous cries of Vox Populi and the rattle of distant musketry. To avoid upsetting the egalitarian susceptibilities the bride's carriage was disguised to look like a cab.

With her distinguished, delightful, attentive Joseph, Emilie settled down to a life of bliss; with the rest of the Chimay family she was less well at ease. The legendary Theresa, ill-dressed, cocooned in rolls of suety fat, glared maliciously out of unblinking lizard eyes on a world that had long since ceased to pay tribute to her beauty. Her children, by various fathers, remained surprisingly uncaptivated by Emilie's loveliness and charm, and, Royalist by sentiment, they resented the Bonaparte intruder. There was great satisfaction when the honeymooners decided to get away from everybody and settle at Ménars, a good fifteen hours' drive from Paris. In time Emilie grew to half-admire and half-understand the dissolute, defiant old woman who was her mother-in-law – but not yet.

Chapter Three:
Rebellions and Gallantry

The July Revolution of 1830, that spoilt Emilie's drive to church, began on the 26th with the publication of ordinances intended to bring about a Royalist *coup d'état*, which was resisted during the following three days with increasingly fierce street fighting in Paris and the eventual mutiny of the troops sent to restore order. On 30 July a deputation of the two legislative chambers invited Louis-Philippe, Duke of Orleans, to assume control as Lieutenant-General of the Kingdom, and the following day he entered Paris from his summer residence at Neuilly – the same delightful château where Hortense had so often visited Caroline more than twenty years before. On 2 August Charles X formally abdicated in favour of his grandson Henri, appointing the Duke of Orleans as Regent. But Louis-Philippe was not now going to yield the throne that he and his ancestors had schemed and tricked through many centuries to obtain. He signed the charter offered him by the Chambers and on 9 August was proclaimed King of the French.

With the wind against them, the vessels carrying news of these events took five or six weeks to make the westward crossing of the Atlantic, though they could return in three or four. When Joseph Bonaparte wrote to Marie-Louise from New York on 10 September, the latest news he had was from the London papers of 1 August. He told her that 'all the major obstacles to the return of Napoleon II to his father's throne will be removed if his grandfather, the Kaiser, will give him the slightest support'.[1] All that was necessary was for Marie-Louise to send her son to France, where Joseph was willing to act as regent for him. That happy dream was soon dispelled by later information, and Joseph then rattled off protests to various Bonapartist generals and the Chambers at their failure to do their duty to his nephew and himself, and invitations to the Kaiser and Metternich to step in and put the Duke of Reichstadt on the throne by force as the only means of averting further revolution, not only in France but also in the neighbouring states, Spain, Italy and Germany. From the Austrians he got no reply; from the French government came a decree renewing the ban on any Bonapartes entering the country.

Madame Mère and Cardinal Fesch, both of whom, like Joseph, had set aside plenty of money to live in comfort, applauded his bold statement of their imperial rights, though in private Madame Mère admitted it was about as effective as a sword thrust in water. Other members of the family, hoping to reach an accommodation with Louis-Philippe which would allow them to pursue claims for compensation in the French courts, were far from enraptured. 'Joseph declaring war on the King of the French from his camp at New York where he is in safety, has ruined everything!'[2] complained Lucien.

Joseph received no flicker of interest from Marie-Louise – recently widowed by the death of Neipperg, but already seeking consolation with her Court Chamberlain, Count Bombelles – nor from the Duke of Reichstadt, now in his twentieth year. Reichstadt's cousin, the intense, mannish Napoleone Camerata, turned up again in Vienna at the

Swan Hotel during November, and followed him when he went for walks in the Prater, but did not speak to him until one rainy night when she caught him unattended on the steps of his assistant tutor's house in the Hofburg. She grabbed his hand and kissed it. Reichstadt, more than a little startled by this outlandish young woman with the grip of a fanatical fencer, was relieved to find the door opening. He slipped inside and Napoleone disappeared into the drizzle – but not from Vienna.[3]

She had parted from her husband and their young son and was her own mistress. From her hotel in the Kärtnerstrasse she sent a letter to Reichstadt urging him to assume his responsibilities like a man, and demanding to know whether he was an Austrian archduke or a French prince. Reichstadt replied that, speaking as neither, he was profoundly touched by her interest but begged her not to communicate with him again. He may have suspected that she was an *agent provocateur* set up by the Austrians, but it is more likely that he was intelligent enough to realize he could do nothing to get back to France, and sybaritic enough to prefer his present way of life at the Austrian court. A few days later Napoleone had a visit from Reichstadt's friend, Major Prokesch, who told her that the duke expected he would one day receive a call from France, but he did not intend to do anything until it came. In the meantime it would be better if the Countess Camerata did not remain in Vienna. She took the hint and left.[4]

In January 1831 Reichstadt made his official entry into society, delayed until now because of fears for his health, at a reception given by the British ambassador, Lord Cowley, the younger brother of the Duke of Wellington. There he met Marshal Marmont, who, having betrayed

Napoleon in 1814 by surrendering his army of 20,000 men to the Russians, was now in exile from France for having fired on the Paris mob in support of Charles X during the July Revolution. The young man and the Marshal, now in his late fifties, struck up a close friendship, Marmont regularly calling on the duke and discussing his father's campaigns. At first these visits took place three times a week, but they later thinned out to twice a month as Reichstadt grew increasingly preoccupied with the battles of the boudoir.

He had inherited his mother's amorous temperament. Rumour alleged that he disported himself so enthusiastically with various ladies of the Court that his frail health was being threatened.[5] In particular, he formed a close association with Princess Sophie of Bavaria, six years his senior and the wife of his uncle Archduke Franz Karl. But he did not allow these affairs to interfere with his formal military duties, and, on a bitterly cold day at the beginning of January 1832, he insisted on taking command of the Vasa Regiment, of which he was colonel, at the funeral of General Siegenthat. As the slow procession moved through the wintery streets he realized that he had lost his voice. He returned to the Hofburg where he made a partial recovery, but the illness would not be shaken off, and by April it was clear that his lungs were seriously affected.[6]

By May he was well enough to face the annual move from the Hofburg to his summer quarters at Schönbrunn. His own apartments were being repaired, so he was allotted a set on the floor below with which he was already familiar, for they were the ones that Sophie usually occupied. She, nearly eight months pregnant with her second child, spent many hours sitting and talking with him, or accompanying him on walks in the park. At mid-summer, Marie-Louise arrived from Parma; her company seemed to act as a tonic for the duke, whose health noticeably improved during the following week. On 6 July Sophie gave birth to a son who was named Ferdinand Maximilian. The gossips whispered that his true father was Reichstadt.

*

The Revolution of July 1830 brought no joy to Hortense at Arenenberg. Joseph's summons to the people of France to accept Napoleon II as their ruler, with himself as regent, was not at all the scenario of which she had dreamed. She cannot have been very disappointed with the lack of response, and she entirely approved of her elder son, Napoleon-Louis', decision not to be involved.[7] He told her of this when she arrived in Florence on 1 November, en route to Rome with Louis-Napoleon. Napoleon-Louis had chosen to live in Florence after his marriage to Joseph's daughter, to be near both his father and his mother-in-law. Hortense spent two happy weeks alone with both her boys, since Louis had gone to Rome to visit Madame Mère. Napoleon-Louis had received offers of support if he raised the Bonaparte standard in either Paris or Corsica. He refused indignantly: 'Would I introduce civil war to my country when my only desire is to serve it with every drop of blood in my body?' Indeed not, agreed Hortense, and besides it would not have been successful. There was also the matter of the one-million-franc suit for the restoration of her property that she was trying to bring before the French courts – she did not want to prejudice that.

Pope Pius VIII died on the last day of November, and throughout the Papal States young revolutionaries saw the interregnum as an opportunity to gain independence. In Rome, where Hortense had now arrived, the authorities watched with alarm as Louis-Napoleon pranced about the streets on a horse with a tricolour saddlecloth; there were rumours that he and his brother were members of the secret republican sect, the Carbonari. Spies reported that 400 insurgents were planning to filter into the Vatican and seize it.[8] The Governor of Rome called on Cardinal Fesch and asked him to persuade Louis-Napoleon to leave the city. Fesch protested his great-nephew's innocence, but next day a colonel and fifty men arrived at the palace, packed Louis-Napoleon into a coach and removed him to Florence 200 miles away.

In the days that followed Hortense came to the conclusion that the odds were against any successful uprising; four weeks after Louis-Napoleon left she wrote to warn him and his brother not to become involved. She then settled down to enjoy the masquerading of the Shrovetide Carnival. On Saturday, 12 February 1831, one of her conspirator friends warned her not to join the carriage procession down the Corso that day because an insurrection was to take place in support of the revolt that had broken out in the Romagna just over a week before. It was a failure, and a week later she, too, left hurriedly for Florence before dawn. She arrived in the Tuscan capital after nightfall, and the following day she learned that her two sons had already gone to join the insurgents.[9]

Louis-Napoleon, always the leader in such affairs, had left her a letter: 'Your affection for us will make you understand.... The name we bear compels us to help the unfortunate people who appeal to us. Make my sister-in-law believe it was I who drew her husband into it – he is grieved at having concealed it from her.' They were on their way, with a rebel band, to lay siege to Civita-Castellana and to release the political prisoners from its massive fortress. Napoleon-Louis had been granted the rank of major in the cavalry; Louis-Napoleon was a captain. If they could successfully storm the palace the road was open to Rome 35 miles away, for while Hortense had been hurrying north to Florence along the Viterbo–Siena road her sons had come south down the eastern road through Foligno and Terni.

In Bologna the rebels had set up a provisional government, in which the Minister of War was General Armandi, steward of the Bonaparte family properties in the March of Ancona, including one owned by Hortense. The Papal authorities had not been as unreasonable as Hortense claimed in suspecting some sort of Bonapartist plot. But her sons' contribution was more of an embarrassment than an asset to the rebel cause (and the source of much concern to their Uncle Jerome, still in Rome, and Uncle Lucien who owed his title of Prince of Canino to the Pope). The rebels had hoped to get aid from Louis-Philippe, who had presented himself as the champion of democracy – but Louis-Philippe would certainly not associate himself with the same cause as the two young Bonapartes. The provisional government decided to recall them. The government of Tuscany, however, refused to allow them to rejoin Hortense in Florence. Austria announced that they would be prevented from returning to Switzerland. From Rome, Jerome and Fesch wrote warning Hortense that the Austrian troops advancing to the aid of the Pope had orders to arrest them and bring them to trial.

Suddenly both her sons were in desperate straits. She decided to try to get them to Smyrna, at the eastern end of the Mediterranean, beyond Austrian reach. She planned to take ship from the port of Ancona, which was in rebel hands, but fortunately discovered in time that an Austrian flotilla was patrolling the Adriatic. As the Austrians advanced by land, closing the ring, Hortense decided that her only hope of sanctuary lay in England. From one of her English friends, Lord George Hamilton Seymour, who was British Minister at Florence, she obtained a passport for 'Mrs Hamilton and her two sons'; she sent a footman to Bologna, nominally with horses for Louis-Napoleon but actually with detailed instructions sewn into the lining of his coat; she carried out a complex manoeuvre entailing leaving, re-entering and again leaving Florence by various city gates in order to get her English passport signed on exit without it becoming too clear that she was heading for Foligno whereas England lay in the opposite direction. She was consumed with maternal anxiety and conspiratorial excitement; it was at times such as these that she was at her best.

She reached Perugia on 13 March and Foligno the next day. There she had to wait until her sons could be traced. Eventually she learned that they were both at Forli, nearly 150 miles away; they had escaped capture by the Austrians, but Louis-Napoleon sent a note to say that his brother could not travel at the moment because he was in bed with a bad cold. Suddenly, overtaken by a frightening premonition, Hortense ordered her coachman to drive northward as fast as he could. She had not gone far when the rumour reached her that Napoleon-Louis had died of measles. The coach clanked and rattled along the old Via Flaminia for another day and night before she found refuge at Pesaro in the palace owned by her nephew, Eugene's son, the Duke of Leuchtenberg, Here Louis-Napoleon joined her shortly afterwards, with confirmation that his brother was dead.[10]

There was little time for mourning, the Austrians were still advancing and had cut the road to Bologna. She moved back down the coast to another of Leuchtenberg's palaces at Ancona, and there, to her horror, Louis-Napoleon developed a rash on his face which quite clearly denoted measles. He too might die; he certainly could not be moved. She spread the word through the town that he was making for Corfu and that she was ill in bed. She booked a passage for him on a boat and had her servants make trips backwards and forward to the harbour pretending to load his baggage. Thanks to a storm, the boat safely ran the gauntlet of the Austrian fleet and any interested observers were convinced that the revolutionary young Bonaparte had escaped.

The provisional government capitulated on 26 March; the Austrian troops entered Ancona three days later. The colonel in charge of the vanguard turned out to be the young lieutenant who had come to Hortense's rescue when the French troops and civilians had harassed her in Dijon in 1815; the army commander and his staff took up residence in the palace, while Hortense retired to a few rooms with her ladies. The Austrians had not the faintest suspicion that Louis-Napoleon was still with her. 'Would you believe it?' Hortense said afterwards, 'I place so much importance on honesty that I was almost remorseful at deceiving those who trusted me.' As soon as Louis-Napoleon was fit enough to travel she charmed a pass from the Austrian general and set off at daybreak on Easter Day, with Louis-Napoleon posing as a servant on the box of her coach and another fugitive, Count Daniel Zappi, as a footman on the back of the following one. Inside were her dame d'honneur, Valerie Masuyer, and Louis-Napoleon's valet, Charles Thélin.

After the general's passport had carried her through the Austrian lines she changed it for the one given her by Seymour; the young men joined her inside, and she continued as 'Mrs Hamilton and her two sons, Charles and William'. On 17 April, a fortnight after leaving Ancona, she was on French soil for the first time for more than fifteen years. She slept that night at Cannes, where Napoleon had landed on his return from Elba. The significance was not lost on her son; from now on he signed himself not Louis-Napoleon but Napoleon-Louis, thus adopting the name of his brother, whose death had brought him one step closer to the Imperial throne. Among his acquaintances and relations, however, he continued to be referred to as Prince Louis.

Still posing as Mrs Hamilton, Hortense arrived in Paris on Saturday, 23 April and put up at the Hôtel de Hollande in the Rue de la Paix. After two days she managed to get in touch with the king, whom she hoped would be favourably disposed to her because she had been of use to his mother and aunt during the Hundred Days – and still had their grateful letters to prove it.[11] The welcome was not effusive. Casimir Périer, the President of the Council, called to ask why she was flouting the law which forbade her or her son to enter France. She gave him one of her engagingly honest stares and explained that since she *had* to pass through France in order to get to England she feared the king might think, if she did not contact him, that her visit had some sinister motive instead of being simply a mother's desperate attempt to save her son.

Next evening Louis-Philippe saw her secretly in a room at the Palais-Royal, so small that Hortense had to sit on the bed with the queen, and Louis-Philippe and his sister, Madame Adelaide, in the only two chairs, while the aide-de-camp, whose bedroom it was, leaned against the door to prevent anyone coming in. Hortense urged the king to lift the ban on the Bonapartes; he hedged, but agreed to help her with the claims she was making for compensation for the property she had left in France. She also obtained from him the promise of a passport to return from England through France to Switzerland, and French government approval for her to remain at Arenenberg with Prince Louis who, as she explained to Louis-Philippe, was unable to present his respects in person because he was in bed at their hotel, suffering from a recurrence of measles. Next day, Périer informed the king that while Hortense was being received at the Palais-Royal 'her son was in conference with the principal leaders of the Republican party, discussing with them the best means of overturning your throne'.[12]

Périer was anxious to get the pair of them out of Paris as soon as possible. He had only recently been called upon to form his ministry as a result of violent legitimist and republican rioting – he did not intend to be forced to resign because of trouble from a Bonapartist mob. Yet that was a distinct possibility. The tenth anniversary of Napoleon's death, 5 May, would bring supporters of his son's cause thronging to their usual rallying point – the column that he had raised to his own glory in the Place Vendôme. If Hortense stepped out on to the balcony of her hotel apartment above their heads, followed by her son, hero of the struggles to liberate Italy, who knew what violent demonstrations and counter-manifestations might erupt and flare through the streets of the city? He persuaded the king to send his aide-de-camp to Hortense on 4 May with orders for her to leave immediately. By luck, or Hortense's skilful management, a doctor was actually examining Prince Louis when the officer arrived. So Hortense was able to postpone her departure until after the great day, but, though she observed the crowd, she remained discreetly in her room.[13]

Whether Prince Louis had genuinely been ill in Paris or not, he was certainly unwell when they arrived in London on 10 May; the rough sea-crossing having brought on an attack of jaundice. They stayed for a few days at Fenton's Hotel in St James's Street, and then moved to a house that Hortense rented at 30 George Street. They had scarcely moved in when Caroline's elder son, the thirty-year-old Achille Murat, called to present his American wife. Their welcome was somewhat less than cordial when Hortense learned that Achille considered himself to be his Uncle Joseph's representative in Europe, had come specifically to watch the progress of events in France, and was already deeply involved in Bonapartist conspiracies in Paris. Achille, boastful and overtalkative, was acidly dealt with in the brief memoir of the year's adventures that Hortense published in 1834; for the moment, she gave him a restrained auntly smile and determined to have nothing to do with his plans. She had no interest in helping him or his Uncle Joseph, or the Duke of Reichstadt whom they both professed to serve; and in any case, as Valerie Masuyer noted: 'The Queen wants to get her million francs back first.'[14]

Hortense had acquaintances in London society – among them the Irish-born Dowager Lady Glengall and Lady Tankerville, the latter French-born and of distinguished lineage, a Gramont on her father's side, a Polignac on her mother's, though Lord Melbourne once described her to

Queen Victoria as 'a frivolous little woman who doesn't know what she is about'. Through them Hortense obtained interviews with members of the Cabinet and Earl Grey, the Prime Minister, whom she hoped to win over as advocates for her claim against the French government. Lady Glengall – whom she had last met nearly thirty years before, taking the waters at Plombières during the Peace of Amiens – also produced two other close relations, even less welcome than the Murats: Leon and Walewski. When invited to meet the former at Lady C'engall's, Hortense pleaded a prior engagement. After meeting the latter, Prince Louis, still full of his Italian adventure, asked 'What's this pretty boy doing here, when they're fighting in Poland?'

England had provided a refuge for Hortense and Prince Louis, but otherwise their stay had not been very comfortable or fruitful; and it had been expensive. Charles de Flahaut sent Hortense a letter of credit. His father, Talleyrand, currently French ambassador in London, promised to issue the passport for her to return through France to Arenenberg, but then withheld it because of riots in Paris. It was not until 7 August 1831 that they eventually landed at Calais as Madame d'Arenenberg and her son.[15]

The direct route home would take her along the northern border, through Charleville, Metz and Strasbourg, but Hortense planned to take Prince Louis on a little sentimental journey through some of the native country that he scarcely knew. She had obtained permission to travel by way of Paris, and their first halt was on the cliffs outside Boulogne, scene of her idyll with Charles de Flahaut, where another of Uncle Nonon's uncompleted monuments – a column more than 150 feet high – marked the spot where the Grande Armée had been assembled for the invasion of England. Twenty miles north of Paris was the great château and park of Mortefontaine that had belonged to Uncle Joseph; closer to the city, at St-Denis, was the school for the daughters of the Officers of the Legion of Honour, of which she was patroness. They had passed the road that would have taken them to St-Leu, a place of unhappy memories not only for Hortense, but for its most recent owner, the Prince of Condé, who had been found hanging from the hasp of one of the windows, but they turned westward from St-Denis to skirt the city of Paris and head for Rueil, where they knelt before the tomb of Louis' Beauharnais grandmother in the parish church. At Malmaison, less than a mile down the road, they were refused admission – because they lacked a letter of introduction from the absent Swedish banker who had bought it from Eugene's widow. With this harsh reminder of changed fortunes they journeyed down to Versailles, then round to Melun and eastward towards the Rhine.

*

Prince Louis' criticism of Alexandre Walewski was less than just. The July Revolution in Paris in 1830 had kindled other uprisings beside the one in Italy. On France's northern border, where the Allies had combined into the Kingdom of the Netherlands the territories once ruled by Austria and the House of Orange, the Belgians of the south resented the preponderant influence of the Dutch of the north. They broke into revolt in August, with the approval of the British government, but to the consternation of Britain's former allies, Austria, Prussia and Russia, now linked in the reactionary Holy Alliance. Tsar Nicholas, who had succeeded his brother Alexander, in 1835, ordered the Polish army to prepare to march against the Belgian rebels. The Poles, instead, exploded into a revolution of their own.

Alexandre Walewski, eager to join the patriot friends of his youth, set out from Paris with a passport describing him as an actor of the Palais-Royal troupe named Dubourt, engaged to appear at the Moscow Theatre. But he no sooner reached Prussia than he found himself in trouble. The border guards had orders to keep a close eye on all travellers going eastward from France, where there was much sympathy for the Polish cause. Alexandre was told that he could certainly proceed; but it was to be with a military escort, which would hand him over to the authorities at the Russian frontier. His adventure seemed ended before it began, for the Russians were sure to hold him, and eventually identify him. Unless he found an opportunity to escape, he could look forward to a long spell in a Russian prison or even exile to Siberia.

It was not until they were approaching the Oder that the chance arose. While the Prussian soldiers were changing horses and getting refreshment at a relay inn, Alexandre slipped off into the forest, abandoning his carriage and baggage. After hours of stumbling eastward through the snow-covered trees, he came to the river and followed it down to a village; but there was no one willing to ferry him across because of the danger of ice-floes. In desperation he invited one of the boatmen into the local tavern and, having filled him with drink, wagered him that he could not row to the other side. The ruse worked; with Alexandre at one pair of oars and the drunken boatman at the other, they made the perilous trip to the opposite bank. In Poland he found friends to provide him with a four-horse sleigh in which he reached Warsaw in safety.[16]

On 25 January 1831 the Polish Diet proclaimed the deposition of the Tsar, five days later, Alexandre was gazetted as an officer in the Free Polish Army and aide-de-camp to the commander-in-chief; within four weeks he had distinguished himself at the battle of Grochow, where he had a horse killed under him and won the Gold Cross of the Military Order of Poland. But it was clear that the Poles could not hope to win without outside help. Their plan was to split the Holy Alliance by offering the throne of their precariously independent kingdom to Marie-Louise's uncle, Archduke Charles of Austria, and to persuade the Austrians to accept the offer by winning the support of Britain and France. In order to achieve their aim, the leader of the rebel government, Prince Adam Czartoryski, decided to send the heroic young Walewski to plead their cause.

Thus, within six weeks of his arrival in Warsaw, Alexandre was setting off through Prussian territory once more, returning to Paris and again posing as an actor – Saint-Albin, a juvenile lead with the French Theatre Company in Moscow. He was again arrested, this time in Breslau, but two hours of questioning failed to shake his story that he was an actor. The police chief, however, was still suspicious and ordered him to prove his claim by appearing in a performance with the local theatrical company; a test which his natural flair for showing-off enabled him to pass with credibility if not distinction. He was allowed to continue on his way and, travelling due west, he pressed on through Weimar and Metz to Paris, where the Foreign Minister, Sébastiani, promised support for the Polish Plan if Britain would agree, and the representatives of Free Polish suggested he should continue on to London.[17]

He arrived there in the last week of March, to the friendly though unenthusiastic welcome from Lord Palmerston, the Foreign Secretary, who frankly admitted that he saw Russia as Britain's natural ally and France as potentially her most dangerous enemy. Undeterred, Alexandre did the rounds of the other ministers, from the Prime Minister, Lord Grey downwards. From Talleyrand at the French Embassy he received shrewd advice to switch the offer of the Polish throne from an Austrian prince to a Prussian, the Austrians having recently expressed their sympathies very plainly by interning an entire Polish army, and the further suggestion that he should enlist the help of Charles de Flahaut.[18]

Charles' fortunes had been greatly improved by the ascent to the French throne of Louis-Philippe, whose days of exile had been much comforted by Charles' mother, Adelaide de Souza. To please her, and in pursuit of his policy of preserving links with the Napoleonic period in the hope that some of the glamour would rub off on himself, the king created Charles a peer of the new realm, appointed him First Equerry to the Heir to the Throne, the Duke of Orleans, and was about to send him as Special Envoy to Berlin. Alexandre came over to Paris from London, obtained Charles' promise of support, and bustled back to London again to present the new plan to Palmerston, who again bent a kindly ear but regretted that no decision could be taken until after the question of a king for Belgium had been settled – in favour of Queen Victoria's uncle (and Louis-Philippe's son-in-law), the handsome Leopold of Saxe-Coburg-Saalfeld who had been the lion of Emilie Pellapra's engagement ball six years before.

Excited by all this to-ing and fro-ing, and convinced that he had a hitherto unsuspected genius for diplomacy, Alexandre promptly despatched a Polish friend to Brussels to hurry things along. In July, though it is difficult to see how the credit could go to either Alexandre or his emissary, Leopold was accepted as King of the Belgians. Alexandre delightedly called on Palmerston – who shared his joy but pointed out that, alas, Britain could not intervene in any Polish question unless Russia invited her to do.[19]

Sadly disillusioned, Alexandre returned to Paris where, in mid-September, he leaned that Warsaw had surrendered to the Russian troops. Poland's fight for independence had failed. Many of her leaders were shot or were sent to Siberia; others escaped to the capitals of Europe, where they set up revolutionary cells. Alexandre found himself being blamed for having bungled his small part in the struggle and for having seen most of the war out in the comfort of London and Paris instead of remaining to fight in his native land.

It was true that his activities in London had not been confined to Whitehall. He was a familiar and popular figure in many drawing-rooms, where Poles were objects of romance; he was a friend of Tom Moore, the young Disraeli, Lady Blessington, Count d'Orsay, and many more. But the most significant of his social encounters was with Caroline Montagu, daughter of the Earl of Sandwich.[20] They fell in love and, after learning of the fall of Warsaw, he went back to London where they were married on 1 December 1831; the bride bringing a dowry of £30,000. Their three-week honeymoon over, Caroline accompanied him to Paris and was presented at Court on the second day of the New Year. On the advice of another prominent British member of Parisian society, Madame de Flahaut, Alexandre wore his uniform as a captain in the Free Polish Army for the ceremony, with the Gold Cross he had won at Grochow, and the national cockade of the failed uprising. The Russian ambassador lodged an official protest.[21]

*

In Paris the Walewskis saw a great deal of the Rothschilds and their business associates and friends, including the Pellapras and the Duke of Caraman, Emilie's uncle by marriage, though neither Alexandre nor Emilie seem to have openly admitted their kinship. At this period in his life Alexandre was careful not to claim any relationship to Napoleon – wisely so, since he had inherited a fortune on the basis that he was the legitimate son of Count Walewski. On one occasion Lady Holland, who was always brandishing her admiration for the late Emperor, exclaimed: 'Oh, how like your father you are!' and Alexandre rudely replied, 'I was unaware, Madam, that Count Walewski had the honour of your acquaintance.' He was, however, on quite close terms of friendly rivalry with another of his left-handed relations, Auguste de Morny, who was often seen with him at the race-course, at the Opera or at Court.

Through Charles de Flahaut's appointment as First Equerry to the Duke of Orleans, Auguste de Morny made the acquaintance of the rest of the king's sons: the Dukes of Nemours, Aumale and Montpensier, and the Prince of Joinville. These royal connections, a bright intellect and graceful manners won him rapid success in society. Like Alexandre, he was seen most mornings riding in the Bois de Boulogne in the foppish uniform of contrasting coloured coat and waistcoat, white gloves, and trousers tightly strapped under the feet. Like everybody else (including the workmen and peasants on Sundays and holidays) he wore a top hat, which he carried everywhere with him, to dining tables, salons and ballrooms, slipping it under his chair for safety.

He danced his way through the figures of the *contredanse*, which had been brought over from England as the country dance and had gone back there as the quadrille; the *cotillon* although this was less popular under the Orleanist regime because it had been brought into favour by Emilie's friend the lively legitimist Duchess of Berry, together with the *galoppe*, a rowdier version of the *polonaise*. The waltz was still considered daring, and the polka, when it came along, was suspect on both moral and political grounds, since anything with a Polish-sounding name was assumed to be dangerously liberal.

Cotillon means petticoat. The dance was so named because of the swirl of the ladies' skirts, but *cotillonner* means not only to take part in the dance but also to chase the ladies. Auguste was dedicated to both pursuits. Membership of the Jockey Club conferred the right to use the Club's box at the Opera; although no member of the Club could claim distinction unless he was keeping as his mistress one of the young ballet-dancers under tuition: *les rats d'Opera*. Auguste eagerly qualified, as a preparation for greater triumphs among the actresses of the Comédie-Française. For other excitements there were the gambling hells, licensed by the police, and bringing both a revenue of eight million francs a year to the State, and very handsome rents to the king, in whose Palais-Royal many of them were located – until the end of 1836 when, in an excess of belated conscience, he ordered them all to be closed down, leaving the field to the private parties organized by impoverished aristocrats.

One of Auguste's dandy friends at this period drew a shrewd portrait of him:

> Well-educated for a man about town, a taste for idleness and the ability to be industrious, complete belief in himself, boldness, courage, composure, clear judgement, wit, gaiety, made more for good fellowship than for friendship, for patronage than for devotion, fond of pleasure, insistent on luxury, both prodigal and greedy, more of a gambler than a careerist, faithful to his personal engagement but bound by no higher principles of politics or humanity.

It was for social reasons that Auguste obtained a commission in the cavalry in December 1830. The army's principal function was to perform police duties at home. To avoid contamination by the liberals, units were constantly being moved from one garrison town to another, so that one of the most familiar sights on French highways was the procession of straggling soldiers trying to catch up with their regiments. Auguste, however, contrived never to be posted far from Paris and, after two years of idling in Staff College, settled into the very fashionable First Lancers stationed at Fontainebleau, looking very handsome in his red uniform with blue facings. But despite his outward inanity he needed something more than success in the ballroom and boudoir; the ambiguities of his birth and upbringing had given him a thirst for the certainty of fame.

There had been some alarms at home. The Duchess of Berry slipped in from Italy and headed a legitimate rising that flickered up from Provençe to blaze with great ferocity in the oldest of dissident provinces, Brittany and the Vendée. Cholera, which swept through France and much of Europe early in 1832, removed the firm hand of Casimire Périer from government. In the ensuing hesitancy republican riots broke out in Paris and endured for two days of bloody fighting, before a new government of Liberal Orleanists was formed, with one of Alexandre Walewski's close friends, the historian Adolphe Thiers, among the ministers. The romantic Duchess of Berry was betrayed by one of her supporters and imprisoned in the citadel of Blaye. Here she numbered among her guards a dashing grenadier, guitarist and ballad singer, Lieutenant Armand de Saint-Arnaud, who was to become famous for other reasons later. And here, too, within the citadel walls, the duchess, a widow for nearly twelve years, gave birth to a baby, to the vast embarrassment of all legitimists, and the great glee of the government.[22]

Emilie had herself become a mother, for the second time, in April 1832. She christened her daughter with her own name and nicknamed her Minette because, with her snub nose and dark Spanish colouring that she had inherited from her grandmother, Theresa, she looked like a little black kitten. Emilie now had her surviving twin, Henry de Brigode, her new baby, Emilie de Chimay, and was to add another son, Joseph de Chimay, in October 1836. She was loved, living in luxury and entirely happy.

As for Auguste de Morny, the itch for distinction was unrelieved. He decided to seek it on the field of battle. 'Talking of tearful women,' the Duke of Orleans wrote to his brother, Nemours, 'Morny is leaving for Africa.'

*

Auguste was following in the footsteps of Alexandre Walewski, who, in August 1833, was gazetted captain in the Foreign Legion, despite an army regulation that non-French-born officers could not be promoted above lieutenant until after seven years' service. The influence of his friends, including General Charles de Flahaut, could not carry him further. His proposed appointment as aide-de-camp to the Duke of Orleans fell through – some said because malicious tongues were making much of the duke's open admiration for young Madame Walewska; and his nomination to the staff of Marshal Gérard was blocked by War Office bureaucrats. To remove some of the official obstacles, Alexandre successfully applied for naturalization as a French citizen in December 1833. On 30 April 1834 his wife died giving birth to their son, Charles. The sumptuous apartment in the Rue de Londres was suddenly chilly. He applied to be posted to his regiment in Algeria.[23]

The Polish companies of the Legion were stationed at Oran, engaged in building a road to Mers-el-Kabir. Alexandre reported for duty with his valet and his cook, and entertained his fellow officers to a series of dinners so magnificent that they appointed him Mess Secretary. For a month they lived like kings – only to discover that their mess bills had doubled. Alexandre's patrician assurance that they need not worry because he would foot the difference was rejected and a new Mess Secretary appointed.[24] In any event, he was already moving on. Now that he was a French subject he was qualified to serve in a French regiment, and, in August 1834, he transferred to the Second Regiment of the Chasseurs à Cheval d'Afrique; and to the General Staff, where the Divisional Commander, General Desmichels, took him as aide-de-camp. Alexandre thus found himself closely involved in the argument that arose between Desmiches and the Governor-General of Algeria over a treaty with the Arab leader, Abd-el-Kader, Emir of Mascara.

Alexandre had a hand in subsequent negotiations, and Desmichels, who sent his report directly to the Ministry of War, at the same time gave Alexandre sick leave and told him to give a personal account to the Minister when he reached Paris. The governor-general protested at his subordinate dealing with the ministry over his head, and Alexandre had a cold reception. Desmichels' recommendation that he should be admitted to the Legion of Honour was turned down; Desmichels himself was sent home.[25]

Alexandre applied for yet another exchange – this time to the 4th Hussars. In the eighteen months since he joined the army, he had won no promotion or decoration, but he had managed to move from the Foreign Legion infantry to colonial cavalry and now to a crack metropolitan regiment. He was given special leave because of the illness of his son, Charles, who died on 9 May 1835. He joined his regiment at Nevers in May, and in the following month went with them to Fontainebleau. Although he did not officially resign his commission until the beginning of 1841, the army saw little of him from now on.

With his friends from the Cercle de l'Union, he had been one of the twelve founder-members in November 1833 of the Jockey Club. By day they rode as gentlemen-jockeys at Chantilly and Le Raincy, in the Bois de Boulogne or on the Champs de Mars. By night they gathered at the Opera, at that time handily placed in the Rue Le Pelletier, the next street to the Club's premises in the Rue de la Grange-Batelière.[26]

Shortly before Alexandre went off to Algeria, his half-brother in illegitimacy, Charles Macon, began to make his name in the National Guard; a less glamorous setting than the Legion or the Lancers, but one that he shortly illustrated with his peculiar blend of conceit and pugnacity. He was now established as Count Leon and openly claiming to be 'the Emperor Napoleon's natural son'. Since gaining control of his own finances he had been getting rid of his money at great speed, and winning an unsavoury reputation on the rackety fringes of Paris society.[27]

As early as the spring of 1832, at the age of twenty-five, he had fought a duel with Charles Hesse, a Prussian by birth who had served the Prince Regent's unhappy wife, Caroline of Brunswick, as equerry and had lost an arm in the 18th Hussars at Waterloo. Hesse was involved in a gambling club set up in the Baron de Rosenberg's apartment in the Boulevard Montmartre. There was talk of Rosenberg doctoring the drinks and Hesse cheating the befuddled guests. When Leon lost 16,000 francs in one evening to Hesse, he first gave him an IOU for the money, then withdrew it, and became caught up in a brawl which ended in a duel at Vincennes.[28]

Leon was supported by several Napoleonic celebrities, including Dominique Larrey, the former Chief Surgeon of the Grande Armée, and General Gourgaud, who had shared much of Napoleon's exile on St Helena and was almost as conceited and touchy as Leon himself. The two duelists, armed with pistols, stood facing outwards at marks set ten paces apart. At the word of command, each took another ten paces, turned and was at liberty to fire immediately or to advance on his opponent and fire at any point before he reached the mark at which he began. Both men marched their ten paces and turned. Hesse fired immediately. The ball missed Leon, who then walked forward five paces, fired and hit Hesse in the chest. Larrey tried to have the wounded man taken to Paris in an ambulance provided by the artillery regiment in garrison at the fortress of Vincennes, but he was too badly injured to be moved and died soon after. Leon was charged with manslaughter but acquitted. When Baron de Rosenberg tried, as Hesse's partner, to collect the unpaid gambling debt, Leon denounced him to the police for running an illicit gambling parlour and he left the country.

Leon, too, felt he needed a change of air. He went down to Italy shortly afterwards, to call on Madame Mère and Cardinal Fesch. Madame Mère, immobilized by a hip injury and almost totally blind with inoperable cateracts, could provide little in the way of a reception for her grandson, but the Cardinal with priestly grace and ambiguity assured him that 'it will give me as much pleasure to see you as it gave me on your last trip to Rome'. This was in answer to a letter written by Leon from Civia Vecchia explaining that he had been detained in quarantine because of the cholera scare. In the same letter Leon promised that he would never again lose 45,000 francs at the gaming tables as he had done recently. If this was intended as a prelude to asking Fesch for money, there is no indication that it met with any success.[29]

Back in Paris once more he had a letter from General Bertrand, telling him of secret clauses in the Emperor's will. The 'legacies of conscience' to his bastard sons (poor Emilie, as a female, got nothing) were to be paid out of the two million francs he claimed that Marie-Louise owed him, and another two millions which Eugene de Beauharnais had received from the sale of silver, jewels and other property which he had held as Viceroy of Italy. But, alas, despite all the efforts of Bertrand, Marchand and Montholon as Napoleon's executors, neither Marie-Louise nor Eugene's heirs had been willing to hand over the money. Leon was to get no more than the shares allotted to him at birth and now largely dissipated. It was a grievance that fermented in his unstable mind, while recklessness and bad luck carried him down in the world.

Early in 1834 he moved from the Rue St-Honoré, where he had lived for the previous two years, to a house in the northern suburb of St-Denis, and took up his duties in the National Guard there with his usual unbridled enthusiasm.[30] The Guard had been a hot-bed of anti-monarchism during the reign of Charles X, who dissolved it in 1830. But its opposition to Charles made it a pampered pet of Louis-Philippe, who regarded it as one of the soundest pillars of his throne. Every taxpayer, or son of a taxpayer, between the ages of twenty and sixty was liable for duty approximately three or four times a year. Officers were chosen by secret ballot; Leon, with his distinguished military parentage and unequivocal looks to prove it, was elected as major and sworn in by the Mayor of St-Denis on 20 April 1834.

Within a couple of months he was locked in battle with his commanding officer, a Colonel Benoist. St-Denis was called upon to provide a detachment of forty-one men for the king's guard at Neuilly, where Louis-Philippe preferred to spend his time whenever he could get away from the Tuileries. Leon applied to the mayor for permission to command this fine body of men, and the mayor consented; whereupon Benoist protested that, although the National Guard was a citizen army under civilian control, the mayor still had the duty to follow military procedures by communicating with the major only through the colonel. Leon leapt on his high horse and soon had everybody embroiled in a thundering row which swept up the sub-prefect in its wake. Despite the distraction of simultaneously prosecuting a law-suit against a man who had sold him a couple of bad horses, and defending one against a man who accused him of cheating over the sale of a picture, Leon kept the dispute on the boil until the last week of July, when the sub-prefect suspended him for two months and some of his supporters came out on the streets in protest. Leon took this opportunity of relief from his official duties to pop over to England and see what could be made out of his Uncle Joseph.[31]

Joseph Bonaparte had returned across the Atlantic in 1832, and taken a large house at Denham, from whence he kept a cautious eye on events in Paris and expended considerable sums in suborning the press, largely through Leon's former guardian, Meneval. Lucien Bonaparte was with Joseph when Leon called; he had met the young man during one of his visits to Rome. Either he had no idea of his nephew's character, or when he warned Joseph of it, the latter turned a deaf ear, as most of the family did to Lucien, who was considered to be too sharp for other people's good. Meneval, who seems to have known nothing of Leon's trip to England, was startled to receive a letter in which Joseph told him that Leon:

was here with me for two days; he looks like the Emperor. He appeared to me to have great spirit and warmth. He wishes to devote his time and energy to getting the Chamber to repeal the law of proscription which weighs heavily on the Emperor's family. He has a natural eloquence and seemed to me to have a thirst for study which is revealed in the erudition that one discerns in his conversation.

Meneval knew better than most that Joseph was a consequential ass (he had been his secretary before transferring to Napoleon), but he was staggered by this appraisal of his former ward's talents and aghast at Joseph's request 'to have him make the acquaintance of the few friends that events have left me'.[32]

On the matter of his share of the Emperor's estate, now reaching the end of its protracted winding-up, Leon got no more than a sympathetic but non-committal hearing from Uncle Joseph, who was never a fool when it came to money. Nevertheless he returned to St-Denis in the latter half of September in the highest spirits, resumed his command and immediately published a protest at the 'illegal and unjust' treatment he had suffered at the hands of his colonel and the sub-prefect. The sub-prefect suspended him again to the accompaniment of more protests. He was then relieved of his duties by Royal Warrant, but he managed to keep the dispute rumbling for another year, when it was finally settled by a new major being elected in his place.

Leon moved back to 15 Rue Talbout in Paris, while at the same time helping to run General Gourgaud's candidature for a seat in the chamber as representative for St-Denis. Gourgaud wrote to him: 'With your powerful intervention I have excellent prospects.... Remember that in working for me you are also working for yourself, for I should be quite happy to quit the chamber to make room for you.' Not unexpectedly, with such distinguished support, Gourgaud failed to get in. It was now the turn of Leon's cousin, Prince Louis, to add a touch of farce to the story.

*

When Hortense and Prince Louis returned to Switzerland in the late summer of 1831, they settled down to a seemingly unadventurous existence. Hortense had reshaped the old battlemented castle into a peaceful country house and laid out flower beds and lawns, where she strolled in the freckled shade of the willows and poplars she had planted. From the terrace she looked out across the Rhine to villages half-hidden in dark woods, to the town of Constance and the main lake, with sometimes a glimpse of snowcapped mountains beyond. Indoors, the principal reception room was decorated in Empire style, like a tent, dominated by a bust of the dead Emperor, and littered with Napoleonic mementoes. Felix Cottreau, whom she had met in Italy and found to be a perfect partner at piano and guitar though a rather indifferent painter of religious and historical subjects, was now her established lover. At forty-eight she had lost little of her charm and attractive looks.

Prince Louis resumed his military studies and, an unflagging, never-satisfied, compulsive, fickle *cotillonneur*, he drifted dreamily from boudoir to boudoir, sampling the erotic delights of Swiss provincial cities. He had scarcely returned when the Poles, impressed by stories of his prowess in Italy, asked him to command a corps of French volunteers in their struggle against the Russians; he refused, on the pretext that support from a Bonaparte would embarrass their cause.[33] His eyes were now firmly fixed on France, as were Hortense's. In November Louis-Philippe's secret police learned of a Bonapartist plot to seize fortresses in eastern France after winning over the garrisons, and uncovering a bank account opened by Hortense with 12,000 francs to pay the conspirators. In 1832 the law of banishment against Napoleon's relations was again renewed.

To some it seemed that the danger of a Bonapartist revival was diminishing, for it was clear that the Duke of Reichstadt could not live much longer. Metternich reported to the Austrian Kaiser on 7 June 1832 that 'I no longer see the slightest hope of recovery', but when he expressed the same opinion to the Austrian ambassador in Paris he added:

> I beg you to call King Louis-Philippe's attention to the person who will succeed the Duke of Reichstadt. I use the word succeed for in the Bonapartist hierarchy there is a succession openly avowed and respected by the party. Young Louis Bonaparte is a man involved in factional intrigues.... The day the Duke dies he will consider himself as called to be head of the French Republic.[34]

He had, indeed, already made his claim. In May that year Prince Louis published a pamphlet, *Political Day-Dreams*, in which he repeated some of the St Helena fictions, including the pretence that Napoleon had instituted his dictatorship only to preserve the liberties of the Republic. He provided the outline of a 'constitutional project' for just such a new empire. It was no doubt the publication of this brochure that had decided Joseph to venture over to England and see what his nephew was up to. A little after dawn on the morning that he set sail from America his other nephew, the Duke of Reichstadt, died at Schönbrunn.

Prince Louis was equally eager to know what his uncle had in mind about the succession to the vacant pretender's throne. In the autumn he went to London with Francesco Arese, a friend he had made in Rome six years before. His pamphlet and his choice of companion – Count Arese was an active Liberal who had served in the Foreign Legion during exile from Italy – brought a letter of complaint from his father, who was trying to live out the rest of his life in peace. Prince Louis, petulant for once, snapped back: 'It really is very distressing to find you vexed with me at every turn, whether I venture to express an opinion or whether I travel from one country to another in search of distraction.... Remember, *father*, that I am twenty-five and no longer a child.'[35] Nor was he any better pleased with his uncle's attitude. For when he asked him what was to be done about the Bonapartist claims, Joseph advised him to go home and get married as soon as possible. 'How can you expect the French to remember us', Prince Louis wrote wrathfully to Hortense, 'when for the past fifteen years the only motive governing the actions of every member of my family has been the fear of compromising himself?'[36]

When he returned home after six fruitless months in England, he found that Hortense shared at least of one Joseph's opinions and was trying to arrange a marriage for him with a daughter of the Corsican-born General Arrighi, Duke of Padua in the old Imperial honours list and a relation of the Bonapartes through Elisa's husband, Bacciochi. It might at least have reduced the expense of the several mistresses Prince Louis was keeping in

Constance and elsewhere; but the general failed to put up a sufficiently attractive marriage settlement and the negotiations fell through. Prince Louis continued with his pamphleteering. In 1833 he published *Political and Military Considerations relating to Switzerland*, which, despite its title, had a lot to say about France and ended with a stirring eulogy of the Imperial army. He was awarded honorary Swiss citizenship and appointed a captain of artillery in the Canton of Berne.

'I know that I am much through my name, nothing as yet through myself,' Prince Louis wrote in January 1835 to his former tutor, Vieillard, 'provoking the same fears through my name in Liberals as well as Absolutists.' But he added that he was determined to climb 'high enough to catch the dying rays of the sun of St Helena'.[37] That they were not dying as fast as they might was thanks in some part to Louis-Philippe. In the hope of basking in their reflected glory he had already replaced the Bourbon lilies on the top of the Vendôme Column with a new statue of Napoleon; he was about to finish off the Arc de Triomphe, which Napoleon had begun in 1806; he had ordered the completion of the Column of the Grande Armée at Boulogne; and he was considering negotiating for the return of Napoleon's ashes from St Helena. With all this encouragement from the opposition Prince Louis could have no doubt that his principal aim must be to identify himself with Napoleon. His first task was to solicit support in the army. He completed his *Manual of Artillery for Swiss Officers* – a reminder that he had specialized in the Emperor's arm of the service – and sent copies to as many French officers as he could claim even the remotest link with.[38] He took to spending a great deal of time in Baden – handy for meeting visitors from garrisons just over the border – and was often accompanied by his first permanent disciple, Jean-Gilbert-Victor Fialin, who styled himself Vicomte de Persigny.

Persigny, tall, dark, intense, had no right to the title of nobility, although he came of a family well respected in the valley of the Loire and had served as a non-commissioned officer in the 4th Hussars, the regiment that Alexandre Walewski was to join later. He was discharged in 1830 because of his extreme republican views and had since wedded these to fervent Bonapartism. It was Uncle Joseph who first came across him in England and sent him to Arenenberg with a note of recommendation. Since leaving the army he had been working in Paris as a journalist. Prince Louis was not slow to recognize his value as a devoted, if sometimes almost too fanatical, publicist. It was Persigny who helped him follow up and cultivate each new military acquaintance that he made with presentation copies of the *Manual*, and to sustain a continuous flow of letters to the newspapers explaining, refuting, expostulating, continually getting space for his name and its association with Bonapartism. He came into Prince Louis' life at just the right moment; for Hortense's influence was waning, not from lack of will but from physical weakness. It was Persigny who provided a great deal of the driving force for the next fifteen years.

Other members of the family were in the news: Uncle Jerome's wife, Catherine of Württenberg, died in November 1835; and Madame Mère in the following February. In May that year, Prince Louis' cousin, Pierre, son of Lucien Bonaparte, tried to shoot his way out when arrested by Papal Carabinieri, fatally wounded one of them and was only with difficulty saved from execution. Aunt Caroline Murat, after years of waiting, obtained permission to return to France for a brief visit. Uncle Joseph, once again in America and plagued with suspicions that things were going on behind his back, decided to return to London, where he rented at house at 24 Park Crescent at the end of August 1836. About the same time the widowed Jerome arrived at Arenenberg with his daughter, Mathilde, to visit his son Napoleon-Joseph, who had been staying with Hortense since his mother died.

There was never much sympathy between Louis-Napoleon and Napoleon-Joseph, whom the family nicknamed 'Plon-Plon'. He was fourteen and already had the dusky skin, morose scowl and pronounced Bonaparte features that reminded his seniors of 'the Emperor on a bad day'. As time went on he was to accentuate this likeness by adopting the familiar posture, leaning forward, hands clasped behind his back, large head on short neck sunk into hock-bottle shoulders, thus making Prince Louis in comparison look more than ever an inexplicable member of the Bonaparte brood. His sister, on the other hand, was intelligent, charming and pretty. Hortense saw an appreciative gleam in Prince Louis' eye, and hastened to make the most of it. For marriage with Mathilde would strengthen his standing as the principal Bonaparte pretender. Jerome, a spendthrift very nearly at the end of his money, was entirely in favour of the union – if Hortense would put up a large settlement for her son and accept a very small one on Mathilde. By the time he left it was agreed that they would soon discuss a date for the marriage, though there was plenty of time on Mathilde's side, for she was only just sixteen. She left in a tiny flood of happy tears, wearing a turquoise ring in the shape of a forget-me-not that Prince Louis had given her.

Prince Louis went back to Baden with Persigny for conferences with an operatic singer named Eleonore Brault-Gordon. She was an imposing woman, twenty-eight years old, the daughter of a former captain in the Imperial Guard and herself an enthusiastic Bonapartist. She had been married briefly to an Englishman named Sir Gordon Archer; she may possibly have met and fallen in love with Prince Louis during a visit to London, and she was almost certainly the mistress of Persigny, but neither he nor she had any hesitation in sacrificing her formidable charms to the cause by seducing the commander of the 4th Regiment of Artillery, Colonel Vaudrey. Vaudrey, aged forty-nine, was known to be nursing a grievance at having been given so little promotion since Waterloo, where he served as a major. Miss Gordon moved to Strasbourg where the 4th Regiment was stationed; she was followed by Persigny under an assumed name. At the end of the summer Prince Louis joined them one evening with the help of a false passport. Before he left he was introduced to some two dozen officers from artillery and engineer units, who all pledged to help him.

It was not wise for him to be away from his known haunts for long, for he was still kept under casual observation by the French secret service. He spent a day or two in Baden, then went back to Arenenberg. He flitted backwards and forwards between the two, plotting, consulting, polishing his plans. Hortense had no need to ask what he was up to, though she pretended not to know. On the evening of Monday, 24 October he told her he was leaving next morning to join a hunting party at Hechingen, fifty miles away, the estate of one of his Uncle Eugene's daughters, Eugenie. Hortense gave him a gold ring, saying 'Wear this, it will bring you good luck.' Inside was the inscription: *Napoléon Buonaparte – Joséphine Tascher;* it was his grandmother's wedding ring.[39]

*

In October 1835, Louis-Philippe sent the Duke of Orleans to North Africa to lead an attack on Abd-el-Kader. Auguste de Morny, still only a second-lieutenant, was appointed aide-de-camp to the general commanding the advance guard of the four-brigade force which left Oran for the Emir's stronghold at Mascara. They took part in some brisk skirmishing on the way and entered Mascara in December, finding it deserted and partially destroyed. On their return march to the coast the weather turned from sun to rain, from rain to sleet and hail. Auguste, weak from fever and exposure, was promoted to lieutenant and sent on sick leave to Paris, where he idled away the spring and summer of 1836 in the elegant dandy round of riding stables or the Bois de Boulogne in the morning; the Boulevard, the Café Tortoni, the Café Anglais, the Café de Paris in the afternoon; the clubs, the theatres, the fashionable salons in the evening.

A friend wrote of him: 'Without being exactly handsome, he had a delicate, kindly cast of features, elegance and distinction; practised at all skills, he was one of our best gentleman-riders; the friend of the Duke of Orleans, and sometimes his successful rival, he scored many brilliant successes with women.' Even to the more critical eye of the journalist Maxime du Camp he appeared to have 'rare distinction, admirable ease of manners, perfect grace. Well-proportioned, of medium height, blond, prematurely bald, with attractive blue eyes, he strolled leisurely through life, the spoilt child of fortune.'

Alexandre Walewski strolled with him. They were frequently seen together, close friends as well as rivals on the racecourses: on one occasion Alexandre knocked himself unconscious for six hours by falling off one of Auguste's horses in a steeplechase at the Duke of Orleans's estate at Le Raincy.[40] It was Auguste's rivalry with the duke in the matter of ladies that brought him the companionship of the woman who was to share his life for a quarter of a century: Countess Fanny Le Hon.

Françoise-Zoe-Mathilde Le Hon was the daughter of an immensely rich Dutch banker and mine-owner named Mosselmann, and the wife of Charles Le Hon, an elderly lawyer and politician. She had been born and brought up in Paris (her grandmother was the Pellapras' friend Madame Gazzani) and, when Le Hon was appointed ambassador to France of the newly-constituted Kingdom of Belgium in 1831, she converted her home – once that of a less fortunate banker, Jacques Récamier – into the Embassy, preserving intact the bedroom with the Empire couch on which Julie Récamier had posed for her famous portrait by David. The new hostess in the Rue du Mail could bear comparison with her predecessor:

> She was as slender as a wasp, yet had splendid shoulders. Her face was attractive even though her features were not regular; magnificent eyes and blond hair of a delightful shade did wonders for it even though it was a little flat and the mouth a little disdainful. Add to that a supreme elegance, toilettes that were admired everywhere, a rare wit, good education, a very serious mind beneath the affectation of frivolity, and you may understand the great success of the Belgian Ambassadress.

Soon after her husband's appointment as ambassador, she became a very close friend of the Duke of Orleans, and it was widely assumed that he was the father of her eldest child, a boy christened Leopold. She was familiar with Auguste (who was three years her junior) because of his friendship with the duke and their meetings at the houses of common friends; but she had a special interest in him because her father had known Hortense well during her unhappy period as Queen of Holland. As time passed she learned Hortense's secret and sent her news of Morny, who had become her lover and was lightly disguised in the correspondence as 'sister Augustine'. Hortense showed considerable affection for 'Augustine' in her replies. 'All I want is to know her to be as happy as it is possible for her to be.... *This letter is for both of you.*' And in 1836 Fanny travelled to Arenenberg to report in person.

It may well be because of what Fanny learned during this visit that Auguste became involved in the adventure on which Prince Louis was embarking when he left Arenenberg wearing his grandmother Josephine's wedding ring in October. The story told by Maxime du Camp, but not published until more than fifty years after his own death and almost one hundred years after the event described, contradicts the formerly accepted theory that Auguste and Prince Louis did not meet until several years later, and that the prince did not discover the existence of his illegitimate half-brother until after Hortense's death. It would have delighted Hortense's romantic heart to know that both her surviving sons were taking part in the great adventure, and she may well have hinted to Fanny Le Hon that Auguste should join Prince Louis without revealing the exact nature of the plan.

According to du Camp's account, Auguste called at the 1st Lancers' barracks in October 1836 and spent some time in the company of a young fellow-officer, an Alsatian named Obermann. At the end of the month he disappeared briefly, returning to Paris on 2 November, leaving again almost immediately for Toulon. From this point onwards the facts are not in dispute: he crossed the Mediterranean to Bône, where he arrived on 12 November; next day he left with the column that was to attack the great Berber fortress perched above the deep ravine at Constantine. The attack failed, but Lieutenant de Morny displayed considerable bravery, saving the life of his commanding officer, and was awarded the Knight's Cross of the Legion of Honour.

Back in France at the 1st Lancers' barracks, Second-Lieutenant Obermann was puzzled, and at first alarmed to receive a visit from a squad of detectives and a *juge d'instruction* who showed him a passport and asked if it belonged to him. Obermann replied that it did. Then what, asked the examining magistrate, had he been doing at the Maison Rouge Hotel in Strasbourg on the night of 29/30 October, when he engaged a room and offered his passport as identification but did not return to collect the following morning? Obermann denied that he had been anywhere near Strasbourg at the time. By good fortune he had been on duty and could produce his captain and a troop of lancers as witnesses. It was not until twenty years later that he learned from Morny the explanation of the mystery.[41]

*

When he left Arenenberg on Monday, 24 October 1836 Prince Louis did not go north to his cousin's estate at Hechingen but north-west to Freiburg on the Upper Rhine.

There he was joined by Colonel Vaudrey and Madame Gordon – an imposing pair who completely dwarfed him – but not by other French officers whom he had hoped would come from Paris. On Friday they moved on to Strasbourg, entering under the cover of darkness just before the city gates were closed at 11 p.m. The Colonel and Madame Gordon went off together after leaving Prince Louis at the lodgings which Persigny had rented in the Rue de la Fontaine.

Saturday was a day of conferences, held in yet another rented apartment in the Rue des Orphelines. Prince Louis' plan was simple and based on a sound historical precedent. He proposed to march on Paris and mount the throne just as Napoleon had done when he returned from Elba. He would be marching at the head of his uncle's old regiment, the 4th Artillery, which he had commanded at the siege of Toulon; as they went along they would be greeted by bands of delirious Frenchmen and joined by the garrisons from other towns: Metz, Luneville, Nancy, Châlons, Lyons, Lille, with whom he and Persigny and other members of the plot had secretly been making contact during the past months. There were, it was true, some differences between Napoleon's march and his own.[42] He had, for example, never been Emperor of the French before; Napoleon's troups were 600 battle-proven grenadiers, who had spent more than a decade in his service, while Prince Louis' artillerymen had never even seen him; many Frenchmen in 1815 had been ready to get rid of the Bourbon king, whom their recent enemies had imposed upon them, but there was no indication that anything like a majority were yet resentful of the Orleans king who had replaced the Bourbons. But to Colonel Vaudrey, bewitched by Madame Gordon, to the Viscount de Persigny, bewitched by the Bonaparte name, and to Prince Louis, bewitched by the legend of Napoleon, these were considerations of small importance.

That night, before he went to bed for a few hours of restless sleep, Prince Louis wrote two letters to his mother, one to be posted if he were successful, the other if he failed. He had already composed, and read to his comrades, the proclamations he was to make to the army: 'Deliver the Motherland from traitors and oppressors, protect the rights of the people: defend France and her allies against invasion – that is the road to which Honour summons you... !' To the People of Strasbourg: 'You have called me to you so that we may conquer or die in the cause of the people.... Tomorrow we march on Paris to deliver the capital from traitors and oppressors!' To the People of France: 'Confident in the sanctity of my cause I present myself to you with the Testament of the Emperor Napoleon in one hand and the Sword of Austerlitz in the other.... From the Rock of St Helena a shaft of the dying sun has lit up my soul; I will keep that sacred flame alive; I will conquer or die for the people's cause.' He signed them all: 'Napoleon', for, as he said 'my name is a banner which should recall great memories to you'.

When the conspirators stepped out into the street early next morning the cobbles were sprinkled with a thin covering of snow, grey in the faint light. All of them wore some sort of uniform, and many had granted themselves promotion. Fifty-year-old Colonel Parquin, who had served in the Chasseurs of the Imperial Guard and was the widower of Hortense's former reader, Louise Cochelet, had become a general overnight. Prince Louis, a captain in the Swiss army, was dressed in a French artillery colonel's uniform of blue with red facings, but wearing a general's hat and a heavy cavalry sabre and sporting the star of the Legion of Honour. He was accompanied by a standard bearer who carried an Imperial eagle on a pole, discreetly shrouded for the moment.

It had been decided that the first regiment to be courted should be Colonel Vaudrey's 4th Artillery, where there was known to be a strong Bonapartist sentiment. Having gained their support, Prince Louis and their own officers would lead them to the opposite side of the town, to win over the 46th Infantry who were quartered in the Finkmatt Barracks. These two regiments would then march to the central Place d'Armes, gathering up the 3rd Artillery and a battalion of engineers whose barracks were nearby. Two remaining infantry regiments, stationed on the outskirts, could be expected to follow the lead of the others, if only because they would by this time be outnumbered and outgunned.

Everything began perfectly. Vaudrey had his men drawn up on the square at the Austerlitz Barracks, aware that some great event was impending though they did not yet know what. Prince Louis entered the gates; Vaudrey saluted him, led him to the centre of the parade ground and presented him to the troops. This was the Emperor's nephew – returned to restore the Rights of the People, the Glory and Liberty of France and the Army – would they support him? There was an immediate roar of cheering and shouts of *Vive l'Empereur!* followed by a roll of drums. The prince addressed them, recalling Napoleon's association with the regiment. 'Yours is the glory of beginning a great enterprise; yours the honour of being the first to salute the Eagle of Austerlitz and Wagram.' He held aloft the staff with the bronze bird unveiled: 'This is the symbol of French Glory! For fifteen years it led our fathers to victory; it gleamed above every battlefield; it passed through every capital of Europe!' There was a great tumult of *Vive l'Empereur!*, with swords and busbies flourished in the air. The first and vital round was won.[43]

The prince's aides hurried off through a flurry of snow to set the second part of the plan in motion: some to carry the news to the 3rd Artillery, the Engineers and the 46th Infantry and get them to parade on the Place d'Armes; others to seize the telegraph office and arrest the prefect and two or three senior officers likely to cause trouble: others to take over the printing presses and rush out the prince's proclamations. The band struck up, the prince took up his position at the head of the regiment and off they marched through the main streets in the direction of Finkmatt Barrack. The guard of the gendarmerie and district headquarters presented arms as they passed; the few citizens already stirring in the streets or at their bedroom windows gave them a goodnatured cheer; the prince called in on the district commander to invite his co-operation and, when it was refused, placed him under close arrest. The tall fierce battle-scarred Colonel (temporary general) Parquin, a very familiar figure from Arenenberg where he was continually springing to attention and yelling: 'Parquin! Soldier of the Emperor!' was given custody of this important prisoner and shortly afterwards managed to let him escape.

The march continued. The plan called for the prince to parade with the regiment on the northern ramparts which dominated the Finkmatt Barrack square from the rear, and harangue the infantrymen from there. But as the artillerymen approached the barracks somebody, from stupidity or overeagerness, swung right into a side street that led directly to the main gate. Instead of being

147

supported by his thousand men drawn up in a line behind him, the prince found himself at the head of a narrow column, filing slowly down the street and through the gate. The officer who had been sent to tell the infantrymen of the artillerymen's decision to support the prince had inexplicably failed to arrive, but the hubbub brought many of them to the windows and down to the square. Prince Louis' supporters chanted *Vive l'Empereur!* Some of the infantrymen took it up. One of them, a former sergeant of the Imperial Guard, ran forward and knelt to kiss the prince's hand. The gesture brought more cheers. The Bonapartist officers moved around among the infantrymen, beginning to form them into makeshift companies, preparatory to marching off to the Place d'Armes.

From the rear of the square, one of the infantry officers shouted: 'Men! They are making fools of you! This person whom they present to you as the Emperor's nephew is a puppet. He is Colonel Vaudrey's nephew!'[44] Suddenly the infantrymen saw the light. It was only too clear from this man's face that, whoever his uncle might be, it was not Napoleon. There was not a single Bonaparte trait to be seen. And why did he speak with a German accent? They were outraged at being deceived and annoyed still more when some of the artillerymen renewed their cries of *Vive l'Empereur!* Scuffles broke out. The infantry formed up to charge the artillerymen, while the crowds that had gathered on the ramparts began to throw stones at the infantrymen. The prince shouted that he never intended to seize power by violence. He was scarcely heard and grossly outnumbered. Driven up against the barrack wall, he surrendered his sword to an officer of the 46th. Vaudrey ordered his artillerymen to return to their quarters. The whole plot, apparently successful an hour before, collapsed in disarray. The Engineers and the 3rd Regiment, already on their way to the rendezvous at the Place d'Armes, turned round and doubled back to barracks. Persigny made a desperate effort to get some guns from the arsenal, failed and disappeared. Somewhere in all the confusion, if du Camp's story is true, Auguste de Morny slipped away and back to Paris, leaving nothing more incriminating behind him than Second-Lieutenant Obermann's passport.

The other prominent rebels were marched off to detention, but robbed of martyrdom in the days that followed by the government's shrewd decision to make light of the affair. When the coup had appeared to be successful, Prince Louis' valet, Thérin, had sent off the 'victory' letter to Hortense, whose reply, urging her son to treat the members of the overturned government with clemency and 'at least spare the Royal Family' was published amid gales of laughter. To make the young Pretender appear even more foolish, he was whisked off to Brittany to be put on a boat for America (with a well-publicized generous gift of 15,000 francs in gold from the king – which was, in fact, a very small fraction of the 200,000 francs seized from him on his arrest), thus appearing to get off scot free while his deluded supporters languished in prison awaiting trial. But this part of the plan recoiled on the government, for when the conspirators were brought into court the unruly Alsation jurors of Strasbourg, after twelve days of damning evidence for the prosecution, declared every one of the accused men innocent and released them to a night of defiant civic celebration.

For a brief moment Prince Louis lost faith in his destiny and wrote to Hortense that he intended to settle down as a farmer when he reached America. But she knew better than to believe this and was already preparing to combat the unfavourable publicity he had blundered into. She travelled to Paris directly she heard the real facts about Strasbourg. There she anonymously offered a publisher the *Memoirs about Queen Hortense and the Imperial Family* written by Louise Cochelet. Since Louise's death in May the year before, Hortense had been editing and revising the manuscript, presenting herself and her son as two misguided patriots, innocent of all guile, devoted only to their country and the liberal ideals of Napoleon. The publisher snapped up the offer and, in accordance with Hortense's stipulation, had the memoirs in print and on sale before the end of November.[45]

The Strasbourg escapade was yet another source of grievance for the rest of the Bonapartes. Joseph, in particular, could scarcely contain his wrath at his nephew's deceit in telling him nothing about the plot. 'He treated his father and his uncles as if we were already dead,' he wrote from London to a friend in New York. 'I am firmly determined not to receive him when I return to America.'[46] All the simmering Bonaparte–Beauharnais feud came to the boil. 'This so-called Bonapartist plot was aimed as much against us as against the present Government', he protested, adding with a bitter reference to the old family suspicions: 'There is not a drop of Napoleon's blood in his veins.'[47]

'Everything you say is true', his brother Jerome wrote from Florence. 'We only know what the papers say here, but that is enough to make one shudder at such a ridiculous undertaking. You can imagine what sort of state his unfortunate father is in. Why did Hortense let him get involved with so many intriguers?' It was clear that there was no advantage to be gained by Mathilde marrying the young man. Jerome broke off the engagement.

Joseph was as good as his word. When Prince Louis arrived in New York, after having been taken as far south as Rio de Janeiro and then up the east coast, his uncle refused to see him. Unperturbed, Prince Louis settled into the Washington Hotel on Broadway with Thélin and Count Arese, and was extensively paraded in New York society. His hosts admired his manners and his modesty, though they were startled, amused or impressed by his habit of invariably discussing his future in terms of 'When I am Emperor.'[48] He was not to enjoy the lionizing for long. On her return to Arenenberg from Paris, Hortense had been forced to consult her physician, Dr Conneau, about symptoms which had long been troubling her. Ironically, she had fallen victim to the Bonaparte family disease: cancer. Conneau told her that she might need an operation, and that she certainly should consult experts.

Louis was at this time still at sea, on his way to America, but she planned to see him once more before she died. To Fanny Le Hon she wrote in December 1836: 'I expect to go to England in the spring, and will write to you from there. Only there shall I be able to see your sister Augustine, and say goodbye to her.' Then she felt her condition worsening and wrote to Louis, warning him and sending her blessing should she not survive. But shortly afterwards she wrote again to say that the specialist had told her that no operation was necessary.

The letter did not reach Louis until 2 June 1837. Scrawled on the outside in Conneau's handwriting were the words 'Come! Come!' For the specialist had, in fact, found Hortense's condition too far advanced for any operation to be successful, although he decided not to tell her this. Prince Louis set sail from the United States on 12 June, having sent a polite note to the President, informing him of his departure and regretting his inability to visit him in Washington. He had never been invited to do so, but this was the sort of courtesy expected of a future emperor.[49]

In the second week of July he arrived in London, where the pretty and vivacious Victoria had recently succeeded her Uncle William IV to the throne. The French, Prussian and Austrian ambassadors refused to give him a passport for Switzerland, but, by impersonating an American friend, he managed to get to Rotterdam at the end of the month and then sailed up the Rhine, deeply plunged into melancholy and resentful of 'relations who shun me and enemies who fear me'. At Arenenberg he found Hortense desperately ill. Conneau's urgent *Venez! Venez!* had been only too well justified. On 9 October she died.[50]

Chapter Four:

Scheming, Losing and Winning

Hortense had asked to be buried in France beside her mother. Her body was embalmed, the permission obtained, the arrangements made, and on the bitterly cold morning of 8 January 1838 her coffin was committed to the vault in the parish church of Rueil. There was only one member of the Bonaparte family among the mourners – Caroline Murat, who had been given leave by Thiers to return temporarily to attend to business affairs. Little more than a year from death by the Bonaparte disease herself, Caroline had greatly changed in appearance but still retained her proud bearing. A whole generation of luxury and misery had passed since she vied with Hortense for supremacy in the Imperial salons and goaded her to jealousy by flirting with young Charles de Flahaut. And here, by irony of fate, Flahaut had appeared once more, pacing in the line of black-coated mourners, paying his respects to the woman who had been his mistress and the mother of his only son.

Since Prince Louis was banned from entering France, much of the work of arranging the funeral had fallen upon the devoted Valerie Masuyer, a tall, elegant brunette in her early forties, her rather plain long face enlivened by expressive blue eyes. The prince had given her permission to see his Aunt Caroline, 'on condition that I tell her nothing of what he is doing or intends to do'[1]; she found her kind and sympathetic, confirming Hortense's view that she did not hate the Beauharnais as much as the Montforts (the title taken by Jerome and his family) did. Of Charles de Flahaut, who called on her a week after the funeral, she formed a much less favourable impression:

He is one of these great diplomats, and did not fail to let me know it. He talked with me for a quarter of an hour, with the most excruciating politeness, about the Queen's last moments, exactly as a gentleman should do when discussing the death of a lady whom he has had the honour to meet – nothing more. He showed not the slightest sign of emotion on his face or in his voice, even when he saw me so overcome that he apologised for having revived memories for me.

Charles's diplomatic career had not, in fact, been making much progress since his brief mission to Berlin seven years before. He was spending more time in England and Scotland, where his wife was known by her title of Baroness Keith, and it was on his return from there in late June 1838 that he brought Auguste de Morny to meet Valerie for the first time. She was fascinated by the young man 'less tall than his father but of just as distinguished an appearance. And I have to remark that he showed unmistakeable signs of his maternal origin. He resembles the Queen perhaps even more than the Prince himself – to such a degree that I could not prevent tears springing to my eyes on seeing him.'

Loyal, discreet Valerie, who did not join Hortense's household until 1830, had not met either Charles or Auguste before, and she tried to give the impression in her memoirs that Prince Louis had no idea that Charles had been his mother's lover and that Auguste was her son. She referred to 'the tears shed by our dear Prince' when, at Arenenberg after Hortense's death, 'he learned what he had known nothing of until then'. It is an unlikely reaction, since he knew very well that his mother was in the habit of taking lovers, and it is not made any more credible by Valerie's statement at one moment that Hortense never gave the slightest hint of Auguste de Morny's existence, and at another that Hortense told her Napoleon had been so furious when he found out that he had made her promise never to see the child.

Auguste, having amply proved his courage, decided that the army and its petty regulations for stupid people – 'just like school' – no longer interested him. Early in 1838 he resigned his commission, settled down in Paris, and became Fanny Le Hon's disciple in business as well as love. Auguste's former guardian, Gabriel Delessert, was a close friend of Fanny, and Gabriel's brother, Benjamin, had played a large part in the development of the sugar-beet industry. Both the countess and Gabriel Delessert advised Auguste to buy a beet factory and plantation near Clermont-Ferrand on his return from Algeria in 1837, and it is more than likely that the countess put up most of the purchase money, 183,000 francs, though some may well have been provided by the small legacy left him by Adelaide de Souza, who died the year before. At any rate the venture was registered as a *société en commandite*: a company in which the countess was, to use the English translation, a sleeping partner.

Although he had no business training Auguste suddenly found himself in his element. At school, he wrote later in life, 'I was the most idle of children, but wonderfully clever. I could not apply myself for a quarter of an hour on end; I could give nothing any profound study. I guessed everything.' At Staff College, 'working in fits and starts, studying only those aspects of the subjects that interested me', he had shown no more application. But now he discovered that his interest caught fire when he was making money. Knowing little of the techniques of the businesses in which he successively involved himself, he reshaped and expanded them by use of his sharp intellect, a modicum of intuition, and a great deal of daring.

He modernized the factory, bought beet plantations to keep it busy and was chosen as one of the delegation sent by the beet-sugar manufacturers to lobby the government when the cane-sugar importers campaigned for equality of taxes (home-produced beet-sugar had hitherto been free from any customs or other duties). It was a losing battle, but the long struggle increased Auguste's reputation for clear thinking and forceful argument and as a skilful negotiator and pamphleteer. It also increased his wealth, for, as smaller, old-fashioned factories were driven into bankruptcy by the new taxes, Auguste bought them up and made them profitable by linking them with his own up-to-date, well-managed enterprise.

He branched out, taking over a couple of factories in Clermont-Ferrand which produced the madder-red dye used for French infantrymen's trousers. He bought shares in Mosselmann's great metal company, named after the Vielle-Montagne mine near Aix-la-Chapelle, and Fanny got him a seat on the board. He began to speculate on the Stock Exchange, fascinated by the opportunity to use his brain when he gambled, instead of submitting to the caprice of cards, dice, or the wheel. There was as much excitement, much more gratification and a far higher percentage of winnings. In 1839 he became a councillor in the Department of Puy-de-Dôme; in 1842 he was elected to the Clermont-Ferrand Chamber of Commerce; and in July of that same year he won a seat in the Chamber of Deputies as the Representative of Puy-de-Dôme.

*

At the time of the Strasbourg fiasco, Alexandre Walewski was still a serving officer in the French army. That month his stepfather, General d'Ornano, recommended him for the Cross of the Legion of Honour. It was the second time the general had put Alexandre's name forward, and the refusal was again curt and uncompromising: 'It would be the grossest injustice', noted the Director-General of Personnel. Alexandre discovered he was suffering from gravel and unable to perform his regimental duties. In September he was formally granted six months' sick leave and at the end of the month called at Arenenberg. Prince Louis was away, but the dying Hortense received him for a few minutes. He returned to Paris determined to leave the army but not yet certain what career he should adopt. After a few months disporting himself with the younger royal set, stag-hunting and attending steeplechases (at one of which his horse, Webb, a 2 to 1 favourite, was handsomely beaten by Auguste de Morny's, Taragone, the owner up), he decided to devote himself to writing.[2]

He had already published a pamphlet *An Observation on the Algerian Question*, which set out (as his own) General Desmichels's theories of peaceful penetration in North Africa. He now bought an evening paper, the *Messager des Chambres*, with the intention of giving editorial support to his friend Adolphe Thiers, a diminutive but aggressive man (Gambetta later described him as 'a bespectacled snake' and Marshal Soult referred to him as 'that little squit'), who had lost his place in the Cabinet in

1836 and was aiming to form an opposition from a combination of both right and left parties. Alexandre was a frequent visitor to his house in the Place St-Georges, where Thiers would discuss editorial policies while shaving; but he was less often seen at the *Messenger*'s offices, a former draper's shop in the business quarter, leaving the day-to-day conduct of the paper to his managing editor. In November he published a second pamphlet, *The English Alliance*, in which he supported Thiers' proposal to ally France with England rather than Russia. 'I say without hesitation: the English alliance is the guarantee of liberty in France,' wrote Alexandre.[3] But nobody seemed to pay much attention, and it was not for a year that Thiers managed to form his coalition and bring down the ministry.

By then Alexandre had lost interest in political polemics and had addressed himself to a purer form of the writer's art. Since returning from Algeria he had won the favours of Anais Aubert, a star of the Comédie-Française. He determined to bring his talents to bear on writing a worthy dramatic vehicle for his mistress. Never one to dawdle, he had his five-act piece ready by the end of 1839, and on 8 January 1840 *L'Ecole du Monde*, a Comedy of High Society, was presented at the Théâtre-Français, with Mademoiselle Aubert in the leading role and the author anonymous on the play bills, but prominently identifiable in the stage box.[4] The fashionable audience greeted the end of the first act with polite applause, which grew listless by the end of the second. From then on the pit took over, with laughter in the wrong places, a few hisses, some whistling and, at the final curtain, howls of derision, which brought the tearful collapse of both the leading lady and the author.

'The newspaper and his play and his mistress and his pretty house in the Rue Blanche and his dinners – have all put an end to his poor 50,000 francs a year', a friend wrote in her diary on 2 February 1840. 'The *Messager* is up for sale, the house has been sold for next to nothing, and the mistress would be too, if he could find a purchaser.'[5] Fortunately it was at this point that Thiers came back into government. He took the *Messager* off Alexandre's hands for 120,000 francs paid out of secret funds and set its owner off on yet another career – this time in diplomacy.

For several years past, upheavals in the Middle East had provided a bone of contention for the major powers of Europe. The principal loser had been the Sultan of Turkey, forced to grant independence to the Greeks in 1830, and during the next ten years deprived of authority over the Lebanon and Syria by the continuing advance of his nominal vassal, Mehemet Ali, Viceroy of Egypt. The undoubted beneficiary of all this had been Tsar Nicholas of Russia, and both England and France were belatedly concerned by the threat to their interests in India and the Mediterranean respectively. Yet they still could not agree upon the *alliance anglaise* that Alexandre had preached on Thiers's behalf and, when the French decided to support Mehemet Ali while England joined Russia, Prussia and Austria in bolstering the Sultan, it was ironically Thiers who had to face the allied threat to French influence and self-esteem – and Alexandre whom he chose for the secret mission by which he hoped to save France's face.

The Quadruple Alliance of Britain, Austria, Prussia and Russia demanded that Mehemet Ali call off his attempts to seize the throne of Turkey from the old Sultan's recent successor, Abdul Medjid, and to return Arabia and northern Syria to Turkish control. If he failed to do so all four countries would attack him. Thiers' plan was to persuade Mehemet Ali to accept France as a mediator and to agree to certain lesser concessions which the Sultan might be expected to accept. France would thus frustrate the Four Powers and substantially increase her standing in the eastern Mediterranean.

It was a plan that, in view of Mehemet Ali's fierce and fractious character, had only a limited chance of success. In case it should fail, Thiers decided to make the approach both secret and unofficial. Instead of instructing the French Consul at Alexandria – Adrien Cochelet, a former state councillor under Napoleon and brother to Hortense's reader – to present the proposal, he sent Walewski as his personal emissary.[6] The choice was calculated to flatter the old warrior, who had fought against Napoleon at Aboukir forty years before and would know quite well that he was dealing with his famous opponent's son.

Thiers gave Alexandre his instructions on 27 July 1840 and the next day Alexandre set off. It was to be a calamitous journey: at Fontainebleau a wheel of his carriage broke; on the road to Vichy a horse fell and nearly killed his postilion; while at Nice (he was sailing from a Savoyard port so as not to attract attention) he fell foul of the French Consul, who spread a great many disobliging stories about him. These were picked up by the opposition press in Paris, where it soon became public knowledge that Alexandre was not going to Corsica, as he had said, but to Egypt, and as Thiers' representative.

As expected, Mehemet Ali was impressed by Thiers' choice of secret agent, but it still took Alexandre a fortnight to get authority from him to negotiate with the Sultan. By the time he arrived in Constantinople the Four Power ultimatum to Mehemet Ali had expired. The Sultan appointed a new Viceroy in Mehemet Ali's place; the British fleet attacked the Syrian ports held by Mehemet Ali's son, Ibrahim. Alexandre returned to Alexandria, where he arrived on 11 October. He wrote to Thiers that he had persuaded Mehemet Ali to order Ibrahim to advance across the Taurus Mountains from Syria into Turkey, but that 'I gained the impression that we had more to fear from timidity than temerity on his [Mehemet Ali's] part; I therefore had to emphasise the need for vigour and resolution.'[7]

Mehemet Ali's timidity was justified, for the British fleet that had been bombarding the Syrian ports now threatened to come down and do the same to Alexandria. Alexandre, sent as a mediator, was becoming an agitator. His solution was to ask Thiers for 'a definite title that will establish my position' (as superior to Cochelet, whom he was busily denigrating), or alternatively to be sent to London, where he claimed to be the intimate friend of all the ministers and 'if there is still any possibility of doing anything, I shall handle it better than anybody else, for I shall be on my own ground'. In the first week of November he announced that he had solved the whole problem by persuading Mehemet Ali to sign a letter placing his fate entirely in the hands of Louis-Philippe.

It was not until the following week that he learned that Thiers had resigned on 29 October because the king refused to support his policy. Alexandre's imprudent reports had fallen into the hands of the new government of Soult and Guizot – proof that while Thiers had been claiming to restrain Mehemet Ali, his personal representative had been urging the viceroy to stand firm even at the risk of war. Alexandre went back to France, greeted by jeers and sarcasm from the anti-Thiers press.[8]

It had been a discouraging sortie into the world of serious endeavour. Doing his best to conceal his wounded pride Alexandre returned to the glamour of the Beau-Monde. He formally resigned his commission in the army and renewed his affair with Anais Aubert. But Anais was twelve years older than he, and he now set out to captivate an actress ten years his junior, though already famous for her performances in the great classical roles. She was Elisa Felix, known as Rachel: small, dark, imperious, wayward, witty, expensive but far from unattainable. 'I cannot remember ever having been a virgin', she once said. Her breadth of interest was indicated by the variety of men whom she had taken as her lovers before reaching the age of twenty-one: the gross journalist and director of the Paris Opera, Louis Véron; the precocious poet and dramatist and former lover of George Sand, Alfred de Musset; the royal and nautical Prince of Joinville, son of Louis-Philippe. Joinville was said to have conquered Rachel the first time he set eyes on her, by sending a note to her dressing-room with the simple query, 'Where? When? How much?'. His effrontery so enchanted her that she responded, 'Your place. Tonight. For nothing.'

Joinville had been very much in the news during Alexandre's mission to Egypt. His father, pursuing his ill-advised policy of trying to glow in the reflected lustre of the Napoleonic legend, had encouraged a measure permitting Napoleon's remains to be brought back to France for burial. The British government gave permission for the coffin to be removed from St Helena, and the Prince of Joinville was sent with the oddly-named *Belle Poule* to transport it to Cherbourg. From there, with great pomp, it was conducted up the Seine to Paris, then carried through the crowded streets amid tears and shouts of *Vive l'Empereur!* and installed in the Hôtel des Invalides, pending the construction of a tasteless tomb.

*

Among the many figures from the past who claimed a place in the ceremony of the Retour des Cendres was Count Leon. He had made a similar demand in 1836 to be present at the long-delayed inauguration of the Arc de Triomphe, whose first stone had been laid in 1806, the year of his birth. Neither of these requests was granted. Although he had recently gained a semblance of respectability by his re-election to a commission in the National Guard as a lieutenant in the Second Company of the Chasseurs, he had been going steadily downhill, both morally and financially, for several years. He suffered from two incurable weaknesses: first, he was incapable of living within his income; secondly, he was unable to resist believing his own fantasies of great fortunes that would, must, one day come to him simply because he was Napoleon's son. And Napoleon's first-born son into the bargain.

The money that Meneval had so carefully looked after for him was soon frittered away. The legacy from Napoleon of 300,000 francs payable from the State forests had been annulled by Louis XVIII. The Emperor's secret bequest of more money to be paid out of sums retained by Eugene de Beauharnais as Viceroy of Italy had never been acknowledged by Eugene's descendants, the Leuchtenbergs, living far out of reach in Russia. His mother was seeking a means of commuting her holdings in the Grand Livre, thus depriving him of the reversion. Yet he went on spending, running up bills for board and lodging, furniture and clothes. He borrowed money, bought goods on credit and immediately sold them for cash at a third of their value; he even managed to get 1,500 francs by false pretences from the State pawnshop.

He was at that time living in the Rue du Mail, not far from the Palais-Royal, but his address was always changing. He had a mistress who was also living with a married clerk in the Ministry of War named Lesieur. 'Madame' Lesieur practised as a mesmerist and gave the proceeds of her profession, and much of Lesieur's wages, to the sombrely handsome Leon. Keeping one step ahead of the bailiff's men with a handful of writs to serve, Leon flitted from one bilked landlord to the next. When they tracked him down to rooms in the Rue Neuve St-Augustin, he quickly arranged to exchange lodgings with a woman occupying inferior rooms on the floor below, with the result that the unfortunate lady had great difficulty in dissuading the process servers from removing her furniture and Leon from making off with her watch.[9]

The bailiff's men at last laid hands on him. In 1837 he was committed to the debtors' prison in the Rue de Clichy for failing to meet a promissory note. After months of argument he was released in the spring of 1838 on a plea that the man who presented the note could not prove that he had come by it honestly; an argument which Leon put forward with a wealth of indignation. But he had scarcely come out when he was put back in again; this time by a moneylender with a claim for 47,000 francs, and he did not re-emerge until the late autumn. While in prison he applied to Meneval for help, who refused and suggested he should apply to his mother. According to his own story, Leon was also in correspondence with Monseigneur Quelen, formerly secretary to 'my Uncle Cardinal Fesch' and now Archbishop of Paris, who approached the Pope with a proposal to have Leon admitted to the priesthood and rapidly appointed to a bishopric. But the archbishop died at the end of 1839 without having succeeded in this remarkable plan – or having had an opportunity to deny its existence.

Leon never managed to explain how he succeeded in paying off his many debts and obtaining his discharge from the Clichy gaol, but he did so – and within a few months was in difficulties again. His landlord in the Rue du Mail ordered him to quit for not paying his rent. He moved to the Rue St Honoré to share lodgings with François-Guillaume Coëssin, a man with the same energetic and optimistic qualities as himself.[10] Now approaching sixty, Coëssin had in his time tried to found a model republic at Cayenne and a new religion in Paris. He was an indefatigable inventor, particularly in the field of hydrodynamics, with a series of improved, but unsold, water-pumps, sprinklers and submarines behind him. His latest venture was an oil-lamp based on a new principle which he claimed provided more light and less smell.[11]

In February 1840, the police informer who was keeping an eye on Madame Lesieur reported that she had told a friend that Leon was going to visit Prince Louis – in London, where he had lived for more than a year. In the summer of 1838 one of the prince's supporters, Lieutenant Laity, had published a pamphlet defending the Strasbourg escapade.[12] The French government had foolishly over-reacted by prosecuting Laity, thus providing a public platform for his Bonapartist counsel. France then demanded that Switzerland should expel Prince Louis. The noisy tantrums, mounting eventually to a threat of war, ensured that when the prince left of his own accord he did so in a blaze of favourable publicity and the halo of persecution.[13]

Leon's story was that he was making the journey to London as Coëssin's representative, hoping to sell the right to the new lamp. There were others who said that the true object of his journey was to spy on Prince Louis and even to assassinate him, and that the French government had released him from prison solely for this purpose. He took with him a letter of recommendation from Count Molé, Louis-Philippe's Prime Minister, another from Meneval, and samples of the Coëssin lamp. He put up at Fenton's Hotel.

His first call was on Joseph Bonaparte, back in England again and living in Cavendish Square. Unfortunately, when Leon had last been in London he had met Dr O'Meara, the naval surgeon who had been one of Napoleon's agents on St Helena, and in conversation with him had made some bitter criticisms of Joseph – to whom O'Meara had relayed them. Joseph had a long memory for that sort of thing. When Leon left his letter of introduction from Meneval, Joseph sent a reply, under open seal so that Leon could read it, flatly refusing to have anything to do with him.[14] Leon was deeply offended, but for the moment did nothing about it because he had become entangled in yet another of the bizarre business propositions upon which he seemed to stumble with such ease. Through another French exile, Colonel Bouffet de Montauban, he made the acquaintance of a pair of Germans, who initiated him into the secrets of a new weapon they had invented. It was a fireball said to be capable of making the sea boil and any nearby ships burst into flames.[15] One of the Germans suggested that Leon, who had been talking of his intention to go to St Petersburg to dun the Leuchtenbergs, should offer the invention to the Tsar, assuming that as good Frenchmen he would prefer the Russians to have this fearsome weapon rather than the British.

This proposal set bells ringing in Leon's head. He had made four fruitless calls on Prince Louis at the house he was renting from the Earl of Ripon at 1 Carlton Gardens. Bouffet de Montauban had told him that Prince Louis regarded him as a spy. He had since discovered that Montauban was a member of the prince's staff, and he now convinced himself that Montauban had introduced him to the Germans and their fiery cannonballs in order to compromise him. He wrote an abusive letter to Prince Louis – 'my little cousin', as he called him – threatening 'by the ashes of the Emperor Napoleon, my father, that your ill manners to me shall one day receive their due punishment'[16] and demanding an answer. Prince Louis, unwilling to be drawn into a correspondence which he guessed Leon intended to publish, sent Parquin to Fenton's Hotel to tell him that he would neither answer his letter nor receive him. That afternoon Leon sent another of his recently made acquaintances to challenge Prince Louis to a duel the following dawn. There was no honourable alternative but to accept.[17]

Leon set out from Fenton's at seven o'clock on the morning of 3 March 1840 accompanied by his seconds and followed at a short distance by Inspector Nicholas Pierce of A Division. At Wimbledon Common, Leon and his friends made for the hollow below the windmill where they were met by Prince Louis and his two seconds: General Parquin and Count d'Orsay. As in all of Leon's ventures, a new argument broke out almost immediately; this time because Prince Louis, as the challenged party, chose the weapons and decided on swords, which Parquin had brought, while Leon insisted on pistols, rightly recognized as much more dangerous weapons. The dispute had no sooner been decided in favour of Leon and the pistols than Inspector Pierce stepped out from behind some bushes, accompanied by another inspector, a sergeant and assorted constables, and arrested the lot.

They were taken to Bow Street Magistrates' Court and released on bail: Barings the bankers for Prince Louis' faction, Fenton the hotelkeeper for Leon's. Prince Louis made a triumphant appearance in a box at Her Majesty's Theatre that night; while Leon, unable to meet Fenton's bill, let alone his bail, moved into lodgings in Bloomsbury until he could raise twenty-five shillings to pay his fare back to France.[18]

*

To most English people the duel on Wimbledon Common, despite the element of farcical melodrama with which Leon managed to marinade it, had served to add a little more lustre to Prince Louis' laurels. Ever since his departure from Switzerland in the autumn of 1838 – 'only the thought of sparing Switzerland from trouble can soften my regret at leaving her' – he had marched from one propaganda success to another, assisted by the inanities and ineptitudes of the French government. He had set himself up in London in suitably princely style. He was reputed to have inherited nearly £5,000 a year from Hortense, and spent lavishly on horses, carriages emblazoned with the Imperial eagle, glittering receptions and public appearances, at which he was always attended by two aides-de-camp. In 1839 he bought two Paris newspapers and also published his *Idées Napoléoniennes*, praising the achievements of the Empire and implying the need for a new emperor who would, with the support of all the people, bring France peace and prosperity. In 1840 the devoted Persigny published *Lettres de Londres*, presenting Prince Louis as the ideal successor to his uncle.

Successful though this was in keeping him in the public eye, it was not a campaign that could continue for long. Propaganda of this kind reaches a peak and then goes into a rapid decline. A move had to be made sooner rather than later, for he was now thirty-two; Napoleon had seized power at thirty and made himself emperor at thirty-four. Fortunately, the inept Louis-Philippe had begun to slide down the farther slope of his own popularity. The Mehemet Ali affair had been a bitter reverse for French diplomacy and pride. The Prince of Joinville had sailed for St Helena to collect Napoleon's body: the inglorious present was about to be reminded of the glorious past. It seemed an excellent moment for Prince Louis to strike. In Paris he had a lively group of supporters based on the Cotillon Club for women and the Buckskin Club for men; in the northern provinces of France his agents were sounding out army commanders; in Carlton Gardens Dr Conneau was secretly printing proclamations addressed to soldiers, civilians and the world, and sewing buttons on uniforms. Dining out one evening in early August, Prince Louis caused a good deal of suppressed merriment by inviting his fellow guests to take supper with him at the Tuileries in exactly twelve months' time.[19]

It was perhaps not as indiscreet as it sounds. His preparations were well advanced and his real hope was to be installed in the Tuileries within a week; it was therefore useful to let those who were spying on him think that he had a later date in mind. In fact, his modest expeditionary force for the recapture of France in the Bonaparte cause left London Bridge at nine o'clock in the morning of 4 August. Its sole transport was a pleasure steamer, the *Edinburgh Castle*, hired for a month at £100 a week. It carried two carriages, nine horses, sixteen dozen bottles of wine, some cases of spirits and a few of the fifty-six men who made up the party. The remainder joined the ship as it stopped at various points down the river and at ports on the Kent coast. The intention was to avoid the suspicion that might have been aroused by embarking all the men at one time. The effect was to cause delay, aggravated by the uncertainty caused by whether the leader himself was to come aboard at London, Greenwich, Gravesend, Margate or Ramsgate – so that at dawn on 5 August, when they were due to make their triumphant descent on Boulogne, they were only just putting in at Ramsgate. To avoid questioning they set to sea again and drifted about in rough weather in the English Channel until early next morning. By this time many of the mercenaries were sea-sick or drunk. They had been given 100 francs apiece and a brief harangue by Prince Louis and the effect of both was rapidly wearing off. At 1 a.m. the *Edinburgh Castle* at last hove to, three-quarters of a mile off Wimereux, and the first wave of invaders set off in the single available boat.

Prince Louis intended to appeal for the support of the army, as he had done at Strasbourg. Early in the year he had sent Parquin and others to Lille, to try to win over the army of the north, to whose commander he offered 100,000 francs and a marshal's baton if the coup was successful, 300,000 francs if it were not. The proposal was rejected but, firmly convinced of the corruptibility of all men, he concluded that the general was merely being cautious and would rally with the whole of his command if one of his regiments were won over. Two companies of the 42nd Foot were stationed at Boulogne; the second-in-command of this detachment, Lieutenant Aladenize, had expressed fervent support for the cause. Prince Louis' plan was to lead them to Calais, the regimental headquarters, and from there to Lille, gathering numbers as they went. The detachment commander, regarded as unsympathetic, was expected to be absent from the barracks on the day of the landing – 5 August.

Thanks to bungling it was actually 6 August. But a messenger had got through to Lieutenant Aladenize, who was waiting for the first boatload, commanded by Montholon, when they landed at Wimereux. The boat had to make several trips to the *Edinburgh Castle* to bring off all the men, dressed in the uniforms of the 40th Foot, a sister regiment of the 42nd. They should have been accompanied by a live eagle, provided by Parquin, which, it was hoped, would hover portentously over a slice of bacon placed in Prince Louis' hat, but the bewildered bird refused to leave the boat.[20] They were challenged by three customs officers who refused to believe the prince's story that his men were members of the 40th Regiment en route from Dunkirk to Cherbourg but forced to land because of a mechanical defect in their steamer. However, since they were outnumbered, there was nothing the excise men could do about it; the invaders formed up and strode off towards the gates of Boulogne.

It was five o'clock in the morning. The sound of marching feet brought citizens to their windows, and a sergeant to the door of his guard post in the Place d'Alton. He saw Lieutenant Aladenize leading the column, followed by an ensign carrying a gold-edged tricolour on which, lacking any battle honours of his own, Louis had had embroidered a selection of his uncle's; then came the

171

prince himself and his staff, all lavishly uniformed, and finally the detachment of the pseudo-40th Foot. The sergeant, impressed by the weight of gold braid, turned out his guard of four men. Aladenize stepped across and urged them to join the column, but they declined. A little farther on, Aladenize spotted an officer of the 42nd, his junior, and called him over to be presented to the prince; but after a few embarrassed words the subaltern slipped away.

They arrived at the barracks in the Lower Town. The main guard turned out and, on Aladenize's orders, presented arms as the prince and his men marched in. While the prince's staff threw money to the early morning bystanders outside in return for shouts of *Vive l'Empereur!* Aladenize called forward some of his own men, whom the prince promptly promoted to sergeant or lieutenant. To the sergeant-major he said: 'I promote you Captain and award you the Cross I have worn myself.' Unhappily, the cross was too tightly attached to his uniform. After some furious tugging which threatened to rend the cloth, he gave up and said: 'Well, all the same I appoint you a Chevalier of the Legion of Honour.' There was general rejoicing – but only for a few minutes. The subaltern, having slipped away, alerted the detachment commander who had so rightly been regarded as unsympathetic. This captain, sword drawn and eyes gleaming, burst in through the main gate, tangled in a scuffle with Persigny, and was disentangled by some officers who had followed him in. He ordered Prince Louis to leave the barracks. The prince, who had warned everybody before disembarking that there was to be no bloodshed, raised his pistol and fired a shot which struck one of the infantrymen of the 42nd Regiment in the mouth and caused the pseudo-infantrymen of the 40th to leave the premises at great speed, unwilling to get involved in a fracas of that seriousness for a mere 100 francs.

They were formed up again with some difficulty in the street outside and, under protest, marched up the hill to the grim medieval fortifications of the Upper Town, scattering pamphlets and silver among the populace and, as they passed the Sous-Prefecture, giving the sub-prefect a reverberating thwack in the chest with the bronze eagle that surmounted the gold-embroidered tricolour. They found the great gates of the Upper Town closed against them. After a halfhearted attempt to break them open with axes, the majority of the party demanded that they should turn and hasten down the hill to the port and some hope of escape. The prince refused: he led them round the walls and out on to the main Calais road to the great column set up by Napoleon on the spot where, emulating the Duke of York, he had marched his men up to the edge of the cliff then marched them away again. It was the scene of those delicious days that Hortense had spent with Charles de Flahaut in the dawn of their love affair. It was the first point of pilgrimage to which she had brought Prince Louis on their return from London nine years before.

The monument, completed by Louis-Philippe, was almost ready for its ceremonial opening. The sentry on guard at the bottom was intimidated into handing over the key, and the gaudy tricolour was raised at the top of the tower, a rallying sign for Prince Louis's fast-fading followers and non-existent supporters. Instead the only figures in sight were loyal royalist soldiers and hastily-summoned members of the National Guard. Prince Louis proclaimed that he would stand and fight to a finish at the foot of his uncle's column. His companions, seeing there was no time for discussion, unravelled his fingers from the railings to which he was clinging, picked him up and bundled him down to the shore, where they swam out to a boat owned by the local life-saving society. Having discarded their weapons they were now at the mercy of the National Guardsmen, who opened fire: 'just like a duck-shoot'. In the resulting hurly-burly one man was shot dead, two badly wounded, the boat overturned, a fourth man was drowned, and the others were captured. Prince Louis, in a borrowed jacket – he had discarded his own in the water – was taken off to the castle at the top of the Old Town. 'Had he been shot it would have been the proper end of so mischievous a blockhead', a local correspondent reported to *The Times* next day.

On 12 August Prince Louis was brought to Paris and put into a cell in the Conciergerie, guarded by three warders day and night. It seemed excessively cautious. This second fiasco, even more farcical than the one at Strasbourg, suggested that he presented no great threat to the security of the State whether he was captive or free. Any plot that he organized seemed to automatically fall apart in his hands. To add a bitter note to his tribulations, one of the two Paris papers that he owned was sued by Leon, now returned from England, for reprinting articles that had first appeared in a London paper in March, accusing Leon of being an Orleanist spy sent to challenge Prince Louis and either kill him or ensure his deportation for breaking the law against duelling, and for publishing a letter from Parquin accusing Leon of having argued about the choice of weapons in order to give the police time to arrive. The editor was fined 1,000 francs and ordered to pay Leon 5,000 francs damages for libel.

Prince Louis himself was brought for trial on 28 September. Dwarfed in the dock by the lanky Montholon, he nevertheless made a good impression by claiming sole responsibility for the offence. When allowed to make a statement, he scored several shrewd points, refused to recognize the authority of the court, and treated it to a range of pungent untruths based on the myths of St Helena and his own *Idées Napoléoniennes*, including 'My Uncle the Emperor preferred to abdicate rather than accept treaties giving France the restricted frontiers which expose her to the contempt and menaces that foreigners dare to offer her today.' He ended with a stirring challenge: ' I represent a Principle, a Cause, a Defeat. The Principle is the Sovereignty of the People; the Cause is that of the Empire; the Defeat is Waterloo. You have recognised that Principle; you have served that Cause; you wish to avenge that Defeat. There is no disagreement between you and me.'[21] This was popular meat to a nation which believed its king and government had allowed it to be humbled a second time by the victors of Waterloo. It brought a sharp reaction from the court. One member of the prince's party received a sentence of two years' imprisonment, Conneau and Montauban five years, others ten or fifteen; Parquin, Persigny, and Montholon were gaoled for twenty years; the luckless Lieutenant Aladenize was transported for life; and Prince Louis was ordered to be detained in a fortress 'in perpetuity'.

On 7 October 1840, the same day that the Prince of Joinville arrived at St Helena in the *Belle Poule*, Prince Louis was taken under escort from Paris to the fortress-prison of Ham, where he was shortly joined by Conneau and Montholon. The latter, Napoleon's chamberlain on St Helena and one of his three executors, was a testy, touchy man in his late fifties. Conneau was lively, always occupied with a hundred new projects, most of which he failed to complete, and totally devoted to the prince, whom he had promised Hortense on her deathbed never to leave.

The fortress was a grim, sturdy building, dating from the fifteenth century, set in marshes sparsely inhabited by wildfowl, and used for the past fifty years as a place of detention for political notabilities. Across the courtyard from the two drawbridges and the entrance lay the quarters allotted to the new prisoner: a sizeable sitting-room, a bedroom, a small spare room. Later he obtained permission to turn this room into a laboratory for scientific experiments. His valet, Charles Thélin, found not guilty at the trial, was allowed to resume his duties in May 1841. There was no way out through the barred windows, and no way in except by passing through the guardroom on the ground floor. The garrison of 400 soldiers provided a twenty-four-hour guard of sixty men. If the prince walked out into the courtyard one soldier constantly followed him; when he obtained permission to stroll on the ramparts he looked down through the persistent mist on the figures of more sentries surrounding the walls. The military governor had the right to open and confiscate any of his correspondence and the duty of visiting four times a day.

When he heard in November that his cousin, Mathilde, had married a rich Russian, Count Anatole Demidoff, he seemed deeply affected. But he was back to his old opportunist self by December when Napoleon's ashes were returned to Paris. 'From the pomp of your funeral, you have cast a glance towards my sombre dwelling', he apostrophized him in a pamphlet for distribution to Bonapartist mourners. 'Remembering the caresses you lavished on me as a child, you have said to me: "You suffer for me, my friend, I am pleased with you".' Napoleon's remains passed on to Les Invalides; Prince

176

Louis busied himself with chemical experiments, an exhaustive *Study of Artillery, Past and Future*, and a steady flow of pamphlets and protests and demands for privileges, in which he was supported by his two companions.

He was allowed to ride a horse in the courtyard, to make a garden on the ramparts and, to have his valet pass in and out of the prison at will. Conneau's complaints about their accommodation resulted in a grant of 600 francs for repairs; Montholon protested that 'The Emperor was not so badly treated by the English in an English prison as his nephew is by the French in a French prison.' Prince Louis scribbled away at his pamphlets. 'I readily admit that there are a hundred writers better than me in Paris, but ask … if they have even managed to move their readers to tears'[22], he wrote to Vieillard in the summer of 1842. Yet *he* had done so, he claimed, because 'the Napoleonic cause appeals to the soul; it arouses turbulent memories, and it is always through the heart, never by cold reason, that one moves the masses'. After all, as he wrote to Lady Blessington: 'With the name that I bear I must be either in the gloom of a prison or in the radiance of power.' It was only a matter of waiting.

*

While Prince Louis continued his campaign to capture the hearts of the French people, Alexandre Walewski continued to woo just one of them: Rachel, who was progressing from triumph to triumph, not only in France but also overseas. 'We are so charmed with Madame Rachel', Queen Victoria told her Uncle Leopold in the summer of 1841, after hearing her declaim at Windsor. 'She is perfect … such a nice, modest girl.'[23] On her return

Alexandre renewed the assault, and presently the lightly-defended fortress yielded.

The association became permanent, or as nearly permanent as these things ever were with Rachel, who confessed that 'I don't mind tenants but I won't have landlords.' It astonished the fashionable world, which could not divine what the vivid, mercurial, quick-witted actress could possibly see in the little pretentions and pomposities of this lover whose distinction plainly lay in his parentage rather than his accomplishments.

Rachel loved him in her fashion, which was turbulent and fickle. He danced attendance, basking in her glory. She quarrelled, telling him 'I never want to see you again, and nothing, nothing in the world, will make me change my mind.' But she did change her mind, perhaps because in the spring of 1843 she discovered that she was pregnant – and strangely delighted. She remained almost as thin and frail as before: 'like a thread with a knot tied in the middle', said her cousin, Judith. To her sister, Sarah, she wrote in June that the unborn child was 'playing pranks and giving me no rest at night, but I console myself for all discomforts, present and to come, with the thought that I am going to have a charming little creature all my own'[24]. But the child was stillborn in November.

The tragedy brought the pair closer together for a while, but by February of the following year Alexandre had been introduced to pretty young Suzanne Brohan of the Comédie-Française by Anais Aubert, his former mistress whom Rachel had displaced. Anais passed the news of the budding affair on to Rachel, who promptly gave one of her most sensational performances. Bursting into a rehearsal at the Théâtre-Français she threw open her cloak, revealing a pair of pistols with which she invited Madame Brohan to take part in a duel forthwith. The dramatic confrontation, with a chorus of fellow actors and stagehands, waxed and waned, flared up again and finally ended with the reconciliation of all the principals and a celebratory love feast which was in its turn followed by the birth of Rachel's second child in November 1844. Alexandre formally acknowledged him as his son, giving him both his christian name and surname. The mother and child were set up in a house at 4 Rue Trudon, where Rachel got through 300,000 francs of Alexandre's sparse balance in refurbishing the rooms.

The quarrels began again. They were not quite as passionate as before – but neither were the reconciliations. In the late summer of 1845 Alexandre went off with Thiers, who was still out of office, on a tour of Spain. He was away for more than a month, and on his return Rachel assured him that despite any stories of 'silly little tricks' that might have come to his ears, she had remained completely faithful to him. In her fashion, perhaps. But Alexandre, no longer in love, was not inclined to be indulgent. He left her in the spring of 1846.

*

In comparison with Alexandre's life during the first half of the 1840s, the activities of his three cousins were humdrum. Even the tortured and tempestuous Leon managed to keep his name out of the newpapers for most of the time. His mentor, François Coëssin, died in 1843, but by then Leon had established himself with another source of occasional loans: General Gaspar Gourgaud to whom he had offered his inauspicious support in the elections a decade before. Gourgaud, the strangest of Napoleon's companions on St Helena, a man of paranoiac suspicions and a temperament as fiery as Leon's, had quit Napoleon after a series of quarrels, denounced him in the hope of endearing himself to the Bourbons from whom he had already deserted during the First Restoration, and switched back to Bonapartism when this second defection failed to bring him any reward. He found a niche independent of both camps when Louis-Philippe usurped the throne of France: as an aide-de-camp in the royal household, a member of the mission that brought back the Emperor's ashes from St Helena, and in 1841 a baron. Despite all of this, he was no match for Leon, who called in at frequent intervals to discuss the glorious past and borrow a few francs for the uncertain future.

These loans, although not repaid, were never enough. Leon continued to brood on the money that Napoleon had left Eleonore, of which the reversion would be his, provided he could continue to prevent her from disposing of the capital. In October 1845 he took the novel step of suing his mother for maintenance – and the court surprisingly awarded him 6,000 francs a year. This decision was quashed six months later, but on a further appeal Leon won – at the reduced rate of 4,000 francs.[25]

Charles de Flahaut had been appointed ambassador to Vienna in the autumn of 1841; and while Charles luxuriated in the life of a diplomat his son, Auguste, was taking his first step into parliamentary politics. It was a time of growing turmoil – and of opportunity. In the elections of 1842 and again in 1846, Auguste stood as an Independent. Although he usually voted with the governing Conservative party, his sharp foresight told him that the inequalities and injustices that had been brought back to France by the Bourbons and perpetuated, despite his promises, by the 'Citizen King', Louis-Philippe, could not remain unchallenged much longer. The opposition was clamouring for electoral reform (the department that Auguste represented had a total of less than 500 electors); the country was going through an economic crisis precipitated by a bad harvest, which was followed by bank failures, industrial bankruptcies and increasing unemployment. Auguste approached both the head of the government, Guizot, and the aged king, urging that they should make some sort of concession in order to avoid an upheaval. Both replied that the only solution was to stand fast against these revolutionary demands.

In his rheumaticky prison on the Somme, Auguste's half-brother continued to keep himself busy with his electrical experiments and the pamphlets in which he rattled away at any subject that he could turn to his purpose: a consideration of the Great Rebellion in Britain, with the implication that he was the William of Orange destined to supplant the King James of Louis-Philippe; a life of Charlemagne, the figure often touted by Bonapartists as a forerunner of Napoleon; a plea, on a subject close to Auguste's heart and pocket, for the protection of the metropolitan sugar-beet industry against the cane-sugar imports from the West Indian colonies; a proposal 'which cannot fail to do me a great deal of good', to do away with poverty by having the unemployed cultivate France's vast tracts of wasteland; a memorial notice on his Uncle Joseph, who died in July 1844 – anything and everything to keep himself in public view.

There were moments when time dragged; on the other hand, he enjoyed distractions not always available to prisoners. In December 1840, Montholon was given permission to have a young Irishwoman, who called herself Countess Lee but who seems to have been Miss

Caroline Jane O'Hara, installed in a pair of ground-floor rooms inside the fortress. In January 1841 she was given permission to spend time with Prince Louis as well as Montholon; but she talked too much on her trips into the town and in September that year the Minister of the Interior ordered that she must leave, although she was allowed back again in the following April. This banishment did not apply to her servant, a local girl of twenty, named Eleonore Vergeot, the daughter of a weaver turned clog-maker. Alexandrine, as she was usually called, was employed by Prince Louis from the summer of 1841 'to attend to his linen'. Early in 1843 she went off to Paris, calling herself Madame Camus (her mother's family name), and there her son Eugene was born on 25 February. He was placed in the care of Prince Louis' former nurse, Madame Bure, as was the brother, Louis, who followed him in March 1845.[26]

The arrangements in Paris were handled by Hortense Cornu, daughter of Queen Hortense's butler and chambermaid, and Prince Louis' godchild (though she was only a year his junior). A small, bright, prickly, warmhearted chatterbox, she had been his close friend in their childhood but a quarrel, and her marriage to the painter, Sebastian Cornu, had kept them apart for more than ten years – until the news of the Boulogne disaster brought her to visit him in the Conciergerie, and later many times at Ham.[27] Besides overseeing the welfare of his two illegitimate sons, she did much of the research for his *Study of Artillery, Past and Future*. There was a suspicion that Hortense Cornu wrote a great deal of the pamphlets that were published under the prince's name, but it seems that she limited herself to detailed criticism, while the more extensive rewriting was carried out by her friend, Gustave Planche, art and literary critic of the *Revue des Deux Mondes*. In addition to her help with his literary efforts, Madame Cornu served as Prince Louis' agent in raising money.

Keeping up appearances in London and subsidizing Bonapartist propaganda in France had brought him almost to the end of his available funds by the time of the Boulogne raid; the shortage may indeed have been one reason for rushing into the folly. In January 1841 he resumed the claim for the restitution of his mother's property in France; later the same year he put up for sale, at a price of half-a-million francs, the Castle of Arenenberg, including the furniture, paintings and most of Hortense's cherished Imperial souvenirs. (When his relations, particularly his cousin, Princess Mary of Baden, protested at this, he replied: 'If the Grand Duchess is upset at seeing them pass into the hands of strangers, she should buy them herself.') She did not; and in January 1843 he agreed to accept less than 70,000 francs for the house and furniture and some of the family treasures. It was not nearly enough to keep the propaganda machine working – a task in which Armand Laity was playing an increasingly important part. He was now visiting the prince three times a week.[28]

During the following year, some of the Boulogne raiders who had been sentenced to five years' imprisonment, were pardoned. They included Conneau, who asked permission to remain at Ham, and Count Orsi, whom the prince sent to London to try to raise a loan. It was not easy. The only person Orsi could eventually persuade to advance 150,000 francs to the prisoner-for-life in Ham was the eccentric and immensely rich exiled duke of Brunswick (who left more than £10,000,000 when he died). Orsi probably met the duke through a Member of Parliament, Thomas Duncombe, a friend of both Auguste de Morny and Alexandre Walewski, who had seconded his secretary George Thomas Smith to the duke. Brunswick agreed to lend the 150,000 francs for five years at five per cent interest on condition that Prince Louis signed an agreement under which the duke would do all he could to establish the prince as President or Emperor of France, while the prince would help the duke to regain the throne of Brunswick that he lost in 1830 and to bring about the unification of Germany.

On the pretext that Smith was interested in buying some of the remaining Arenenberg tapestries, pictures and a diamond necklace, and that Orsi was acting as his business agent, the prince obtained permission for a visit by both of them in June 1845. The pass, had, as usual, to be signed by the governor of the fortress, Major Demarle, and approved by the Minister of the Interior; because of Orsi's known complicity with the prince, the minister insisted that Demarle should be present throughout the interview. Since the prince could communicate freely and secretly with the outside through Thélin, the only difficulty raised by Demarle's presence was the actual signing of the agreement. This was overcome by Orsi having it written on a piece of silk, which he passed to the prince, and received back with his signature, when he shook hands on arrival and departure As soon as he returned to London with Smith the 150,000 francs were deposited with Barings, the prince's bankers.[29]

Prince Louis now began plotting to escape, working through English friends in London and Valerie Masuyer in Paris. With typical secrecy it was not until his plans were far advanced that he told Conneau of his intention, and

Montholon, though he had shared the prince's imprisonment for five years, was not told at all. In May 1846 a gang of workmen was brought into the fortress to repair the prisoners' quarters and the staircase leading to them. The prince and Conneau watched their movements closely and noted that the men were rigorously inspected by the sentries at the main gate when they arrived in the morning and again when they left in the late afternoon; but there were occasions during the day when they carried out rotten planks and joists and other rubbish, and the surveillance was then markedly less keen. The governor, who was suffering from rheumatism, had fallen into the habit of not getting up before 8 a.m. It was decided that the prince should try to make his break at about 7 a.m. on Monday, 25 May. Thélin bought a short single-breasted jacket in Ham, the sort worn by servants of the local well-to-do middle-class families. Madame Bure's son acquired a set of working clothes in Paris – overall trousers, a coarse shirt, apron, scarf and cap – and when these arrived, looking too distinctively new, Conneau set to work on them with a pumice stone and dirty water, a job that occupied him for a whole day.

Prince Louis was up early on the Monday morning. He dressed himself in the jacket that Thélin had bought in Ham and, over that, the workman's trousers and shirt that Bure had sent from Paris; he stepped into a pair of clogs that added a couple of inches to his height, shaved off his moustache and whiskers, rouged his normally pallid cheeks and put on a wig and the cap. Thélin went out to the men working on the staircase, invited them into a ground-floor room for a glass of brandy, and then hurried upstairs again. The prince picked up a plank of wood that had served as a bookshelf, balanced it on his shoulder, stuck a clay pipe in his mouth, and set off downstairs preceded by Thélin. With the superstitious sentimentality that marked many of his actions, he took his pet dog, Ham, with him – led by Thélin; in his pocket he put the letter written at his birth by Napoleon to Hortense, and the letter Hortense had written to him on her deathbed. If he were stopped for questioning after he escaped from prison, either of these documents would ensure his immediate re-arrest.

There were two guards on the door leading into the courtyard. Thélin spoke to the man on the left while the prince walked past, the plank on his shoulder hiding his face from the one on the right. He was out in the bright light of the square, nerves a-quiver. The unaccustomed pipe fell from his mouth and he had to halt, bend down and pick up the pieces before running the gauntlet between the duty officer on one side of the courtyard, who was fortunately reading a letter, and on the other side the clerk of works, who failed to notice that he had an extra carpenter in his gang that morning. There was a group of soldiers at the main gate. This was the most dangerous moment of all. Disguising his voice he asked for the wicket to be opened so he could pass through on to the drawbridge. One of the men, a drummer, was staring at him, puzzled. There was a burst of shouting and snarling behind him. Thélin had put up a diversion by teasing and fooling with Ham, who showed signs he might give the game away by bounding up to his master. The soldier's eyes swung round to the pair of them; the doorkeeper unlocked the gate; Prince Louis was out. He forced himself to walk slowly, still carrying his plank, and saw Thélin hurry past him, pulling the dog on its lead. Skirting the centre of the town, he made for the cemetery where he got rid of the plank.

In his quarters at the fortress, the sitting-room fire had been lit by Conneau, who put a kettle on it to boil and set out his medicine bottles and jars on the table. To the orderly who came in to tidy up at a little after 8 a.m. he said that the prince was unwell and had decided to stay in bed. The orderly reported that the local priest, who came in every Monday to say Mass and take breakfast with the prisoners afterwards, was waiting downstairs. Conneau pretended to have forgotten this regular appointment; he went into the bedroom, mumbled for a while, then came out with a letter that the prince had written the previous night, apologizing for his sudden indisposition and asking the priest to come back on Tuesday. The orderly went off with the letter, which he showed to the governor in accordance with standing orders. The governor sent word that he would like to speak to the prince; Conneau strolled across the courtyard to explain that his patient, though not in a serious condition, was too unwell to be disturbed. At midday he had the orderly clean the sitting-room and himself went into the bedroom where he paced up and down holding an half-audible conversation with nobody.

At the cemetery the prince had been picked up by Thélin in a cab. When they reached St-Quintin he dismounted outside the town, hid his working clothes in a ditch, passed through on foot, and on the other side was again picked up by Thélin, this time driving a post-chaise. They reached Valenciennes at a little after 2 p.m. and drove straight to an inn, where an Englishwoman and her daughter had arrived the previous day. Mrs Crawford and Miss Laura Crawford had, in fact, recently visited the prince at Ham to discuss the final link in his line of escape; and during his brief stay at the inn had received from Mrs Crawford the passport issued to her husband, who had already slipped back to England without it.[30] He and Thélin then went to the station, where they hoped to catch the 4 p.m. train for Brussels.

By now Conneau had received a visit from the governor and had managed to convince him that the prince, though in better health, was still in no condition to be disturbed, so the governor went away without entering the bedroom where Canneau had taken the precaution of putting a dummy in the bed. It was just as well, for at the station at Valenciennes the time was going painfully slowly, particularly when a former guard at Ham, now a railway employee, recognized Thélin and got into conversation with him. At last the train came in. Thélin and the prince took their seats. At the customs-post they were not even asked to produce passports; at Brussels they changed immediately into a train for Ostend.

At Ham the governor called again at 7.15 p.m. Conneau went through his pretence of speaking to the prince, but getting no reply because he was sleeping. The governor peeped round the door at the recumbent figure in the close-curtained room then settled back for a further chat. It was not until lights-out that, overruling Conneau's objections, he went into the bedroom and up to the bed – and discovered that he had been fooled. Conneau was manacled and taken off to the garrison guardroom at Péronne.

*

Like Prince Louis, Alexandre Walewski had recently left France – though for a different reason. 'I've quit Paris because I was in one of those moods which demand a change of existence', he wrote to his half-brother, Rodolph d'Ornano, from Turin in March 1846. 'Society bores me, my club bores me, there is nothing for me in politics. I could get married, of course, but to whom? I am difficult to please, though I realise I no longer have any right to be. I am thirty-six already, my fortune is far from considerable, and yet, and yet ...' He called on his Uncle Jerome in Florence, then went on to Rome where he communed with the old masters of painting and sculpture in the Vatican, the Capitoline Museum and the Villa Borghese before returning to Florence with his mind made up: he would marry again, and he knew who his bride should be.

He had met her before, during the period of disillusion after his luckless mission to Egypt and before he took up with Rachel. She had then been 'a tiny beauty, blonde as March corn', with grey-blue eyes and a skittish disposition. She was now, at twenty-four, becoming almost a senior female citizen in a society that favoured early marriages. Her mouth had grown a little larger, her nose a little more imposing. Her dowry was expected to be modest, but her mother was a Poniatowska, claiming kinship with Stanislas the last King of Poland (who was her grandfather's uncle), and her father, Marquis Ricci, was said to be descended from both Dante and Machiavelli – excellent qualifications for the wife of a man who fancied his talents in literature and politics. And he, matching the family's Italian Polish aristocratic descent with his own Colonna-Walewski title (even though he had nothing but Laczynska-Bonaparte blood), was an acceptable suitor to both daughter and parents. On 3 June 1846 Alexandre Walewski married Anne Ricci in Florence.

The elections of the following month failed to bring Thiers back to power, but with the help of other friends Alexandre managed to resume his diplomatic career with the seriousness befitting a married man. This time he was given an unofficial mission, though not a very enviable one. He was sent to Buenos Aires to negotiate with the Argentine dictator, Juan Manuel de Rosa, whose protracted war against Uruguay was causing difficulties for the French and British trade with both countries. Alexandre's wife accompanied him and, on 12 May 1847, gave birth to a daughter who lived for less than eight weeks. By then the joint mission had failed. Alexandre returned to Paris in October 1847 – one more unsuccessful errand behind him. Nevertheless he was retained in the Diplomatic Corps. His letters of accreditation as Minister to Copenhagen were signed on 22 February 1848.

*

While Alexandre was away in South America, the government headed by Guizot came under renewed attack; this time not because of Louis-Philippe's timid foreign policy but because of scandals in high places. In July 1847 Jean-Baptiste Teste, who had held the Ministries of Justice and of Public Works, was charged before the Chamber of Peers with having accepted bribes to the amount of 94,000 francs in return for granting a salt-mine concession to a financier named Parmentier. The case came to light because Teste failed to fulfil his part of the bargain and Parmentier thereupon sued the go-between who first suggested his offering the bribe to the minister. That go-between turned out to be General Despans-Cubières, a former Minister of War and one of the band of Napoleonic military men who had frequented Madame Pellapra's salon when Emilie was growing up. Worse still, Emilie's father was accused of having been the go-between's go-between – the man who handled the negotiations between Parmentier and the general. Teste's defence against the charge of bribery was that he had never received the money and knew nothing about it; Parmentier was just as insistent that the money had been paid. Consequently, the general and Pellapra were charged with obtaining the sum by false pretenses and presumably sharing it among themselves. Pellapra disappeared, but his wife, Françoise, was able to produce accounts and correspondence which clearly showed that Teste had been paid. The opposition newspapers made great play of this evidence and poor Emilie, though her father was saved the ignominy of a prison sentence, was deeply ashamed by it.

No sooner was this scandal out of the way than a new one erupted, involving the man who was Hortense's former banker and Auguste de Morny's former trustee, Gabriel Delessert. The Duchess of Choiseul-Praslin died in suspicious circumstances, and her husband was believed to have murdered her. A warrant was issued for the arrest of the duke, who committed suicide before it could be served; and it was alleged that it was the Paris Prefect of Police himself, Gabriel Delessert, who had warned the duke and thus given him time to escape before being brought to court. A new uproar about corruption, protection and concealment broke out in the newspapers.[31]

Auguste had long been perturbed by the loss of public confidence in the government, and its blindness to the need for change. In the first issue for 1848 of the influential *Revue des Deux Mondes* he published an article entitled 'Some Reflections on Current Politics', which repeated his warnings of trouble to come if the government did not agree to reforms. 'I do not believe a revolution possible ... but let us have no illusions ... a revolution will no longer benefit any political party – it will only benefit communism.' He called for changes 'in industry, in commerce, in finance – every sort of reform that may contribute to the welfare of the masses and better the conditions of the working classes.' He outlined some of them: crèches, free education, care for the poor, state industries for the unemployed, workers' savings banks, old-age pensions, worker representation on industrial tribunals. It was addressed to deaf ears. The king and Guizot stood firm.

On 22 February 1848, the same day that Alexandre Walewski was appointed Minister to Copenhagen, the barricades went up in Paris. The traditional French coalition of students and workmen thronged the streets, howling for reform and Guizot's resignation. The National Guard refused to march against them and Guizot resigned. It was a great triumph. Next day the crowds were thicker and noiser, and this time many were shouting not for reform but for a Republic. Shots were fired, more than twenty people were killed. That evening their bodies were paraded through the streets by torchlight, while the bells rang out a tocsin call for revenge. By morning the King had decided to abdicate, making way for a provisional government headed by the liberal, Lamartine, and the socialist, Louis Blanc, who at once set about reforming the electoral laws, enfranchising all males of twenty years and over, so that the people could choose a constitutional assembly.

Persigny, released from his twenty-year prison sentence by the revolution, sent Prince Louis an urgent summons to come to Paris and seize the opportunity offered by the confusion; he borrowed money from Prince Jerome which he spent on a much-needed pair of trousers and the cost of fly-posting proclamations urging the people to 'Remember the Glories of the Empire! Only Prince Louis-Napoleon, Heir to the Victor of Marengo and Austerliz can rescue France cast into the Abyss by a guilty Monarchy!'[32] The people, remembering Strasbourg and Boulogne, remained unaroused. Prince Louis, arriving at midday on 28 February, held a series of consultations at his hotel in the Rue Richelieu with Persigny, Jerome, Vieillard, Laity and others and concluded that for the moment it was better to try to join the provisional government than openly oppose it. While more posters were being distributed bearing his portrait and the single word *Lui!* ('Him!', and also, with a slight mispronunciation, 'Louis'), he sent Persigny round to Lamartine with a letter: 'The people of Paris having, by their heroism, destroyed the last vestiges of the foreign invasion, I hasten from exile to take my place under the flag of the Republic. With no other ambition than to serve my country, I announce my arrival to the Members of the Provisional Government and assure them of my devotion to the cause they represent.'

Even Lamartine was not gullible enough to be taken in by that. Prince Louis received an official reply assuring him that there was no objection to his remaining in France, but in view of the difficult situation the government must ask him to stay out of Paris until things were more calm. Throughout the 29th the Prince debated what to do. Persigny was all for refusing to leave, so that the provisional government, who had no more mandate to govern than Prince Louis himself, would have to expel him or put him in prison, excellent propaganda in either case. Prince Louis did not agree. That night he sent

Persigny back with his reply: 'After thirty-three years of exile I thought I had gained the right to find a lodging on my native soil. You believe that my presence in Paris is a matter of embarrassment; I therefore withdraw for the moment. In this sacrifice you will recognise the purity of my intentions and of my patriotism.'[33] At 4 a.m. on 1 May a special train took him to Boulogne where he caught the Channel steamer for Folkestone. In London he settled again to the comfortable life he had enjoyed since his escape from Ham.

His father's death in July 1846 had provided him with a welcome increase of capital; publication of the first volume of his *Study of Artillery* (the remaining six volumes were written later by somebody else) brought him election to the Army and Navy Club; he was a familiar figure in hunting and horse-riding circles; he took a house in King Street, but it was noticed that he spent most of his days and nights just the other side of Piccadilly, at Miss Harriet Howard's home in Berkeley Street. Miss Howard, whose real name was Elizabeth Ann Haryett, was a beautiful young woman of twenty-three, who had failed as an actress, but succeeded handsomely as the mistress of a Major Martyn by whom she had a son in 1842, and who left her with a large trust fund invested mainly in London house property. The major's cousin by marriage, Lady Blessington, introduced Miss Howard to Louis in June 1846 and they were very soon living openly together. It was a busy summer. In July he wrote to Hortense Cornu: 'I have seen Rachel and I have been enchanted by her.' He followed her on tour and she, too, became his mistress before her return to France. It was only a few months since she left Alexandre Walewski; she was shortly to take up with Jerome's son, 'Plon-Plon'. She could truly claim to be an impassioned Bonapartist.

Foreseeing a time of difficulty, and that more was to be gained by waiting on the sidelines until things got worse, Louis did not offer himself as a candidate in the elections of April 1848. (Leon, who dropped his self-conferred title of count in accordance with the Republican spirit of the time, stood without success at St-Denis.) During the course of the month Louis did play one active rôle: he enlisted as a special constable and went on duty at London Bridge on 10 April, the day the Chartists presented their petition to Parliament. The anticipated riots did not take place. But in Paris there was still turmoil.

In his New Year article Auguste de Morny had warned that 'those who start revolutions never finish them.... The torrent breaking through its banks sweeps everything away indiscriminately.... Yesterday's liberator is denounced as tomorrow's tyrant.' For four months, while revolutionary tremors rocked the rest of Europe, Paris too was stumbling to the brink of anarchy. The Executive Committee, the provisional government under Lamartine, bowed to the socialist claim of 'the right to work' and established National Workshops, in which the otherwise unemployed were paid one franc a day. But though the government set up the workshops it failed to find the work, or else provided tasks that were evidently unproductive. One wag suggest that the thousands of applicants – 115,000 by the end of May – should bottle off the Seine. The middle classes, scandalized at the waste of money, demonstrated in the streets. The working classes came out in a demonstration six times larger. The mob burst in on the deliberation of the newly-elected Constituent Assembly and was with difficulty driven out by the National Guard.

Persigny, Laity and others clamoured for Louis to return and take advantage of the disturbances in which the Bonapartist supporters were making their voices heard. Louis refused. If he was to follow Napoleon's example he must pose as the disinterested saviour of the nation not the representative of one faction – and the pot must get closer to boiling point. For this reason he again kept out of the June elections; but Laity, hearing that the Prince of Joinville was considering standing as an independent law-and-order candidate, thus stealing Louis' political clothes, proposed Louis for the Paris constituency, while Persigny nominated him in the provinces. He was elected for Paris and three departments. But by now the provisional government had become thoroughly alarmed by the street rioting led by the Bonapartists allied to other bully-boys from Les Vieux de la Vielle (the soldiers of the Old Guard) and crack companies of the National Guard. The government ordered all prefects to arrest on sight 'Charles-Louis-Napoleon Bonaparte: aged 40, height one metre seventy (5 feet 7 inches - an overestimate), chestnut hair and eyebrows, small grey eyes, large nose, medium mouth, thick lips, blonde moustache, oval face, pale complexion. Special peculiarities: head sunk into shoulders, arched back.'

The Assembly debated whether to admit Louis or to uphold the provisional government's ban. 'Plon-Plon' produced a letter from Louis, written before the elections, saying that even if elected he would not for the moment take his seat. Fast on the heels of this came another letter: 'If the people impose a duty upon me, I am prepared to carry it out.'[34] But by the time this reached the President of the Assembly, Louis had learned that Persigny and Laity had been arrested and that the Bonapartist demonstrations were doing more harm than good. He sent yet another letter, expressing his pride at being chosen and his regret that 'the hostility of the Executive Power forces me to refuse the honour'.

He had called off his supporters just in time. On 21 June the government declared that the National Workshops, costing 170,000 francs a day, had become centres of sedition and would be closed. The workmen, many of whom came from the provinces, had the choice of returning home or joining the army. Two days later the east end of the city flared into civil war. In the Faubourg St-Antoine and the Faubourg St-Marceau across the river the barricades went up – 300 of them. The Assembly conferred dictatorial powers on General Cavaignac, the Minister of War, who sent in cavalry with drawn sabres, infantry and artillery with small arms and cannon – and orders to use them. Within four days 8,000 prisoners had been taken, 1,000 soldiers and 10,000 rioters were either wounded or dead. The rebellion was over, though martial law continued for two months more.

Because the system allowed one candidate to stand for several constituencies, supplementary elections had to be held in September in the thirteen departments where the successful man had decided to sit for another constituency. The election of the President of the Republic was to be held on 10 December. This was the post that Louis was aiming for, but he accepted Persigny's argument that it would now be of advantage to secure re-election to the Assembly – presenting himself as the representative whom the people were determined to have despite the opposition of the corrupt politicians at the helm. In August he announced his candidature: 'I should regard myself as shirking my duty if I did not respond to the appeal of my fellow-citizens.' This time he sent money from London (Miss Howard was said to have contributed £80,000) for intensive propaganda, posters and circulars – and was elected not to four seats but to five. He arrived in Paris on 24 September, and was introduced to the Assembly by Vieillard the following day as Deputy for the Department of Yonne. He waited for more than a month, orchestrating his publicity and feigning reluctance before announcing his intention of standing for the presidency – 'a candidature that I have not sought'.

The other candidates included Cavaignac and Lamartine, but it rapidly became clear that recent events would propel a Bonaparte into office, whatever his personal qualities. The middle classes had a fear and hatred of the Republic, and the possible return to the Red Peril of the great Revolution sixty years before. The rural voters, by far the largest section of the electorate, combined a fear of the Paris mob, which had so often imposed excesses on the rest of the nation, with a fuddled dream of past and perhaps future glory. 'How could I not vote for this gentleman? said one peasant. 'I whose nose was frost-bitten at Moscow?' Of the principal opponents, Lamartine had made a poor impression during the provisional government, Cavaignac was loathed by the working-class socialists, whom he had defeated at the barricades, yet distrusted by the middle class for his outspoken republican views. Many of the middle-of-the-road politicians privately supported Louis in the belief that he would be more malleable than the others.

With little against him save some jokes, and much in his favour based on the traditional recollection of how the first Bonaparte imposed order after the excesses of the Revolution, supported by an excellent propaganda machine (he now had six news-sheets in his control, each published at a low price or distributed free), he swept to victory with a majority three times that of his nearest rival. Suddenly, astoundingly, the ugly duckling, the 'mischievous blockhead' had changed into the presidential swan. After taking the Oath of Allegiance to the Republic on 20 December 1848, he told the Assembly: 'My duty is clear. I shall fulfil it as a man of honour, and I shall regard as enemies of the country any who try by illegal means to change what the whole of France has established.'

He looked inoffensive enough. Victor Hugo drew this portrait of him: 'Still young; dressed in black; pale faced: a large long nose, moustache, curly lock of hair on a narrow forehead, small lack-lustre eyes; timid and uneasy in appearance.' He wore a goatee beard, of the kind later to be called 'Imperial', but the moustache was not yet pommaded and twisted into two long stiff narrow spikes as if pleached on invisible wires. He moved with a faintly crablike gait, dragging his left leg. When discussing such physical abnormalities it is usual for French biographers, as a matter of national pride, to diagnose venereal disease. They may well be right. On the other hand it could have been an inherited rheumatic condition of the sort from which his father, Louis, suffered. It might even have been a habit formed by imitating a rheumatic condition with the intention of convincing people that King Louis was indeed his father.

The black clothes delighted Thiers, one of the several moderates who saw themselves as mentors and possible successors to this timid young man, for the President was barred from immediate re-election. Thiers, a tiny man who would have looked ludicrous in regimentals, recommended wearing civilian dress on all occasions. Louis listened with his usual grave attention, and next time appeared in the uniform of a lieutenant-general in the National Guard. He would have been foolish to do otherwise. From Bonaparte to De Gaulle the French people chose to be governed for more than one-third of the time by men in uniform. For Prince Louis his general's uniform was a constant reminder of his relationship to Napoleon. He set about appointing a large military household, to which he did not forget to add a large civil household, and a stable of one hundred horses.

*

The overthrow of the Orleanist monarch and the violence of the days that followed convinced Alexandre Walewski that Paris was no place for him. He took his wife to Florence, where their second child, Charles, was born in June 1848. The uncertainties of the revolution and his earlier prodigalities made it difficult for him to live in the style to which he had accustomed himself, so that he learned of the result of the December ballot with much pleasure and promptly returned to bask in the presidential sunshine.

There were many others making similar journeys: Taschers and Beauharnais, Murats and Bonapartes, notably the Montforts, Jerome, Plon-Plon and Mathilde, of whom Hortense had once remarked, 'They are not without generous feelings, but they are sometimes a little absent-minded', and to which Valerie Masuyer acidly added, 'Their memories suddenly returned on the day that the Head of their House assumed power.' They discovered that Prince Louis did not intend to make any great distribution of prizes until he was more securely established. Alexandre, for instance, got only the post of

French Minister to Tuscany, an assignment that he had eagerly and vainly canvassed from Guizot, but which he now almost resented as being very less than his deserts.

With the ill-luck that dogged so many of his confrontations with history, Alexandre arrived in Florence in February 1849 to find that the populace had been having a revolution there too. The Grand Duke of Tuscany fled. While trying to decide to whom he should present his credentials, Alexandre managed to affront the revolutionaries, the Austrians who sent in an army to quell the uprising and the grand duke who lurched from one side to the other and managed to return to power in July. But it would now take more than diplomatic blunders to check the upward flight of a Bonaparte. In April 1850 he was transferred from Tuscany to Naples; in February 1851, he was appointed ambassador to Spain, and in June he was awarded the prize plum – the Embassy in London.

*

Louis' victory brought great relief to Auguste de Morny, who had suffered considerable financial set-backs during the recent uncertainties and upheavals, and was intensely fearful of the future. Even now that his half-brother had the presidency, his anxiety persisted. During the elections of May 1849 for the Legislative Assembly that was to replace the Constituent, he wrote to his stepmother in Scotland about the 'alarming strikes' made by socialism and its probable success at the polls:

If this happens there will be nothing left to do but pack our things, get up a civil war, and ask the Cossacks to come and help us! I smile in writing this, and I expect your national pride will be up in arms against me, but I give you my word, if you were to come into contact with Socialists you would infinitely prefer Cossacks.... The Empire is the only thing that can save the situation.'[35]

The assumption that the new President of the Republic would try to re-establish the Empire his uncle had founded was implicit in everything he had done and said – including his solemn denials. For Auguste it could not come too soon: he assiduously cultivated his links with Louis. 'I see him once at least and often twice a day', he told Baroness Keith. 'He discusses everything with me, both persons and events.' And he diligently nudged him towards dictatorship.

Charles de Flahaut, father of Auguste and perhaps of both of them, came to Paris in the autumn of 1849 and commented on the kindness with which the President received him: 'He took me by the hand and said that I was mixed up with all his oldest recollections.'[36] It was the eve of the first of Louis' moves against the power of the Legislature. Under the Constitution he could not dissolve it, so instead he dismissed the whole ministry and appointed puppets of his own. In their choice he had been largely guided by Auguste, who then prepared for higher things by taking elocution lessons from his mistress, the actress Judith, and from Samson, the leading actor of the Comédie-Française.

Charles was back in February of the following year, to solicit a pension as a general and to negotiate the sale of his house in the Champs Elysées. He stayed meanwhile in Auguste's house, which was next to the Countess Le Hon's. 'The President exercises a sort of fascination over me', he wrote to his wife. He was impressed by Louis' unruffled calm, an imperturbability that often irritated Auguste. In by-elections at this time Paris returned three rabid Socialists, and Auguste warned Louis: 'When your Presidential term comes to an end in 1852 the problem will be the same as it is today, except that you will have less strength, society will be less afraid, and you will not be able to drive as good a bargain.'

It was an odd relationship between two basically antipathetic men. Of his first interview with Louis as President, Morny said: 'I was convinced that we did not like each other very much. If it had been merely a matter of pleasing myself, I should not have gone back. But I had to see him again out of a sense of duty, as much for his sake as for that of the country. I became the intermediary between him and the moderate party.' On Louis' part there was even more reluctance. A man may brag at times about his father's infidelities, seldom about his mother's. Auguste was a constant reminder of Hortense's frailty. And if she could have one illegitimate son. why not two? He was not unaware of the whispered comments on his resemblance to Charles de Flahaut. But he had spent no more than seven of his forty-one years at large in France and was in need of as many friends and advisers as he could get; while Auguste, living beyond his depleted means (he was on the verge of having to sell his house, and was arranging for Christie's to auction the pictures that he had sent for safety to England), was, despite his protestations of duty and disinterestedness, desperate to get a firm hand in control, and one friendly to the sort of business enterprise at which he excelled. 'From the moment the President was elected,' he confessed later, 'I was obsessed with the idea of a Coup d'Etat.... I never saw any other possible solution.'

Meanwhile, amid the promise of bounty for Bonapartes and their bastards, the unfortunate Leon remained chronically out of luck. His business and political ventures had been pursuing their familiar storm-tossed course: inadequately subsidized by loans from Gourgaud, he moved from one lodging to another, barely a pace ahead of his unpaid landlords' bailiffs. In June 1849 he had asked the Assembly for a grant of one million francs for the Société Pacifique that he had recently founded with the aim of 'organising a series of productive works that may provide the French People with the means of living by the labour of their hands'. It sounded remarkably like the National Workshops all over again, and remarkably unlike the sort of thing of which Leon had any first-hand knowledge. He got nothing.

That same year he stood once more as parliamentary candidate for St-Denis, and once more failed. At the end of March 1850 he applied for an interview with the President – but the President, no doubt with memories of their last meeting on Wimbledon Common, sent word through his Principal Private Secretary, Mocquard, that he was too busy. Leon set about interesting the Pope in the religious propositions put forward by his late friend, François Coëssin.

Chapter Five:
Coup d'Etat

On the evening that Louis assumed his duties as President he entertained a few friends in his new home, the Palace of the Elysée. They were the Old Guard, veterans of Strasbourg and Boulogne and all the years of exile: Persigny, Mocquard, Vaudrey, Laity and the rest. They were installed in posts of importance or profit and joined by even older acquaintances: Plon-Plon, for instance, who was appointed ambassador to Spain, though he was recalled within a few weeks for making a speech attacking the President. There was a constant undercurrent of bad feeling between intelligent but cross-grained Plon-Plon, who set himself up as the leader of the left in the Assembly, and Louis who saw him as a rival and deeply resented the fact that he called himself (with every justification since it was his first name) Prince Napoleon. 'Personally,' Louis wrote to him, 'I always call myself "Louis" to distinguish myself from my relations. In fact I would gladly be called Napoleon Nebuchadnezzar Bonaparte in order to have a clearly marked personal identity.'[1] Napoleon had caused a great deal of confusion in the family by his edict that every male member of his family should carry his name: and it had, after all, no more effect on their conduct or character than had Madame Mère's whim of naming all her daughters after the Virgin Mary.

Plon-Plon marked his return to Paris by making very rude remarks about Louis' suspected illegitimacy. He did this in the presence of his sister, Princess Mathilde, Auguste de Morny and Louis himself, who was with difficulty restrained by the other two from coming to blows with him. Auguste reported the incident to Charles de Flahaut, who replied, 'I am sure nothing could be more certain' that Plon-Plon's insinuation of bastardy was false, adding with the studied nonchalance of one establishing an alibi: 'We were in Prussia at the time.'[2]

It was not long before Louis was given an opportunity to fulfil his promise to bring law and order to the country, and even to its lawless capital. When the leaders of the socialist riots of May 1848 were brought to trial in January 1849 and their supporters showed signs of taking to the streets, the President at once declared martial law, brought out the troops, and ordered them to open fire on anybody making the slightest attempt to set up a barricade. In June, when the Socialists and Republicans protested against French troops being used to drive Italian nationalist rebels out of Rome, Louis again silenced them by the immediate and ruthless use of force. Then he set off on a tour of the provinces. Wherever he went he promised whatever was wanted, whatever would bring the most votes: 'Canals, railways, public works, measures to alleviate the plight of agriculture, bring life to industry and commerce' but only 'if you give me the means to accomplish them ... by your support in strengthening Authority.' The eager departmental councillors demanded that the Assembly should repeal the clause forbidding the re-election of the President; the Tenth of December Society, a pseudo-charitable Bonapartist organization, sent its thousands of members out on to the boulevards to thwack the message home with their iron-tipped clubs.

By November 1850 Louis was complaining in a speech to the Assembly that 'today it is permissible for everybody, except me, to wish to hasten the revision of our fundamental law. I alone, bound by my oath, restrict myself to the limits it has set me.' The Assembly had no intention of letting him serve for a second term. The elections of 1849, which had replaced the Constituent Assembly with a Legislative Assembly, had returned a great number of monarchist deputies, but they were divided between those who wanted a restoration of the senior Bourbon line and those who supported the Orleanist – and they included several leading figures, each of whom was prepared to continue with the Republic provided he became President. Before Louis was halfway throught his tenure of office it was apparent that he would not be able to extend it by legal means.

From his legitimate Bonaparte relations Louis received little useful support. On his Uncle Jerome's side, Plon-Plon was an open enemy; Mathilde retained some affection for the early days when they had been engaged, increased perhaps by her disastrous marriage to Demidoff, but was influenced by the traditional Bonaparte hatred for the Beauharnais. Of his Uncle Lucien's many children only two played much of a role in politics: Louis-Lucien, who was brought up in England and became a right-wing senator after arriving in Paris at Louis' coat tails; and Pierre, a hot-head of the left. Of his aunts, Elisa's sole surviving child, Napoleone, who had tried to arouse the Duke of Reichstadt's dynastic passion, had sunk into eccentricity; Caroline's eldest son, Achille, settled in America, his brother, Lucien, spent more time and energy on social pursuits than in the Assembly. So it turned out that of all the family the two members most eager to serve Louis were his illegitimate relations, Alexandre Walewski and Auguste de Morny.

As time grew shorter he found himself relying on Auguste more and more, still resenting their relationship yet admiring Morny's intellect and energy. In February 1851, he offered Charles de Flahaut the French Embassy in London, before giving it to Alexandre Walewski. Charles refused on the ground that he had sworn never to serve under the Republic: an argument which, as Auguste pointed out in a letter, would shortly have no validity. 'Since the establishment of the Presidency, the Republic exists only in name', though he admitted that 'the solution of the matter must be extra-legal'.[3]

Morny, eager, lively, the antithesis of the apparently lethargic Louis, was all for action and fearful that the contest would go by default or that, if Louis decided to resort to force, he would do so too late. In March Auguste wrote to his father: 'I am much afraid we are tending towards the "Reds" – the spirit of loyal resignation shown by the Prince, the strict observance of the Constitution, and the general blindness are all taking us straight towards that end.'[4] Charles came to Paris for a closer look at what was going on. Louis invited him to dinner and detained him afterwards to greet an old servant named Florenton. It was one of those ambiguous, unexpected gestures at which Louis excelled, for Florenton was the coachman Charles had sent to Hortense from Geneva when they were attempting to meet in August 1815.

To Auguste's despair, Louis still seemed unwilling to make positive plans for action, though he continued to give the impression that he intended to remain in power.

On Sunday, 4 May, the third anniversary of the proclamation of the Republic, Charles noted that the cold, rainy weather had not prevented the Socialists from celebrating – with 'a good number singing and hollowing in the Champs Elysées' outside his house. But another observer remarked that the festivities mirrored 'the horrible weather. Nobody feels joyful, anyway. Business is bad, spirits are low, and, faced with the seriousness of the situation, lovers of peace and order are more divided than ever.' In July, when a proposal to revoke the ban on a second term was debated in the assembly, it failed to get the three-quarters majority necessary for a change in the Constitution.

Auguste, walking with Louis in the garden of the Elysée Palace, drummed home the lesson. 'My dear Prince, this is the final phase. There can be no more hesitation. I don't know how you envisage the future, but for me there is only one solution, in your interest and that of the State: a coup d'état.' To Auguste's relief and delight Louis replied: 'I share your opinion and I am seriously considering it.' He was, in fact, already planning and preparing for it.

There remained the question of timing. After Auguste's conversation with him, Louis was all in favour of striking as soon as the Assembly rose for the autumn recess; but Auguste, who had hitherto urged him on, now advised holding back until the Assembly resumed its sittings – when the opposition could be rounded up and muzzled with ease. The intervening period could be well spent in fanning the fears of the middle classes. More publicists were engaged to spread the rumour of an imminent Socialist take over, none more successful that Auguste's friend, Auguste Romieu, whose pamphlet, *The Red Spectre of 1852*, chilled the marrows of the bourgeoisie with its predictions of revolution, anarchy and ruin. 'The Army alone can save us ... A leader will soon arise ... whoever he may be his role is simple: to impose with a firm hand the most absolute dictatorship ...' and finally, straight out of Auguste's letter of more than two years before: 'only the cannon can decide the problems of our century – and it will decide them, even if it comes from Russia'.

When Alexandre Walewski departed in July 1851 for London to take up the ambassadorship that Charles had refused, Louis made it clear to him that he intended to retain the presidency though he did not reveal any of his plans for doing so. On his arrival, Alexandre was able to assure his old acquaintance Palmerston, and later Queen Victoria herself, that Louis was determined to counter the stirrings of revolt in France by continuing in office. Both Victoria and her Foreign Secretary expressed their approval.

By September the talk of Paris was not of whether Louis would stage a coup d'état, but when he would strike. In October he appointed new ministers, including General Saint-Arnaud as Minister of War. This was the most significant of his moves. Armand-Jacques Leroy de Saint-Arnaud had been recruited to his cause in the early summer while serving in Algeria as a brigadier. In July he had been promoted lieutenant-general, and shortly afterwards given command of the Second Division of the army based in Paris. Now the topic of conversation was: which coup would come first: the President against the Deputies, or they against him?

Louis did not move. From London Alexandre wrote that all the English newspapers 'have come round in your favour. Public opinion ... absolves you in advance for anything that your integrity, zeal and patriotism force you to undertake … in the interest of the country.' Despite the prodding, Louis hesitated. After Strasbourg and Boulogne he could not risk another tumble; this time, breaking his oath to preserve the Constitution, he would be committing treason and would pay for it with his life. At last he moved – and no doubt remembering the near-disaster of the Brumaire coup d'état when Napoleon had panicked and was saved only by the courage of Lucien and Murat, he decided to entrust the helm to the cool, steady hands of Auguste.

Typically, it was neither directly nor in writing that he approached Auguste. He sent Persigny with the verbal message that he had long ago realized that 'you are the only man capable of carrying it out. But he has not until now dared to ask you to help him in this enterprise because it is too great a service to ask of anybody – to risk his neck.' Auguste replied: 'I am proud to be the Prince's choice. Tell him he can count on me – unconditionally.' He called on Louis that afternoon and at once began to draw up the final plans.

Charles de Flahaut came over on 5 November to put his shoulder to the wheel, arriving exhausted at 10 p.m., only to find that Auguste was out at the Opera with Fanny Le Hon. He need not have hurried, for the days continued to drag by while the precise moment of action was discussed, decided, revised, reconsidered. The Assembly, which had reconvened on 4 November, was debating a measure which would reintroduce a law passed, but not officially published, in 1848, giving the President of the Assembly, not the President of the Republic, the right to take over the army in an emergency. On the final day of the debate, 17 November, Auguste waited with Saint-Arnaud in an

211

anteroom. If the motion was passed, Saint-Arnaud would bring in his troops immediately and arrest the Deputies. To the relief of the conspirators, the vote was 'No', but even after this scare it took more than a week before Louis could be brought to name the day: 2 December, the anniversary of Austerlitz and of Napoleon's Coronation as Emperor. The only members of the conspiracy to be told were Louis' private secretary, Mocquard, his equerry, Colonel Fleury, Charlemagne-Emile de Maupas, recently appointed as Paris Prefect of Police, General Saint-Arnaud, Persigny, Auguste de Morny and Charles de Flahaut. On the 30th these began to warn subordinate conspirators to be ready for action, though still not giving them the date. At dinner at Fanny le Hon's that night, Auguste said: 'It'll all be over soon.... And then we'll know how to conduct the affairs of State – with a purse in one hand and a whip in the other.'

*

The 1 December 1851 fell on a Monday and, in accordance with his usual custom, the President held an evening reception at the Elysée Palace. Auguste attended a performance of *Bluebeard's Castle* at the Opéra-Comique. One of his lady friends greeted him with: 'They say the President is going to sweep out the House. What will you do?' He smiled and replied: 'I know nothing about it. But if there is any sweeping I shall try to be at the handle of the broom.' Before the end of the performance he slipped away to the Elysée where the guests had departed and Louis had retired to the pretty little Silver Boudoir where Leon had been taken to see his Aunt Caroline forty years before. Gathered around him were Saint-Arnaud, Maupas, Persigny, Mocquard and Colonel de Béville, the

President's orderly officer. From a drawer of his desk he took an envelope, inscribed in his own hand with the single word 'Rubicon'. It contained the plans and instructions on which he and Auguste had worked for weeks in secret: among them a decree dissolving the Assembly, the declaration of Martial Law in Paris, proclamations from the Minister of War to the army and from the Prefect of Police to the civil population, an order appointing Auguste as Minister of the Interior and a list of seventy-eight persons to be arrested at dawn.

When they had been read out, Auguste turned to the others and said: 'Gentlemen, we are risking our hides in this. You all understand?' 'Mine's pretty well worn out already,' said Mocquard 'I've not much to lose.' Béville left at once for the State printing works in the Marais, where the workers had been told to stay behind for a special night shift, and a company of gendarmerie guarded the doors and windows with orders to shoot any who tried to leave. As soon as the proclamations had been printed Béville took them to Maupas at the Prefecture of Police, where they were distributed to the bill-posters. Saint-Arnaud warned General Magnan, Military Governor of Paris, that the operation was on, then went home to catch a few hours' sleep. Persigny joined Colonel L'Espinasse, commanding the 42nd Infantry (of Boulogne fame) who, with another regiment quartered with them at Les Invalides, were roused at 5 a.m. and marched the short distance to the Palais Bourbon, which they surrounded. The rest of the infantry of the three divisions composing the Paris Command were marched to strategic points, followed three-quarters of an hour later (lest the noise of hoofs and harness should rouse too many people) by the various regiments of light and heavy cavalry.[5]

The Silver Boudoir had emptied. Auguste turned at the door and remarked to his half-brother: 'Well, you can be sure of having a soldier on guard outside your door tomorrow morning – whichever way it goes.' He drifted off to the Jockey Club, where he played cards into the small hours in case he was under observation.

Louis sat down at his desk and wrote a short note: 'I should be very glad to have your company on horseback this morning about eight o'clock.'[6] He sent it off by messenger to 'General Flahaut at M. de Morny's, Champs-Elysées'. Strange, lonely Louis – at this most critical hour of his life he sought comfort in the companionship of his mother's lover, while he entrusted the most powerful office in the State to their bastard son.

About 4 a.m. Auguste left the Jockey Club and went home to change. He called at Fanny Le Hon's house to collect her younger son, nineteen-year-old Leopold, and then got into a two-horse carriage driven by Charles de Flahaut. In drizzling rain, they clattered through the dark streets, deserted except for the rag-pickers moving from one pile of rubbish to the next, lantern in one hand, spiked stick in the other. In the Place du Palais-Bourbon, Auguste checked with Persigny and L'Espinasse that the troops were already encircling the Chamber of Deputies, then drove back to the Place Beauvau, where the Ministry of the Interior faced the Elysée Palace. The street sweepers had succeeded the rag-pickers; it was just 7 a.m. A squadron of cavalry saluted Auguste as he stepped out of the carriage with Leopold Le Hon. Charles returned to the house in the Champs-Elysées, where the President's note and a horse awaited him.

Auguste and Leopold ascended to the bedroom on the first floor where the Minister Thorigny, wakened by the noise below, had put on his dressing gown and picked up his bedside candle. In the thin light Auguste bowed, offered his apologies for disturbing him and informed him that he was, from that moment, no longer in charge of the ministry. Thorigny made no attempt to argue; Auguste walked off to take possession of the office. Outside and through all the streets of Paris the last posters were being stuck up, signed by the President and the new Minister of the Interior. A separate proclamation announced the President's intention to reform the Constitution and restore 'The system created by the First Consul at the beginning of the century, which formerly brought France peace and prosperity and will guarantee it again.'

By the time that Auguste took official control he had troops lined up through the heart of Paris from the Champs-Elysées and the Place de la Concorde to the Tuileries Palace and the Town Hall. Soldiers guarded every belfry from which a tocsin might be rung; in districts where the National Guard could not be relied on for support, the drums had been pierced during the night and water poured on the gunpowder. During the past hour scores of politicians and soldiers, Thiers and half a dozen generals among them, had been arrested in their beds and taken off to prison. Deputies arriving at the Palais-Bourbon found a ring of soldiers denying them entrance and, when they protested, they too were marched off to gaol.[7]

At 10 a.m., when Louis took his delayed ride through the streets accompanied by Charles de Flahaut and others, the cafés were open for business as usual and all seemed calm. Leopold Le Hon brought Rachel to call on Auguste at the Ministry that morning and they found him in the bath, dictating to two secretaries. There were other visitors who found him equally calm: about three hundred Deputies had re-assembled at the Town Hall of the Tenth Arrondissement in the north-east of the city, and voted the deposition of the President and the immediate release of their colleagues. Two of them bravely put in an appearance at the Ministry of the Interior with an order to Auguste to surrender himself to the law. He treated them to one of his charming smiles and replied: 'If you call the people to arms, and if I find any Deputies on the barricades, I will have them shot – every single one of them.'[8] A battalion of light infantry that had surrounded the Town Hall marched the Deputies off to prison, whence some were sent to Ham. 'General Post', said Auguste with another gentle smile as he ordered that Cavaignac should be given the quarters formerly occupied by Louis.

'Calm in the suburbs, agitation in the Boulevard des Italiens and Bonne-Nouvelle', Leopold wrote from the Ministry to his mother that evening. 'The opinion is that there is no danger.' Fanny Le Hon had a right to be kept informed: no documents were ever found to establish how much she invested in the coup, but family tradition put it at not less than a million francs. Although an avowed Orleanist, her fear of a swing towards socialism – to say nothing of fifteen years of illicit love – induced her to support Auguste.

As Leopold predicted, the night was calm. 'Auguste has been heroic,'[9] Charles wrote to his wife early in the morning of Wednesday, 3 December, sending the letter in the diplomatic bag to Alexandre Walewski in London. It was clear by now that success or failure would depend on Auguste's clear head and firmness of purpose, for the opposition was beginning to show itself. Dawn revealed new posters speckling the streets of Paris: 'To the People!

Louis-Napoleon Bonaparte is declared an outlaw. Martial Law is repealed. Universal Suffrage is restored. Long Live the Republic! To Arms!' It was the signal many had been waiting for. Paving stones were levered up. Barricades were erected in the boulevards and side streets. The troops sent to dismantle them were fired on. A Deputy, Jean-Baptiste Baudin, determined to prove his republican ardour, climbed a barricade improvised out of an overturned bus, a milk cart, a baker's van and a few sacks of rubbish near the Place de la Bastille, and was shot dead. A mob gathered outside the Stock Exchange; there was a cavalry charge in the Boulevard Montmartre.[10]

Auguste summoned Saint-Arnaud, the Minister of War, and Magnan, commanding the Paris District for a conference at the ministry that afternoon. He told them to draw up a second and final warning: peaceful-minded citizens were advised to stay indoors, as for the others: 'any individual found carrying arms will be subject to the full rigour of military law'. Such was the wording when Saint-Arnaud handed the draft to him. Auguste struck out the last eight words and substituted 'shot'.

In the next room the telegraph chattered reports from the provinces. From the Prefecture of Police, where Maupas was losing his nerve, came appeals for artillery and more troops, and warnings of an Orleanist invasion. Auguste read them and scribbled 'I don't believe it' on them. Instead he ordered Magnan to withdraw all troops to their barracks. Let the opposition have time to rally and concentrate during the night; then they could be dealt with next day in bulk instead of penny packets. 'My Chief is at the Elysée and I cannot leave because I am deputizing for him', Leopold wrote to his mother that evening. 'They say there will be a battle on a larger scale tomorrow.'

There was. In the morning Leopold sent another note to his mother: 'Magnan has all his dispositions made', he told her. 'May Heaven help us to administer exemplary punishment on this final burst of demagogy.... Have you any Prefects or Sub-Prefects you want appointed? Send me their names at once.... Write to Eugene [his elder brother] and tell him I have found a place for his friend.' That crisp, bright afternoon General Magnan marshalled his troops on the boulevards and took the barricades by storm, at a cost estimated at between 300 and 600 dead and wounded. 'Insurrection overcome.' Leopold telegraphed to Charles de Flahaut's wife in London. To his mother he wrote, 'Everything is calm now; the rioters have been tamed.' During the hours of darkness troops searched houses in the insurgent districts and shot many of the occupants out of hand.

On the morning of 5 December, Auguste telegraphed instructions to the prefects and senior army officers of all departments:

All armed insurrection in Paris has ceased, thanks to vigorous repression. The same energetic measures will have the same effect everywhere. The gangs which are committing pillage, rape and arson are outlawed; there is to be no parleying with them, no calling on them to surrender – they are to be attacked and dispersed. Any who resist must be shot in the name of Society legitimately defending itself.

By Saturday morning, 6 December, it was all over in Paris. 'It was a tremendous game to play and which necessity alone could justify'[11], Charles wrote to his eldest daughter, Lady Shelburne; and as soon as they had the upper hand Auguste and Louis played the game very roughly. On 8 December they issued under their joint signature a decree sentencing all members of secret societies, past or present, to transportation to penal colonies, similar sentences for any who were banished from Paris and returned without permission, all to be carried out without trial. In his instructions to the prefects to proceed with this purge, Auguste added that, since the words Liberty, Equality and Fraternity had now become associated in the public mind with disorder and civil war, they were to be effaced from all public buildings.

Official statistics showed that 26,000 persons had been arbitrarily arrested. The true figures were no doubt a great deal higher. 'Poor Auguste', wrote Charles to his wife on 10 December, 'has inspired hatreds that will never end.'[12] And the hatred was not confined to the Socialists. Years later, arriving at a party where the guests numbered many Orleanist politicians, including the Count d'Haussonville, Auguste found himself cold-shouldered. Most of the guests left the room while he was talking to his hostess, who thereupon ran into the hall to try to persuade them to return. 'Ah!' said d'Haussonville to her, 'so you are coming with us?'

Auguste could afford to shrug it off. He had a firm grasp on France and every day made it firmer. The Bonaparte legend, the promise of promotion, and direct bribery assured the support of the army. Of the National Guard he was not so certain. Louis offered the command to Charles, who on Auguste's advice declined it. Auguste circularized the prefects, ordering them to discharge or at least disarm any guardsmen whose loyalty was in any way doubtful. 'Auguste shows activity, ability and firmness above all praise', wrote his admiring father on 17 December.

'Notwithstanding the pressure of business, he remodels his administrations, diminishes the number of employees, increases the salary of those retained – in short, shows a master mind. His orders for clearing Paris and France of those scoundrels who have caused all the revolutions and disasters are firm, and for the first time, instead of being called *des hommes égarés* [misled people], they are branded with their deserved designation of *bandits* and *coquins* [rogues].'[13]

As promised, the electors were asked to vote on a referendum: 'That the French People desires the maintenance of the authority of Louis-Napoleon and delegates to him the necessary powers to establish a Constitution on the lines proposed in his proclamation.' These were almost exactly copied from Napoleon's consulship: A President with complete executive powers for a period of ten years, a council of State to initiate laws at the President's direction, a Legislative Assembly to vote on them, and a Senate, nominated by the President, to keep an eye on the Constitution. The President's power, or his ability to manipulate affairs, was virtually unchecked. The electors voted seven-and-a-half million in favour of the new Constitution, only half-a-million against. Louis moved from the Elysée to the Royal and Imperial Palace of the Tuileries.

Auguste sent Charles de Flahaut back to London at Christmas to report on public opinion there. Although the typically ruthless Bonaparte violence should have been anticipated in Britain, it had, in fact, come as a considerable shock. The bloodshed and arbitrary arrests had aroused fierce criticism in the press and in Parliament, and the queen had requested that the British ambassador should carefully refrain from showing support for either side. But when the ambassador, Lord Normanby, passed on this message to the Quai d'Orsay he was briskly informed that Palmerston, the British Foreign Secretary, had already informed the French ambassador of 'his complete approval of the President's actions'.

It was another of Alexandre Walewski's little mishaps. Palmerston had made the remark in confidence as a personal opinion; Alexandre had relayed it to Paris as official, and had exaggerated its importance.[14] The upshot was that Russell, the Prime Minister, demanded Palmerston's resignation, and the queen, who did not care for Palmerston, invited Alexandre and his wife to spend three days at Windsor, where Prince Albert organized a hunt in their honour. Charles was able to report that the British government had every intention of remaining on friendly terms with the newly-constituted Republic, although the queen's enthusiasm was tempered by her family ties with the House of Orleans.

*

On 1 January 1852 Louis entered the garlanded Cathedral of Notre-Dame, dressed for the first time in the uniform of a lieutenant-general in the regular army, to lead the nation in gratitude to God for the success of the coup. The great rose window was obscured by a banner inscribed '7,500,000' – the number of votes that had been cast for him. The congregation rose and shouted *Vive Napoléon!* A group of aged veterans put on their old uniforms and marched past the new leader. The weather was very cold and misty, glittering with hoar-frost – exactly like the day when the Emperor was consecrated, they remarked happily. The new coinage was already minted, with Louis' effigy on one side and the Imperial eagle replacing the

Gallic cock on the other. From his lodgings in St-Denis, Leon issued a proclamation to his former comrades of the National Guard, calling on them to support Louis. Auguste, no doubt coincidentally, issued a decree disbanding them.

For Auguste it was not to be a happy new year. Louis, now that he had achieved supreme power, was acting rather strangely towards the brother who had done so much to put him there. 'He has no real friendship for anyone', Auguste wrote bitterly to Charles before January was out. 'Less perhaps for me than for others – and then my peculiar position is an annoyance to him and yours makes the matter still worse.... He is suspicious and ungrateful, and only likes those who obey him slavishly and flatter him.'[15]

The truth was that Auguste had been too successful at the key post of the Ministry of the Interior. He knew it, showed that he knew it and was now too free and insistent with advice. He had made too much, too openly, of their relationship as half-brothers, a kinship that was more and more frequently touched upon in English newspapers, where there was also comment on the resemblance of Louis to Flahaut. He was protesting too vehemently at Louis' proposal to confiscate the property inherited in France by the family of Louis-Philippe, who had died in 1850; a project which he disliked because of his own and Fanny Le Hon's old Orleanist loyalties, and also because he considered it mean and silly. He was, in fact, acting too much like a legitimate member of the family, and the senior brother rather than the junior one. Louis listened to the protests, said nothing, and went about his ways, settling himself firmly into power. Auguste was now dispensable. Louis decided to bring in Persigny, of less intelligence and unquestionable loyalty. He would give him the Ministry of the Interior, at the same time reducing his power by setting up a separate Ministry of Police under Maupas. Auguste could have the Foreign Office.

'I wish you were here with me', Auguste wrote to Charles on 14 January 1852. 'I have been much worried by serious matters about which I have not dared to write.... I shall do my duty to the end, but so long only as I can do so with honour.' He was pressed for time and had to hurry off to a meeting of the Council.[16] In a separate letter Fanny Le Hon gave Charles a long account of the dispute which had begun on the 9th and reached its crisis on the 11th with an angry interview between Auguste and the President, in which Auguste insisted that the Orleanist confiscation would look like petty vengeance and would antagonize many of Louis' supporters by its breach of the rights of private property owners. He was the more incensed because, now that the ruthless repression was completed, he was trying to heal the wounds and unite all sections. He sent instructions to the prefects that they should seek the help 'of men esteemed by the public, concerned more with the interests of the country than with party strife. sympathetic to the sufferings of the working class' and that they should point out to their officials that 'the best policy is kindness towards people.... Bureaucrats must not believe that they are appointed to raise objections, hinder and go slow'.

On 23 January the *Moniteur Universel* announced the decree of confiscation of the Orleans property, the appointment of Persigny to the Ministry of the Interior, and the resignation of Morny. 'He could not find anyone else for the 2nd of December, so he made use of me', Auguste wrote bitterly to his father on 26 January. 'I

223

risked my life; I accomplished my task, but what matter; I am in the way; I am neither a slave nor a sycophant, so I am cast off as useless.... I feel very sad and deeply wounded.'[17] He refused the offer of a seat in the Senate, and gave the same reply on Charles's behalf – perhaps rather to the latter's dismay for under the new Constitution the post was worth 30,000 francs a year.

Charles, unwilling to lose any future golden eggs, wrote to Louis assuring him that 'nothing would have been more repugnant to my ideas or to my feelings than to have shown any active opposition' to the President's actions. He also sent Auguste a letter warning him against influences hostile to Louis – by which he evidently meant Fanny Le Hon, who was widely believed not only to have incited Auguste into opposition because of her Orleanist sympathies, but also to have compounded the offence by careless gossip. 'Believe me, it will be best to show friendly feelings towards the President and to make him *forgive* you for the services you have rendered.... If you take my advice, you will not utter a single word which would justify people in suggesting you had a grievance.'

It was difficult advice to follow, for no sooner had Louis made the conciliatory gesture of offering Auguste the Presidency of the newly-created Legislative Body, which replaced the Chamber of Deputies, than he was forced to withdraw it by the threat of Uncle Jerome (keeping up the feud of Bonaparte versus Beauharnais) to resign the Presidency of the Senate if Auguste were appointed. Louis offered to send Auguste as ambassador to Russia, Austria or Spain instead; Auguste indignantly refused. He returned to his affairs both business and social. At the end of March he went to a party given by Rachel at her delightful little house in the Rue Trudon. The company was agreeable:

two of his fellow ex-ministers, a financier, the directors of the Opera and the Comédie-Française. The surroundings were luxurious: 'Pictures, sculptures and bronzes everywhere, magnificent silver, servants both numerous and well-dressed. The whole house gilded like an eighteenth-century court dress.'[18] The hostess, witty, tempestuous Rachel, saw so much of Louis when he was first elected to the Presidency that the cartoonists depicted her as 'The Angel of the Elysée', but Leopold Le Hon was now her recognized protector, and Alexandre Walewski a forgotten figure of the past.

Though he had benefited more than Auguste from Orleanist patronage and bounty, Alexandre made no protest to Louis about the confiscation of their property. He intended to preserve his bread with the buttered side up, convinced that there was jam to come. Louis was poised for the last steps that led to Napoleon's throne. There had been natural speculation that he would do so ever since the coup d'état. In the early spring of 1852 he confirmed his intention to Alexandre, who was on a visit to Paris. When he returned to England Alexandre at once began urging him on: 'I cannot conceal from you the extent of my regret that you have not yet proclaimed the Empire. Everybody expected it; everybody would have accepted it.... It would be infinitely better to act sooner rather than later.'

The rumours, often set in motion by Louis' own agents, continued to grow stronger. The day after Rachel's party for Auguste and the others the spectators at the Sunday review in the Tuileries were convinced that the troops were about to shout *Vive l'Empereur!*, but they went no farther than *Vive Napoléon!*. In July, when Louis visited Strasbourg, there was the same anticipation, the same carefully-nurtured disappointment. Uncle Jerome, glowering enviously in the background, put about the story that King Louis had filed a declaration of non-paternity when Hortense became pregnant in 1807, and Plon-Plon told acquaintances that he had a collection of thirty-three letters all throwing light on the scandal.[19] In the circumstances it was not surprising that when Jerome, after a tour of inspection of the French ports, asked the President for more money to cover his expenses, Louis told him he had already given him a lump sun of two million francs and an annual pension of 300,000 – and he did not intend to give him any more.

'You have nothing of the Emperor about you!' shouted Jerome.

'You are mistaken', said Louis, answering back for once. 'I have his family.'[20]

By October, he was coming more into the open. At a banquet in Bordeaux, during a tour of the southern provinces, he uttered what was to become one of his more famous untruths: 'The Empire means peace!' It became clearer daily that the French wanted to believe it. On his return to Paris, the Senators, Deputies, Judges and Court officials who received him at the station shouted *Vive l'Empereur!* Cannon fired one-minute salutes and church bells rang as he drove to the Tuileries beneath triumphal arches inscribed 'To the Emperor Louis-Napoleon'. When he attended the Théâtre-Français a week later, the audience rose to stand bareheaded and shout *Vive l'Empereur!* At the end of the performance, Rachel stepped forward to recite verses dedicated to him. A few days later there were similar scenes at the Opera. Everything was being beautifully stage-managed throughout the country, and on 7 November 1852 he approved a decree of the Senate that the people should vote whether to ask him to become their Emperor for life. A fortnight later they did so, by a majority of thirty to one. The dream was achieved – his and Hortense's. After all these changes of name – Charles-Louis-Napoleon, Little Oui-oui, Louis Napoleon, Napoleon-Louis, Prince Louis – he was on 1 December 1852 proclaimed Napoleon III.

Charles de Flahaut now accepted a seat in the Senate and came over from London to offer his congratulations. Writing to his wife he asked her to warn Alexandre Walewski 'that I believe he has enemies at the Foreign Affairs, but that the P. is satisfied with him and knows the perfections of his wife'. There had been previous criticism of Alexandre in the Quai d'Orsay partly because of jealousy aroused by the preferential treatment he received from Louis, partly from a genuine doubt whether he had the intellectual equipment to perform his duties adequately. Earlier in the year Auguste had written to Charles, 'you must take care that Walewski is not too English…. for what have they done for us in any corner of the globe? Nothing!'[21] Charles had replied defending him: 'He has a good political brain; he understands the meaning of high diplomacy.' but this view was not widely held on either side of the Channel.

Alexandre was at the moment concerned with securing the succession to the Imperial throne. Napoleon III was forty-four years old and still unmarried. 'We are getting on', Alexandre had written to him in March 1852. 'I have the honour to be your contemporary and, at our age, marriage is not a thing that one can put off for very long.' However, he now found exactly the right bride for the Emperor: 'eighteen years old, very pretty, fairly tall, regular features, admirable teeth, beautiful eyes and a remarkably pale complexion'. Moreover, the young lady, Princess Adelaide of Hohenlohe-Langenburg, was a niece of Queen Victoria: the marriage would strengthen the ties between the two countries.

Alexandre put the idea up to Lord Malmesbury, the British Foreign Secretary, who foresaw difficulties because Adelaide was a Protestant and Napoleon a Catholic. But religious beliefs have been known to change in such matters. Malmesbury mentioned the suggestion unofficially to the queen, who received it 'very graciously', Alexandre reported to Paris. Perhaps only a man of his determined enthusiam could have read much encouragement into the queen's comment that 'she made it an invariable rule never to intervene in the affairs of the German branch of her family. Princess Adelaide has a father and mother who can be very easily approached.' Alexandre recommended that the Emperor should send an emissary forthwith.

Napoleon replied through his own Foreign Secretary, Drouyn de Lhuys, that nobody could be better fitted for this delicate negotiation than Alexandre himself. He must take leave from the London Embassy and go to Germany to discuss the proposition with the prospective bride's father. Within a week Alexandre was on his way, having informed the startled Prince von Hohenlohe that he wished to see him on a matter of weight and urgency. He broke his journey in Paris, fortunately for all concerned. For there he learned that the Emperor had decided to marry the 26-year-old Eugenie de Montijo. For a moment it may have seemed to him that the Emperor's treatment of his suggestion had been somewhat flippant, even contemptuous.

He returned to London in a reflective mood.

*

Eugenie was descended on her father's side from a long line of grandees, on her mother's from a less distinguished mixture of French and Scottish tradesmen. She had been a figure in Parisian society for several years, a frequent guest at the Delesserts and Flahauts, and much admired for her fair skin, tawny blonde hair, blue eyes and slender build. According to Louis' Uncle Jerome there had been a time in 1850 when she was considered a suitable bride for Plon-Plon. But Louis, when Jerome mentioned the project to him, said: 'Don't even consider it, uncle. Napoleon is worth better than that; one may sleep with women of that sort, but on no account marry them.'

A year or two later, when the President began to pay attention to her, her mother gave her the excellent advice to welcome his advances but to set a limit to his progress. Louis was not accustomed to difficult conquests, nor was he a man of patient disposition in these matters. He called in the palace architect at Compiègne and had him cut a concealed door in a wall of one of the bedrooms. He then invited Eugenie and her mother down for a hunting party. Eugenie, a slim Amazon in a tight riding habit over a wide skirt and long pantaloons, patent leather boots with spurs, ostrich-plumed felt hat and pearl-studded whip, bewitched all the men. She was awakened one night to find Louis standing beside her bed. She invited him to take a chair and remarked with some severity: 'I thought I was in the house of a gentleman!' Louis begged, pleaded, wept and raged but without success, and eventually retired unsolaced through his secret door.[22]

He was now determined to triumph, one way or another. By early January 1853 there were the strongest rumours that Mademoiselle de Montijo was to be the future Empress. Politicians and place-seekers tumbled over each other to seek her favours. On 15 January, Louis sent her mother a formal request for her daughter's hand and then officially informed the Council of State, the Senators and Deputies of his decision to marry. It was a strangely defensive speech, in which he described himself as a parvenu among the monarchs of Europe and argued that it was as well that he was not marrying into one of their royal families because 'in the last seventy years foreign Princesses have ascended to the throne only to see their families dispersed or exiled by war of revolution'. Then, referring to his beloved grandmother Josephine, he added: 'Only one woman seems to have brought good fortune and lived on in the memory of the People and that woman, the kind and modest wife of General Bonaparte, was not of royal blood.' There were mixed reactions to the announcement. Some felt France slighted because he had not aimed higher; others claimed that he should at least have chosen a Frenchwoman.

On 22 January 1853 Eugenie and her mother moved into the Elysée Palace. The civil marriage on 29 January 1853 was repeated the following day in Notre Dame. Princess Mathilde, who would have been Empress herself but for the contretemps in 1840, informed her dinner guests that 'Eugenie is not at all beautiful by daylight; white make-up doesn't suit her; she was painted like a tart; she got hot and the rouge streamed down her cheeks.'[23] Her brother Plon-Plon, according to his own story, restricted himself to remarking to Louis: 'Oh, so one *does* marry them?'

The Imperial honeymoon did not last long. Louis later claimed that he remained faithful for six months, but by February Miss Howard was making a point of stationing her carriage along any route the Emperor and Empress were expected to take and bowing to the Emperor who replied with a salute; within a month or two it was common knowledge that they had resumed their relationship. She had come to Paris soon after Louis was elected to the Presidency and had taken a house whose rear entrance gave on to the Avenue Marigny just across the road from the Elysée. This became his second home and there she brought up his two boys by Alexandrine Vergeot as well as her own son by Major Martyn. At the time of his marriage Louis sent police to break in during her absence and ransack the place for any of his letters that she might have kept. She was upset by this but the grant of a million francs and the title of Countess de Beauregard induced her to overlook it. However, the reconciliation was not to last long. Louis was already wandering in several directions; she, in May 1854, married an Englishman. During the course of that year the account was closed with the payment of a further four million francs.

The Empress found the physical side of her marriage rather irksome; but she delighted in weaving royal fantasies with herself as heroine. Very early on it was noticed that she had a particular interest in Marie-Antoinette. During a visit to the Louvre within a month after her wedding, her eyes were seen to fill with tears as the unhappy queen's farewell letter to her daughter was produced and read to her.[24] A little later, walking in the park at Saint-Cloud with Valerie Masuyer, she told her: 'I always recall that it was here that that noble woman spent the last relatively peaceful hours of her life before the final catastrophe. It was here that she said farewell to the flowers, the trees, nature that she loved so much. And it was from this enchanting palace that she returned to the Tuileries to witness the downfall of the monarch.'

At the end of April Eugenie disappointed the country and rejoiced the rest of the Bonaparte family by having a miscarriage. In July, when she accompanied the Emperor to the Opéra-Comique, one of her over-dramatic dreams almost came true: the police arrested armed men in the theatre suspected of waiting to shoot the Emperor as he left. Next month the Imperial couple went off to Dieppe, which Emilie's friend, the Duchess of Berry, had made fashionable as a watering place. The Empress was happy – it gave her a chance to show off some of the vast collection of clothes that she was already amassing. Princess Mathilde, who accompanied her, was less content. 'I never wished for the fall of Louis-Philippe', she told her friends. 'I was happier under his reign than I am now.'[25] There was perhaps a touch of Louis-Philippe in the air by they time they returned to Paris to face the problems of the meagre harvest, the high cost of cereals, and ructions in the Faubourg St-Antoine over the price of bread.

*

Auguste de Morny was still out of office. 'I am far from finished,' he assured everybody, 'but I am saving myself for difficult times. I have no need of the advantages that follow from power. The Emperor has placed me high enough - I shall wait for the moment when a new, energetic spirit is needed.'[26] There had been no open break between the half-brothers, and Auguste's presumed influence with the Emperor did much to forward his business plans and to protect him in dubious ventures.

On the day the Empire was re-established Auguste was awarded the Grand Cross of the Legion of Honour; and on the same day a great scandal broke over the disposal of shares in the newspaper *Le Constitutionel*. Dr Véron, who was joint managing director with Auguste, had earlier recommended holders of the 180 shares to sell them to a financier Jules Mirès, who was bidding for the company, at the price of 4,000 francs per share. But it was discovered that the original offer had been 10,000 francs a share. Véron had persuaded Mirès to reshape this while paying the same total: the shareholders being given 4,000 a share and the remainder, more than a million francs, being paid to Véron and Auguste as compensation for loss of office. The indignant shareholders called an extraordinary general meeting, only to find that Véron had made off with all the relevant papers.

Because of Auguste's involvement, they appealed to the Emperor, but he refused to intervene, so in June 1853 they began a civil action to recover the money. The trial produced some interesting new examples of how the pair had been running the company. Organizations could, for instance, buy favourable editorials in *Le Constitutionel* for a payment of 100,000 francs to Véron, who exercised day-to-day control of the paper and who gave Morny 25 per cent commission on all business of this kind that he introduced. The legal proceedings dragged on throughout the year before the shareholders were finally convinced that they could never penetrate the protective screen surrounding Auguste. They withdrew the charges against him and concentrated on Véron who, in March 1854, was ordered to repay to the shareholders not only his own share of the million francs but Auguste's as well.[27]

The base for much of Auguste's influence in the financial world – apart from his connection with the Emperor – was the Société-Génèrale de Crédit Mobilier, a bank created for the purpose of drawing on the vast amount of small savings of the middle and lower-middle classes; these the bank invested in the large industrial enterprises which had been growing up over the past decade and needed more capital than the old-fashioned family banking houses could supply. Auguste, as a member of the board, had no scruples about demanding shares at a low price from those firms which asked him to support their applications for loans. Some of them he re-sold at a profit; others he retained and added to, and then demanded a directorship. His special interest at this time was in railways. France had lagged behind England in this, as in other industrial development, but was now making an effort to link up her centres of production by rail instead of relying solely on roads and waterways. In April 1853 the Emperor gave permission for the Crédit Mobilier to back the proposal of an Anglo-French venture, the Compagnie du Chemin de Fer Grand Central de France, to issue 180,000 shares at 500 francs each, for the purpose of constructing nearly six hundred miles of railway line, with Auguste as chairman of the board of directors. In December the Emperor authorized the issue of a further 30 million francs worth of shares for the purpose of taking over existing lines from the Rhône and Loire Railway Company. Auguste soon extended his interests to related industries: coal, iron and steel.

In May of that year Leon, too, had gone into industry. The Société Pacifique that he founded four years earlier had not been a success, despite his offer of shares in it at five francs apiece, payable in cash or kind, and his more

234

direct appeal to 'all well-meaning persons' simply to send him five francs by post office order. His new venture was launched by the organization that he had taken over on Coëssin's death in 1843: the association of those Children of God who according to Saint Luke are 'equal unto angels'. It was an ink factory, which he set up on the Ile St-Denis. In the prospectus Leon and his fellow Children proclaimed their intention of establishing their head office in Paris – in the house in the Rue de la Victoire where Napoleon spent his early married years with Josephine. They never got there; and the ink factory was soon no more.[28]

*

In mid-November 1853, Emilie Pellapra returned to Paris with her husband and her mother. Her father-in-law had become a Dutch citizen after Waterloo, when his principality of Chimay in the Ardennes ceased to be French territory; but a fresh adjustment of the borders in 1830, when Chimay became part of the new Kingdom of Belgium, decided him to return to France, where he died in 1842 at the age of seventy. Although the family retained their other property in France and a townhouse in Paris, they made their home in Brussels, and it was as a semi-official representative of his king, Leopold of the Belgians, that Prince Joseph de Chimay had come to confer with Napoleon III. They arrived at midnight and were not in bed until 2 a.m.; Emilie, although flattered, was not altogether pleased when Jerome Bonaparte called in the morning and sat on talking into the afternoon. The Chimays were due to join the Court at Fontainebleau next day and she had a great deal of unpacking, packing and repacking to supervise, as well as catching up on her lost sleep.[29]

Chimay's mission was to try to persuade Napoleon to repeal the decree confiscating the Orleanist property which, nearly two years before, had resulted in Auguste de Morny's resignation and was still a cause of resentment to Leopold, who had married Louis-Philippe's daughter, and to Queen Victoria, who was Leopold's very devoted and admiring niece. This second consideration had a close bearing on the plan which Emilie's Uncle Jerome had spent so long discussing with her: that, if Napoleon III returned to Victoria's good graces by restoring the Orleanist property, he might – if he could be persuaded into it – propose the marriage of Princess Mary, the daughter of Victoria's cousin, the Duke of Cambridge, to Jerome's unlovable son, Plon-Plon. It was all quite speculative at present, for there were doubts whether Victoria would allow an English princess to occupy what would be a secondary place at the French Court. There was the difficulty, too, of a Protestant princess marrying a Catholic – even so casual a one as Plon-Plon.

On arrival at Fontainebleau the Chimays were given an apartment in the Galerie des Cerfs, and were suitably impressed by a plaque in their bedroom commemorating the murder there of the secretary of Queen Christina of Sweden two hundred years before. This was one of the last occasions when the Court moved to Fontainebleau in the late autumn. Soon the regular pattern became the Tuileries for Christmas and the New Year, St-Cloud in the spring, Fontainebleau in the summer, back to Paris for Napoleon's birthday, 15 August, then to the Villa Eugenie at Biarritz for the rest of the fine weather and from there to Compiègne until mid-December. It was at Compiègne and

Fontainebleau – because they were too far from Paris for a day-trip and large enough to accommodate many guests – that the week-long receptions were held. The guests would arrive in the Imperial train, to be met by the Imperial red and green brakes that transported them to the palace with their vast collection of luggage containing the morning dresses, afternoon dresses, walking-out dresses, riding dresses and evening dresses, each of which must never be worn more than once during their stay.

The daytime entertainment, if there was no hunting, included walking in the forest at Compiègne, boating on the lake at Fontainebleau, rustic frolics and, in wet weather, dancing and games indoors. At seven, the guests paraded to the dining room between two rows of soldiers: after their creation in 1854 the Emperor's Cent Gardes, in sky-blue uniforms with jackboots, steel cuirasses and helmets. After dinner, the Emperor and Empress circulated among their guests, while an equerry ground away at a mechanical piano for any who wanted to dance, or some of the brighter spirits performed charades. The glory of being invited compensated for the boredom, but there was a general feeling of relief when the host and hostess retired and the guests gathered in each other's apartments to relax, gossip and smoke until the early hours.

Napoleon was in no hurry to be confronted with the problems of the Orleanist properties and Plon-Plon's marital future; it was not until nearly the end of their week's stay that the Chimays were granted their first formal audience. Emilie found their majesties 'very gracious. The Emperor was charming to us, and the poor Empress, changed beyond recognition, is altogether a nice creature.'[30] It was too much to expect that she could entirely live up to Emilie's standards. 'She lacks something that does not come of itself', Emilie wrote to her daughter Valentine, who had stayed at home with the two boys in Brussels (little Minette had died young, Joseph, born in 1836, had been joined by Valentine in 1839 and Eugene in 1843); 'just what I try to give you, although I do not design you for a throne – the air of a great lady, the dignity which only childhood habits can bring into being.' Not, she hastened to add, that she wished to criticize 'the warm handshake which the poor Empress so cordially gave me'.

The Imperial couple were, of course, both captivated by Emilie's own distinction and charm. She almost managed to forget how common they were as they played hide-and-seek in the forest and the Emperor leaped up to pluck a sprig of oak-leaves to accompany the violets from the Empress's bouquet which Emilie was sending to the children. This, however, drew criticism from Chimay – they were a well-matched disapproving pair – who remarked unfavourably on the frisky behaviour of 'this ruler of 36 million men'. Chimay made no progress on the issue of the sequestered Orleanist estates, but he reported to Leopold's private secretary that Napoleon was in favour of the marriage between Plon-Plon and Princess Mary, but hesitant about saying so openly, for fear of being snubbed. The Emperor believed that Victoria's opposition to a religiously mixed marriage was a pretext to disguise her reluctance to have her family connected with the upstart Bonapartes, but he would, of course, welcome the alliance for the added strength it would give to the French Throne. He invited Chimay to discuss the matter fully with Drouyn de Lhuys and sent a telegram to Alexandre Walewski in London, summoning him to the conference. As was to be expected, the plan eventually fell through, happily for the

British people, for Princess Mary instead married the Duke of Teck and, in due course, became the mother-in-law of George V, first monarch of the House of Windsor.

On Monday the visit ended. The chief usher, on behalf of the servants, called at each apartment and presented the guests with prepared signed receipts for the amount of the tips at which he had assessed them. Emilie put on her travelling clothes, her eighteen gowns were packed away and the Chimays returned to Paris in a torrential rainstorm. Three weeks later the Imperial couple again took up residence at the Tuileries, where the devout, but superstitious, Eugenie became an enthusiast for table-turning – a supernatural phenomenon introduced to society a year or so before by the Marchioness de Boissy, who, as Countess Teresa Guiccioli, had once been Byron's mistress. The Emperor was concerned with more serious matters. He was about to take his first full stride along the path trodden by his uncle, Napoleon: to offer France the excitement of military glory in contrast to the boredom of bourgeois pacifism that had contributed to the downfall of Louis-Philippe.

*

In 1740 the Sultan of Turkey had agreed to most of the Holy Places in Palestine being controlled by Catholic monks under the protection of France, but in the course of time the privileges of the Latin monks were usurped by their Greek Orthodox brethren protected by Russia. During his term as President, Louis had moved towards demanding the restitution of French rights. On his election to the Imperial throne his antagonism towards Russia was increased by the Tsar's deliberate snub in addressing him as 'my friend' instead of 'my brother' – the accepted form between crowned heads of state. Louis managed to squeeze a quip out of it – 'one has to accept one's brother but one chooses one's friends' – but he had a long memory for grievances, and in March 1853 he instructed Alexandre Walewski to draw the British government's attention to 'the danger there will be in letting Russia increase her prestige in the Orient and her influence at Constantinople'. If he could set the allies of 1815 at each other's throats he would have gone some way towards avenging the humiliation of Waterloo, and this, with the help of bad feeling and suspicion, he managed to do.

The Tsar proposed to the British ambassador (that same Sir George Hamilton Seymour who had provided the passport for Hortense and Louis to escape from Italy more than twenty years before) that since the 'sick man [Turkey] is dying', Britain and Russia should give him a shove into the grave and share the inheritance between them, Russia assuming sovereignty over Serbia and Bulgaria, Britain taking Egypt. The British government refused and published Seymour's report. The Tsar demanded that the Sultan should recognize him as protector of all Greek Orthodox Christians in the Ottoman Empire, which in effect meant almost half the population. Napoleon sent a French fleet to join the British ships stationed at the eastern end of the Mediterranean.

While the warlike measures proceeded, Alexandre returned to his old game of cutting the rungs from beneath the feet of the man above him. Just as he had tried to undermine Cochelet's reputation at Alexandria he now launched an attack from London on his chief at the Quai d'Orsay, Drouyn de Lhuys. He told the British Foreign Secretary to warn his ambassador in Paris of 'the necessity of often seeing the Emperor, and not trusting to the

Minister'. To the Emperor he made his position quite clear: 'If the sincerity of my devotion and the unity of views which binds me heart and soul to your policy should chance to suggest to you the thought of confiding the Ministry of Foreign Affairs to me, I should be proud to accept.' For the moment he got only a reprimand for talking too much to the British press and, when he offered to resign, a friendly but firm note from Napoleon: 'I have few representatives whom I can trust as much as you. So let me hear no more of your quitting, or of misunderstandings with Drouyn de Lhuys.'

In June 1853 the Tsar sent his troops down to the Danube, occupying Moldavia and Wallachia; in October the Sultan declared war; in November the Russians destroyed the Turkish fleet in the Black Sea. In February 1854 France and Britain sent the Tsar a demand that he should evacuate the Turkish territory his troops had invaded. He did not do so, and at the end of March they declared war on him.

There was a pause while the allied armies assembled along the Bosphorus. They then launched an attack on the Russians on the Danube, but found them already gone. The allies pressed on after them to the Crimea, which they reached in mid-September. Napoleon, after spending a month at Biarritz with Eugenie, journeyed to Boulogne in September to review the troops he had gathered near his uncle's famous camp, and to receive a visit from Prince Albert – his first meeting with the Prince Consort. By the time that the Emperor returned to Paris, the allied troops were poised for their first victory on the River Alma. He put down a little harassing fire of his own on Uncle Jerome, letting a rumour filter through that he was taking legal advice on the possibility of rescinding his uncle,

Napoleon's decree that had annulled Jerome's first marriage to an American girl, Elizabeth Patterson. This would have had the effect of suddenly demoting Plon-Plon from second place in succession to the throne to fourth place, after Miss Patterson's son and grandson.[31]

Speaking at the Lord Mayor's Banquet in November, Alexandre expressed the hope that at that moment the allied flags were floating victorious over the walls, or rather the ruins, of Sebastopol. But they were not, and winter was about to descend on the ill-provisioned troops. On the heels of bitter cold and near-starvation came cholera, although the New Year brought a revival of hope with the efforts of Miss Nightingale in the hospitals, the appointment of the energetic Palmerston as Prime Minister, the entry of Piedmont on the allied side with 18,000 troops, and, in March, the death of Tsar Nicholas.

Meanwhile Auguste de Morny returned to the public view. In June 1854 Napoleon had given the Bonapartes another prod by appointing Auguste to the Presidency of the Legislative Body from which Jerome's threat of resignation had previously barred him. Unlike Alexandre, Auguste had not touted for public office and was genuinely in two minds about accepting it: 'I assure you that I am profoundly touched and grateful for this new mark of your confidence but I am in no way suited for this post, I shall not fill it to your satisfaction, and I am certain in advance that I shall dislike it too much to remain in it.' He wrote a second note of excuse to the Emperor the same day, but finally agreed to be persuaded. The fact was that he was fully and happily occupied with his social life and his business affairs. He was the driving force of the Grand Central Railway, informed on every detail of its operations from the construction of the carriages to the surveying of the routes and the forging of the spikes to hold the rails. However, he soon found the Presidency of the Chamber very much to his taste, and served his Imperial master all the better because, from the outset, he managed to convince the Deputies that he was their representative not the Emperor's.

His success prompted the Paris correspondent of the *Morning Chronicle* to report an intriguing rumour at the end of January 1855: Napoleon was contemplating recognizing Auguste as his legal brother:

The illegitimacy of the Count de Morny was at all times a matter of doubt. There was no divorce, or even separation, between his mother, Queen Hortense, and her husband King Louis.... He had always maintained his own legitimacy.... Recent events which have occurred in the east [Plon-Plon had thrown up his command of a division in the Crimea and returned to France amid whispers of cowardice], together with the fact that there appears no chance of a direct heir to the Imperial Throne ...

had prompted the Emperor's decision, according to the *Chronicle*'s man, who sounds like somebody very close to Auguste himself.

There was some urgency, since Napoleon had been talking a great deal about going to the Crimea to assume command of the French army. Auguste was at pains to give the impression that he disapproved of the Emperor's desire to 'wear his uniform in war as well as peace', as he described it to Valerie Masuyer. He expressed the fear that a military set-back would be blamed on the Emperor. To the Empress, who was urging Napoleon to go, he pointed out that, 'the Regency which will have to be confided to King Jerome seems to me to be one of the most awkward hazards in the affair'. Though the Empress had her own ideas on that point.

In the end, the Emperor stayed at home. Nothing more was heard of legitimizing Auguste, who continued outwardly content, busy with finance and politics, yet still finding time for all his usual social engagements, such as the magnificent fancy-dress ball given by Fanny Le Hon on the eve of Ash Wednesday. Their long-standing affair had settled into a sort of matrimony, undisturbed by Auguste's frequent infidelities and subsidiary mistresses. He treated Fanny's children as his own (as indeed at least one of them was), and he took the younger son, Leopold, firmly under his wing, sending him to Spain in March 1855 to negotiate for an extension of the Grand Central line across the Pyrenees to Madrid, and in June obtaining a seat on the board of the company for him.

*

In the spring of 1855 the Emperor took up the invitation that the Prince Consort had offered him at Boulogne six months before and set off with Eugenie in a thick fog across the Channel. At Windsor he attended a review of the Household regiments and a State Ball in the Waterloo Chamber, took part in a joint Council of War and was invested with the Order of the Garter. In London he accompanied Queen Victoria to the opera and the Crystal Palace. There had been difficulties between the British and French commanders in the Crimea. The British government had the gravest qualms about Napoleon's proposal to go to the theatre of war, where he would have to be offered command of the British troops as well as his own. Alternatively, Austria had sponsored a conference in Vienna to discuss the possibility of peace, and the French were suspected of being willing to accept terms that were much too favourable to the Russians.

By the end of the visit all these doubts had been dispelled, for Napoleon was a great charmer when he wanted to be. On the first day she met him, Queen Victoria noticed his 'quiet frank manner' and found Eugenie 'very pleasing, very graceful and very unaffected, but very delicate. She is certainly very pretty and very uncommon-looking.' (An opinion that would have surprised Emilie.) At home the Empress had appeared somewhat differently to one of the queen's ladies of the bedchamber: 'She is certainly pretty and graceful, it is an odd face with eyes rather too near together but they are a beautiful shape and she has a very short upper lip and good skin, and it is very real beauty of its kind. [She] now and then launched into gossip and a shrieking voice and great animation. She must be very amusing when at her ease.'

Ten days after the visit had ended, Victoria was still pondering on the true character of 'this most extraordinary man' and wrote a long memorandum in an attempt to clarify her thoughts. 'He is evidently possessed of *indomitable courage, unflinching firmness of purpose, self-reliance, perseverance* and *great secrecy* ... and at the same time he is endowed with wonderful *self-control*, great *calmness*, even *gentleness*.' It is clear that she was still under the influence of the pale myopic eyes which, once the lids were lifted, stared with a sort of loving intensity, the simple sincerity that had enchanted Josephine and enraptured many young women. At times he managed to look almost winsome, a difficult effect to achieve with so large a nose. 'The Emperor is as *unlike* a

Frenchman as possible, being much more *German* than French in character': a comment which, coming from Victoria, could be construed only as a compliment. He had, however, by no means completely bowled over the highly intelligent queen. 'How far he is actuated by a strong moral sense of *right* and *wrong* is difficult to say.' She considered the trail of lies, deception, broken oaths and ruthless repression and came to the charitable conclusion that 'in all these apparently inexcusable acts he has invariably been guided by the belief that he is *fulfilling a destiny* which God has *imposed* upon him.'[32]

If Victoria had been impressed with Napoleon, Eugenie was positively electrified by Victoria. The sight of a woman controlling affairs from the throne instead of the boudoir, the authority with which she handled her ministers and the most vital affairs of State, gave Eugenie the desire to take up politics. It was another interest to add to her table-turning (she had shocked many people at Court the previous Hallowe'en by organizing a party to summon up the spirits of the dead), her charades and her wardrobe. She demanded a place on the Council and was granted it – because Napoleon disliked scenes. Very soon she had favourites, bugbears, and a highly mischievous faction of her own.

In the interest of the Entente, Napoleon now reversed his approval of the terms negotiated in Vienna by Drouyn de Lhuys, leaving that unfortunate man in such an embarrassing position that he resigned, and Alexandre at last received the summons to take over the Ministry of Foreign Affairs. It was a very distinguished post but, as Drouyn had found out, not an easy one. Napoleon was devious, hesitant and distrusting. He dealt with affairs without his ministers' knowledge, over their heads, behind their backs. He constantly encouraged them only to mislead them, supported them only to let them down. The humilitations had been too much for Drouyn to stomach; Alexandre's stronger digestion was to allow him to stay in office for five years – and even then he went only because he was pushed.

Queen Victoria and the Prince Consort paid a return visit to Paris in August, to see the Universal Exhibition that Napoleon had opened in May and to be shown the other sights of Paris. The Parisians and half-a-million foreign visitors cheered her every appearance. The streets were festooned, arcaded and emblazoned with banners of greetings, arches of triumph and the arms of the two countries. 'I am *delighted, enchanted, amused*', she wrote to Uncle Leopold. 'I think I never saw anything more *beautiful* and gay than Paris.' The Empress was not much seen, for she was again expecting a child and her doctors were guarding against any chance of a second miscarriage. Victoria found her 'dear and *very charming*' and confirmed her first impression that the Emperor '*is* very *fascinating*'.[33] She could not bring herself to say the same of Alexandre Walewski, who had been rather too busily bounding about, basking in the dual regal radiance; she found him a pushful, bumptious ass.

Alexandre was not very popular with any of the English these days; nor they with him. His commitment to Thiers' policy of the *Alliance Anglaise* had faded with Thiers' loss of influence after the coup d'état. Alexandre was now preaching an eastern alliance, with Austria, Prussia and even Russia. So much so that when the Emperor suggested trying to get independence for Poland considered among the peace terms, Alexandre protested that there was little hope for it and the proposal would 'disquiet Germany'.

Since he was so ready to betray the interests of his mother's and his own native land, it is not surprising that he should show little loyalty to that of his first wife. He had been given Drouyn's job because Drouyn was in favour of peace and opposed to the British desire to carry the war to an unequivocally victorious conclusion. No sooner was Alexandre in office than he propounded exactly the same policy. In September 1855, when the news arrived of the fall of Sebastopol, he again urged the Emperor to accept a negotiated peace: 'For who could deny that France comes out of this increased in stature and Russia diminished? Your Majesty will have gained all that the Emperor of Russia has lost and, more especially, it will be France *alone* who has increased her reputation in this struggle.' He assured the Austrian ambassador that he was confident he could win Napoleon's support, even though 'the English, who have not shone in the Crimean War and who will put a magnificent fleet to sea in the spring, will be very inclined to open a third campaign'. And to Napoleon he wrote on 18 January 1856:

If the interests of France and England were nearly identical before the capture of Sebastopol, they are very much otherwise since that great day. At the decisive moment, we took Malakoff, the English failed at the Redan [the two strong points of the fortress]. Since then, our military prestige has increased while theirs has decreased still further. Having attained the real objective of the war, we can only lose by continuing it.

It was a volte-face which no doubt surprised even Napoleon. But he finally accepted Alexandre's assessment

– indeed, may have been working for it all along, one could never tell – and the British Cabinet eventually agreed.

Earlier in the year, the Emperor had decided to settle the outstanding commitments under his uncle's will which the Bourbon and Orleans governments had refused to recognize as a valid charge on the State funds. Among them was the sum of slightly more than a quarter of a million francs for Leon, but since it was clear that he would fritter it away almost as soon as he got it, the Emperor decreed that the capital, after deducting 45,000 francs to pay Leon's outstanding debts, should be put in trust and invested at 3 per cent, the interest to go to Leon during his lifetime and afterwards to Alexandre Walewski if Leon had no children. Leon was thus assured of an annual income of 6,000 francs, which would have delighted many men.[34] But not Leon, who wanted to recapture the feeling of having a large lump sum to trickle through his fingers. There was nothing he could do about the trust fund, but, as he pointed out in a letter to Alexandre, the 45,000 francs were due to be paid to his creditors by a lawyer on his behalf, whereas 'there are certain debts of honour and of sentiment which can and should be settled only by myself: otherwise I should offend the proper feelings of sundry creditors whom I hold in especial esteem'. He asked Alexandre to appoint a time when he might call to discuss the matter. The last thing the Foreign Minister wanted was to have a visit form his scruffy quarrelsome half-brother. He did not reply. Silence and the cold shoulder were never a defence against Leon. After a fortnight he wrote again. Alexandre replied that official duties denied him the pleasure of receiving Leon but 'as for the paltry loans I was happy enough to be able to make, do not give them a thought, I beg you; there will be time to settle up later'. Which was not really what Leon had in mind.

He had recently been refused a loan of 3,000 francs by the Emperor, to whom he already owed 7,000 francs. He could scarcely expect any more at the moment, but it was no doubt with a view to the future that he sent a note of congratulation in October 1855 on the official announcement that the Empress was five months pregnant. A few days later he himself became the father of a son. This was as yet no threat to Alexandre's succession for, in the family tradition, Leon had not married the mother of his child. She was Françoise Jonet, the daughter of a man variously described as Leon's estate manager or his gardener.

Chapter Six:
Adventures

To Alexandre Walewski's delight, January 1856 opened with intimations from the new Tsar that he would like to discuss peace terms. This meant not only that Alexandre's policy had prevailed but also that, since the peace conference was to be held in Paris, it was he who would preside at the discussions. The delegates gathered in March. On the 16th a one-hundred-and-one gun salute announced the birth of an heir to the Imperial throne. On the 30th the guns boomed again for the signing of the peace treaty, a ceremony performed with an eagle's feather plucked from an unfortunate caged bird in the zoo at the Jardin des Plantes. During the night Alexandre's wife became a mother for the fourth time – a daughter, named Eugenie for the Empress. On 2 April he was awarded the highest decoration in the Legion of Honour: the Grand Cross. From the British government he received the reluctant, but obligatory, gift of a snuff-box bearing a miniature of Queen Victoria. He asked permission to have this converted into a bracelet for his wife. Victoria's tart comment was that she had no objection at all: she would rather be on Madame Walewski's arm than in her husband's pocket.

Auguste de Morny was equally pleased with the ending of the war. He had opposed it for at least two reasons: he favoured an alliance with Russia rather than with Britain, and he believed that war of any kind would be bad for business. On this second point he was proved to be right. Although the Spanish government granted permission for him to extend the Grand Central line across the Pyrenees to Madrid, the French government announced in March that it did not intend to licence the issue of any new shares during 1856 – and, despite Auguste's influence with his half-brother, he could not persuade him to give a special dispensation. Money was tight because of the war, share prices had fallen and interest rates risen. Grand Central was running out of capital with its rail network uncompleted.

Auguste showed no signs of perturbation. As President of the Legislative Body he had his official residence at the Hotel de Lassay next door; and here he lived in a princely splendour that in many ways outshone the vulgar Imperial displays at the Tuileries, St-Cloud, Fontainebleau and Compiègne. In the Long Gallery that led to the dining room hung some of the collection of masterpieces which he had never quite been forced to auction through Christie's and which had remained for a long period on the walls of the Flahaut's London home to the increasing anxiety of his stepmother, who feared that when eventually removed they would leave unfaded patches on the walls.[1] In the Oriental Room were displayed a mass of treasures from Persia, China and Japan. In his large high-ceilinged bedroom portraits of Charles de Flahaut and Hortense de Beauharnais faced each other from opposite walls, proudly displayed to visitors as witness to his parentage, for he also used this room as an office and often conducted business while still in bed.

It was for his elegance and charm as well as his pro-Russian sentiments that he was chosen by the Emperor as

Ambassador Extraordinary at the coronation of the new Tsar. Plon-Plon had coveted the post but, as the Emperor said to Mathilde: 'He can play the fool as much as he likes in Paris, but I'm not having him do it in St Petersburg and discrediting us in the eyes of Russia.' Before Auguste left there were two ceremonies for him to attend: the christening of the Prince Imperial at Notre Dame on 14 June, and the wedding of Louise Le Hon to the son of the former Tuscan ambassador in Paris – an event that was forthrightly announced in a Milan newspaper as 'the marriage of Mademoiselle Le Hon, daughter of Countess Le Hon and Count de Morny, to the son of Count Poniatowski'[2]. At the end of July 1856 Auguste left for Russia with a great train of servants, silver, china and pictures. Sometime before his departure Eugenie had a word with him, at the Emperor's prompting, about the portraits of Charles and Hortense in his bedroom. 'If you were to be less his brother, he would be more your friend', she said. Auguste's reply was to have hortensias painted on the panels of the magnificent coach that he took with him to Russia, and beneath them the motto *Tace sed memento* ('I remain silent but I remember').

He arrived in St Petersburg during the night of 5 August. Two days later he was received with noticeable warmth by the Tsar. When he left for Moscow on the 22nd there were 110 persons in his party. In the rivalry among the British, Austrian and French Embassies to put on the finest shows at the coronation and the series of balls which followed, Auguste prided himself on having been the most successful – he converted the courtyard of his palace in Moscow into a ballroom, and the Tsar and Tsarina did not leave until 2 a.m. Certainly he was the only one of the ambassadors to receive the highest Russian decoration: the

Cross of St Andrew. But this was partly due to the Tsar's desire to drive a wedge between the French and British governments.[3]

Auguste stayed on in Russia after the coronation. He had, when appointed as Ambassador Extraordinary, resigned from his various business interests with the alacrity of a man dropping a handful of hot potatoes, and it appeared that he would be very ready to remain at the Embassy permanently. In his reports to Alexandre at the Quai d'Orsay he warmly supported the Tsar's claim for a reinterpretation of the the Treaty of Paris (arising from a confusion over two places of the same name in Moldavia) and insisted, since he knew this was an enticement for the Emperor, that 'Russia is the only Power which will ratify any expansion of France. I already have been given assurance – ask as much from England!' Napoleon read the dispatches, nodded, gave Alexandre the impression that he approved of Auguste's proposals – then quietly went off on his own line. He secretly showed the reports to the British and Austrian ambassadors to prove how loyal he was to them; and kept Persigny informed at the London Embassy. There was a popular story doing the rounds of the time of a visit that Cowley, the British ambassador, was making on Alexandre when the Vienna courier arrived. Alexandre opened the dispatches and gave them to Cowley to read, but begged him not to let the Emperor know he had seen them. That afternoon Cowley called on the Emperor, who had the dispatches in front of him. Napoleon gave then to Cowley to read, begging him not to let Walewski know he had seen them.

Persigny had made the mistake of advising the Emperor against marrying Eugenie – with the result that when the wedding did take place he found himself gradually sliding into disgrace. He lost the key post of Minister of the Interior at about the time that Auguste, who had recommended the marriage, was given the Presidency of the Legislative Body. Brought back to favour with his appointment to succeed Alexandre at the London Embassy, he nevertheless bore a grudge against both Alexandre and Auguste – and lost no time in letting British ministers know that their former admirer, Walewski, had thrown his weight behind a Russian alliance, while telling Napoleon that Alexandre was responsible for spoiling Franco-British relations. Alexandre replied by slipping an unsigned article into *Le Constitutionel* in November 1856, supporting the Russians in their continuing quarrel with the British.

Authors of anonymous articles did not remain unknown for long in the police states of either Napoleon I or Napoleon III. The Emperor sent Alexandre a sharp reprimand for acting without consulting him: 'In future I wish to see every dispatch that you send, and the original of every dispatch that you receive.' Alexandre expressed himself 'deeply hurt' by this 'unjust letter', put all the blame on Persigny 'an ambassador who works openly against his own Government and boasts about it', and offered his resignation. The Emperor did not accept. Instead, he began moves to destroy another project close to Alexandre's heart – an alliance with Austria.

He had secretly chosen Italy to be the arena for his next military adventure. It was a country that had always had a special appeal for the Bonapartes. They were of Italian origin: Napoleon III's cousin had been King of Rome; his Aunt Elisa, Grand Duchess of Tuscany; his Aunt Caroline, Queen of Naples; his father had spent most of his exile there; so had his grandmother; and it was there that he had first come close to warfare with his anticlimactic escapade in the insurrection of 1831. It would be foolish to credit him with sincerity in his protestation of devotion to the cause of Italian independence and unification. He had sent French troops to bolster the Pope's rule over the Papal States in 1849, partly to gain Catholic votes in France, partly to prevent the Austrians becoming the Pope's sole protectors. But Victor Emmanuel, King of Piedmont and Sardinia, had contributed troops to fight beside the French and British in the Crimea and was asking for a reward; which Napoleon was willing to give him because any unification of Italy under Victor Emmanuel would be at the expense of Austria, the country whose soldiers had chased him in Italy, the country that had been at the centre of continental opposition to the Bonapartes.

Early in July 1856 the Emperor went off to take the waters at Plombières, a spa much favoured by his mother and his grandmother, Josephine. A short time before Dr Conneau had persuaded him to see a specialist and, for the sake of secrecy, had brought over a British surgeon, Sir William Fergusson, who found him to be suffering from 'neuralgia, sciatica, dyspepsia, fatigue, irritability, insomnia, contraction of the fingers, loss of appetite and decline in sexual potency'. Fergusson informed the British ambassador that 'great alterations of character may take place – apathy, irritation, caprice, infirmity of purpose are upon the cards as the result of an exhausted nervous system and diseased organs'. Despite this gloomy diagnosis and prognosis, and perhaps thanks to the waters of Plombières, Napoleon returned in quite spritely vein to Paris to resume an affair with the Countess of Castiglione, who was suspected of having been sent expressly by the

King of Piedmont and Sardinia to exchange her amorous favours for the Emperor's political ones.[4]

That autumn there were rumours that Alexandre Walewski had been gambling unwisely on the Stock Exchange and had to be rescued by the Emperor.[5] When the latter returned from reviewing his troops at Vincennes, there were some shouts of *Vive la Republique!* from workers in the St-Antoine quarter, but the police soon had them locked up. From St Petersburg came word that Auguste had arranged to build a railway for the Tsar. This was followed by news of quite a different kind that set the fashionable world buzzing: Morny was to marry the young and dazzlingly beautiful Princess Sophie Troubetskoy; she was just eighteen, he nearly thirty years older. She had dark eyes, very fair hair, a turned-up nose and a dowry of half a million francs provided by the Tsar. She was small, impulsive and, when not in a temper, enchanting.

*

On hearing of the engagement the Emperor is said to have exclaimed *'le faquin!'* (the cad!). Countess Le Hon said much the same thing, bitterly and with threats of revenge; her husband remarked reprovingly, 'I always said, my dear, that man would cause us both trouble.' After their twenty-year affair, Auguste had broken the news to Fanny with the words: 'I am marrying. The Emperor wishes it and France wants it. While I was in office the police reports were always urging me: Get married! Get married! I hope and wish that my wife will have no better friend than you, and that you will not lose the habit of taking the road to Nades [his chateau in the Auvergne]. Do not answer this; simply telegraph me the two words "I approve".'[6]

Fanny certainly did not approve. She hurried to the Emperor to lodge complaints about the manner in which she had been discarded, and to drop hints that unless she received considerable compensation she would sue Auguste, which would entail revealing such embarrassing details as the vast sums contributed by the Mosselmann interests to the coup d'état. The Emperor assured her of his sympathy; when a number of her friends called that evening to offer their condolences and assess how she was taking the reverse, she received them with her usual grace and charming smiles. Before they left she let them all know that she had entrusted most of her fortune to the dastardly Auguste – and intended to get it all back. Though she did not tell them so, the figure she had mentioned to the Emperor was six million francs.

Undeterred, Auguste got married in January 1857 amid a flurry of telegrams and couriers between Paris and St Petersburg. Alexandre wrote to Auguste suggesting that he should accept the Emperor as mediator and arbiter. The Emperor himself confirmed the proposal in a personal letter. Auguste, a man of firm principles where his own money was concerned, contended that, although Fanny and her family had been his benefactors in the days before the coup d'état, the boot had usually been on the other foot since then; he had used his position to help her and her family, and had, in fact, given her large sums of money – at least two-and-a-half million francs – and could produce her grateful letters to prove it. This may or may not have been true, but the last thing the Emperor wanted was for either party to publish any documents at all.

His particular worry was that, whether or not Fanny had a strong enough case to go to court, she might out of simple spite give all her papers to her friends the

Orleanists. He wrote to Auguste offering a carrot and a brief flourish of the whip: if Auguste would agree to accept him as arbiter he would create him a duke, Duke of Nades, he suggested; on the other hand, if they could reach no agreement, he might not reappoint him as President of the Legislative Body when he returned from Russia. Auguste was unimpressed: he did not much care for the title (though he was more than ready to accept a dukedom), and he suspected that the Emperor was bluffing – after all, depriving him of the Presidency in which he had scored so notable a success would merely set off yet another scandal.

The Emperor was unable to report any progress to Fanny; Fanny put round a rumour that the embarrassing letters from Auguste about the coup d'état were already on their way to the Orleanists in London. The Emperor sent for Piétri, the Prefect of Police, and explained some of his difficulties; Piétri sent for one of his most reliable agents, a Corsican bravo named Griscelli who had previously been the Emperor's bodyguard. Griscelli went in search of Leopold Le Hon and told him bluntly that he was suspected of having sold his mother's papers to the Orleans family. Leopold, in a difficult position between his patron and his mother, indignantly denied the suggestion: 'They are in a box in mama's bureau!' Griscelli put a police cordon round the Le Hon house and took Leopold straight to the Tuileries to repeat all this to the Emperor, who invited him to write a note to his mother, asking her to hand over the papers. It was not a request that could be refused.

Armed with the note, Griscelli went to the countess's house, where he was greeted with a stream of reproaches. Fanny believed that Leopold had been arrested. She was confirmed in this impression by his letter asking her to surrender the box of documents. 'Never! Never!' she screamed so loudly that Piétri, who had discreetly waited downstairs, came hurrying in. 'I yield to force', she cried, making a dash for her bedroom. 'I shall protest before Europe against this regime of the sword and the police spy!' Griscelli followed her and took the box of papers. The unhappy Leopold wrote to Auguste begging him to compromise: 'People are misrepresenting my mother's attitude to you. Let us not be impetuous – think of Louise [his sister, of whom Auguste was the father]. Let us settle quickly anything that could give rise to scandal. Let us act with thought for the past – for the welfare and honour of us all. I want to be a loving son *and* a devoted friend!'[7] For his services Leopold became a Chevalier of the Legion of Honour and fickle public attention turned to other, newer scandals. The Emperor, deducting Auguste's claim on Fanny from Fanny's claim on Auguste, arrived at the figure of 3,500,000 francs, which he persuaded Auguste to consider paying and Fanny to contemplate accepting, though there were rumours that in the end he was reduced to paying it himself.

If so, it was well for the Privy Purse that his current affair with the Countess of Castiglione was being financed by the King of Piedmont and the king's chief minister, Cavour, who was the countess's cousin. She had recently moved into a house just off the Champs Elysées with her husband, a presentable young man, who escorted her to all her public engagements and readily informed even the most casual acquaintances, 'I am a model husband – I never see or hear anything!'[8]

But other people kept their eyes open, including would-be assassins. Early in April 1857, three men attacked a small coupe as it drove out of the Castiglione house at 3 a.m., and only the quick-wittedness of the coachman, who whipped up the horses so that they reared and knocked the assailants down, prevented them from getting at his passenger – the Emperor. Eugenie was embarrassed by her husband's conspicuous infidelity and let ministers know that she did not wish the breath-takingly beautiful Castiglione to attend any more official functions. The countess received no invitation for the next ball, at the Ministry of Marine, but nevertheless turned up as the personal guest of Princess Mathilde, who was taking revenge for not having been invited by the Empress to recent Court dinners. The Emperor, however, took the hint and returned to an even more scandalous affair – with Anna-Maria Walewska.

*

Paris was by now beginning to show the effects of the great rebuilding programme which the Emperor had entrusted to Georges-Eugene Haussmann when he appointed him Prefect of the Seine in 1853. Louis-Philippe had been a busy building king, finishing off the many grandiose projects left incomplete by Napoleon I: for example, the Arc de Triomphe and the Madeleine. He had thrown new bridges across the Seine and repaired old ones, planted trees along the quays, cleared the Place de la Concorde and set up the Obelisk, extended gas-lighting, cambered the roads so that the gutters ran at the sides instead of down the middle. But he had not made any great change to the plan of the city and the narrow tortuous streets whose history went back to medieval times. Haussmann's task was to blast broad boulevards through the ancient houses and the mean huddled hovels, thus creating elegant vistas to delight the tourist, and any Imperial artilleryman who might feel the need to administer another tranquilizing whiff of grapeshot to the unruly mob. The massive operations caused so much chaos and distress that by 1856 one weekly magazine was already complaining that 'by building new houses they are making the city uninhabitable'. It was true that Haussmann knocked down a great number of houses – nearly 25,000. On the other hand he built three times as many. Unfortunately, the new homes were so costly as to be beyond the reach of the families that had lived in the old ones. There was a sifting out of the former mixed population, the poor drifting out to the circumference, the rich coming closer to the centre – and the old aristocracy keeping itself to itself, disdainful of the vulgar smart set that danced attendance on the upstarts at the Tuileries.

The most prominent member of that set, for several years to come, was Anna-Maria Walewska, a small woman of great presence and charm, famed for the alabaster perfection of her torso, much of which was visible in the evenings when fashion genially decreed that ladies should bare most of their bosoms. When Victor Emmanuel dined at the Tuileries in 1855 it was noticed that he could scarcely keep his eyes off the countess's bust, repeating to its owner: 'Oh, how beautiful you are! Oh, how I do love beautiful women!' It was a compliment from a man who knew what he was talking about, for the energetic king was coarsely rumoured to have seduced half the female population of Piedmont, thus establishing himself as one monarch who could truly claim to be the Father of his People. The Countess of Castiglione had been one of his easier conquests, before he sent her to Paris to charm the Emperor; whether he shared Napoleon's good fortune as far as Anna-Maria was concerned is not known.

Napoleon's affair with Anna-Maria probably began to burgeon in 1855, and may well have provided one of his motives for bringing the Walewskis from London to Paris in that year. Although there were whispers about their association in 1856, it was not until early 1857, when the countess gave a masked ball and appeared as Diana the Huntress, that the Emperor made something of a public declaration. He paid almost no attention to the Countess of Castiglione, who was daringly revealing as the Queen of Hearts, but followed Anna-Maria everywhere. When she appeared a few nights later at a ball given by Princess Mathilde, again wearing her Huntress costume complete with quiver and arrows, Napoleon exclaimed with heavy gallantry, 'Take that bow away for fear she pierces too many hearts!' From this time onwards Anna-Maria had difficulty in concealing her proprietorial interest and her jealousy of rivals.

During the summer of 1857 Napoleon was angling for an invitation to Osborne to explain away the differences that had arisen due to France's ever-changing policies in eastern Europe. Queen Victoria was preoccupied with various domestic matters, including the marriage of her niece Charlotte of Belgium to the Archduke Maximilian of Austria; she was worried about events in India where the Mutiny was at its height; and she was entirely disenchanted with Napoleon. But she eventually agreed to Palmerston's proposal that she should invite Napoleon and Eugenie over in August. 'The Emperor wants Madame Walewska to be one of the party', reported the British ambassador. 'There is a regular flirtation between her and his Majesty.' This, he implied was why the Emperor had given Alexandre the Grand Cross of the Legion of Honour studded with magnificent diamonds, 'while such men as [Marshal] Vaillant, on whom fell the brunt of the Crimean War, are passed over'. Napoleon's request was granted and Anna-Maria accompanied the Imperial couple to their rather cool reception at Osborne.

Alexandre was now unpopular all round: with Britain and Austria for having supported Russian demands; with Russia for having failed to get them accepted. 'His incompetence had never been more obvious', reported the Austrian ambassador. The British ambassador described him as 'empty-headed and big-bellied'. It was true that Alexandre was putting on more weight than was good for him and looking more and more like a Bonaparte, less and less like a gentleman.[9] Indeed with his over-solemn moon-face and his chubby legs encased in tight wide-checked trousers, the Foreign Minister of France resembled a minor comedian turned proprietor of a provincial music hall.

The riddle of why he continued in office was not difficult to solve. In October 1857, for instance, when the Imperial family travelled by train to Compiègne, Eugenie, Alexandre and other members of the party sat in one half of the Imperial coach, the Emperor, Anna-Maria, Princess Mathilde and a companion in the other. The last two were on one side of the coach, the Emperor and Anna-Maria on the other, concealed behind a swing door. 'The door swung with the movement of the train', recorded Mathilde, 'and let us see my very dear cousin astride Marianne's lap, kissing her on the mouth and plunging his hand into her bosom.'[10]

The princess still believed in the innocence of Alexandre seated a few feet away. 'Marianne [though christened Anna Alexandrina Caterina Cassandra, the countess was usually called Anna-Maria, Marianne or Marie by her French acquaintances] is a thorough little rogue who manages to make herself the friend of the Empress while sleeping with the Emperor: but she is scared to death of her husband and I would swear that Walewski is ignorant of everything.' If so, it was strange that he did not hear of the secret staircase specially constructed between the Emperor's quarters and the bedroom that Anna-Maria always occupied at Fontainebleau. And what did he make of the money orders that the Emperor drew on Baring Brothers of London in favour of Anna-Maria? They were discovered a dozen years later, together with others in favour of the Duchess of Cadore. The duchess was his acknowledged mistress. What special services had Anna-Maria rendered that impelled him to reward her as well as her husband?

'You ask me about the Duchess of Manchester and La Walewska,' the British ambassador reported in November 1857:

I never saw anyone in such a state as the latter during the whole week at Compiègne. The way in which she threw herself at the Emperor was the theme of everybody's conversation. She had neither eyes nor ears for anyone else and, as Walewski is proverbially jealous and must have seen what was passing, I leave it to you to guess the innuendoes respecting him. There was nothing particular in the Emperor's attentions to the Duchess of Manchester, but it was evident to everyone that Madame Walewska could not bear her being at Compiègne.

In 1858 Napoleon gave the apparently complaisant Walewski a vast estate in the Landes estimated to bring in 100,000 francs a year. Mathilde was horrified by the effect on public opinion. 'I have had letters from Germany that testify to the discredit he has fallen into since it is assumed that he is being paid as the husband of a favourite. And God knows he has no suspicion of his wife's infidelity.' Count Horace de Viel-Castel, the diarist, to whom she confided her dismay, noted the following day that 'nobody here believes, as the Princess does, in the innocent ignorance of Walewski', and commented that, 'in the United Kingdom they are very glad to have a pretext for despising our Minister of Foreign Affairs, and they are saying: "Count Walewski is no longer a gentleman" '. Indeed Charles Greville, Clerk to the Privy Council, went a good deal further, calling Alexandre 'an adventurer, a needy speculator, without honour, conscience or truth; and utterly unfit both as to his character and his capacity for such an office as he holds'.

Many people subscribed to the view that Alexandre was wittingly and willingly cuckolded by his wife who was 'worth her weight in gold' to him as long as she remained Napoleon's mistress. Miss Howard, now at the end of her own association with the Emperor, had no doubts: 'It's a family tradition. The Foreign Secretary urged his wife to follow in his own mother's footsteps. No wonder if she practises what her lord and master preaches. Each reigning Bonaparte must sleep with a Walewska.'[11]

But Eugenie, who had been on terms of close friendship with Anna-Maria for several years, did not seem to share even the general certainty that an affair was in progress, though she could not be unaware of the rumours – since the countess herself brought them to her notice. At the time of the scandal over the Landes estate, Anna-Maria came to her and, as Viel-Castel recorded, 'with the most superb duplicity, she said to her: "I am compelled to ask Your Majesty to cease inviting me to your private soirées, because people are accusing me of being the Emperor's mistress, and I do not wish this calumny to injure me in Your Majesty's opinion. Pray banish me from your person until all these horrid rumours have died down."' This so moved Eugenie that 'she kissed her and their intimacy is now closer than ever'.[12]

It was only when Anna-Maria was too openly possessive in her attitude that the temperature cooled. A few months later Eugenie was seen to be treating her distantly and on the other hand showing friendly attentions to 'an American woman in whom the Emperor is said to be interested'. But the chilly spell passed. Anna-Maria was the prime mover in renewing the opulently-staged quadrilles that the Emperor's mother, Hortense, and his Aunts Caroline and Pauline had made such a dazzling feature of Napoleon I's Court. By March 1858 she was back to borrowing Eugenie's jewellery again, and addressing the Emperor in public as '*tu*', to the horror of Princess Marie of Baden, who also heard her 'creating a scene' with him for having flirted with another woman.

*

During the course of the year 1857, Alexandre had, briefly as usual, been in correspondence with his half-brother, Leon. In June, when Leon was once more making an unsuccessful attempt to get a seat in the Assembly, he approached Alexandre with a request for an interview with the Emperor for the purpose of expressing 'the admiration inspired in me by the glory of his achievements, and the

267

assurance of my devotion to his person'. He also desired to offer his regrets about 'the insinuations [of spying and provocation] which were directed against me in 1840 and above all the duel which was a consequence of them'. He claimed that 'I have cruelly expiated my fault by the deprivation for so many years now of the honour of entry to His Majesty's presence. I should like to atone by placing my life at his service.... I have enough strength and energy to fulfil worthily whatever task may be confided to me.' Alexandre replied by return, telling him to apply directly to the Emperor.[13]

Leon did so – delivering his letter in person to the Tuileries. But he did not reach the Imperial presence; neither did he get a reply. Despite his protestations of a desire to serve, and despite the regular income he was now getting under Napoleon I's will, it was clear that his main interest in getting inside the Tuileries was to ask for another loan. In December he approached Dr Conneau, who had acted as go-between before. His lack of success no doubt depressed him, but refusals in money matters never drove him to the point of breaking off communications. On 15 January 1858 he wrote to Conneau once more: 'Please tell the Emperor and the Empress of the joy I feel at their escape from a dastardly attempt on their lives. I thank Divine Providence for this further blessing.... May the perpetrators be eternally damned.'[14] This particular dastardly attempt – there had been at least two earlier ones in which the Emperor showed his habitual courage and imperturbability - took place as they drove up to the entrance of the Opera in the evening of 14 January 1858. Four Italians, led by a man named Orsini, son of one of Napoleon's comrades in the rising of 1830, threw bombs at the Imperial carriage, missing their target but causing death and bloody carnage among many of the escort and onlookers; in all 150 people were injured.

Auguste was by this time back in the presidential chair of the Legislative Body: the Emperor had refused to let him remain in Russia as ambassador, but had delayed his return to Paris until what he called 'the dirty business of the Grand Central' had been settled by selling off the company to two rival concerns, with, of course, an administrative post for Leopold Le Hon and a block of more than 30,000 shares for Auguste. At the ceremony in the Throne Room of the Tuileries to congratulate Their Majesties on their fortunate escape, Auguste was loud in condemnation of Britain, where the assassins had plotted their coup and where the bombs had been made. During the month that followed he pressed through the Chamber a series of laws by which Napoleon tightened even further his grip on the country: fines and imprisonment for inciting hatred or contempt for the government; deportation without trial for any individuals previously convicted of political crimes; or for any found guilty in the future. L'Espinasse, the soldier who had arrested the Deputies on the morning of the coup d'état, was appointed Minister of the Interior charged with carrying out this *Loi de Sûreté Générale*. Alexandre Walewski headed the stormy confrontation with Britain and demanded the extradition or punishment of the assassins' accomplices.

The protest was ill-founded as it was noisy. Nobody had less right to complain about England's traditional policy of granting asylum to political refugees than Louis-Napoleon Bonaparte. As one Frenchman of the opposition remarked: 'Louis-Philippe would have been equally justified in holding England responsible for the Boulogne expedition in 1840.' However, as a conciliatory gesture, Palmerston, who had been Prime Minister for the past three years, brought in a bill making conspiracy to murder a felony instead of a misdemeanour, and one of Orsini's accomplices was sent for trial. But Alexandre's protestations now became so offensively violent that the House of Commons rejected the bill and Palmerston was forced to resign: the second time he had found himself out of office thanks to Walewski. Alexandre, intoxicated with his own rhetoric, demanded to know: 'Does the right of refuge mean raising murder to the status of a doctrine? Is hospitality the due of assassins?' There were murmurs of war between the two countries, and a stolid but deeply affronted British jury found Orsini's accomplice not guilty despite the overwhelming evidence against him.

The confusion, and the crisis, was highlighted by another of Alexandre's typical feuds within his own department. He had long been jealous of Persigny, whom Napoleon had admitted to the secret of the coup d'état while excluding Alexandre. Persigny in turn, as French ambassador in London, corresponded directly with his old friend the Emperor over the head of the minister, whom he covertly attacked by giving information to the British press – the same tactics that Alexandre had used against Drouyn. Persigny assured his friends in London that Alexandre was intent on bringing about war between France and Britain, and threatened to resign. Alexandre accepted the resignation, though it had not been made officially, and Napoleon sent Marshal Pelissier, hero of the Crimea, to London as a replacement. The bad feeling between the two countries was soothed a little in August, when Queen Victoria and the Prince Consort spent a day at Cherbourg with the Emperor and Empress.

The Emperor needed to get on good terms with Britain, for
he was now about to embark on his long-planned
intervention in Italy. In May 1858 he sent Conneau,
Italian-born of an Italian mother, to Turin to invite Cavour
to a secret conference at Plombières in July. At Plombières
he promised Cavour that he would provide military
support to Piedmont against Austria if Victor Emmanuel
would give his daughter, Clotilde, as bride to Plon-Plon,
thus at last getting a Bonaparte of his own generation
married into a royal family. It was not until September that
he told Plon-Plon of his plans, explaining that he needed a
military triumph to distract attention from the economic
recession that had followed the Crimean War, and adding:
'Keep this secret from everybody. The Empress [who as a
devout Catholic feared that the war for independence
would spread to the Papal States] suspects nothing, neither
does Walewski.' Only at the end of the year did he tell
Alexandre something of what had being going on,
whereupon Alexandre warned him that a war against
Austria would make him unpopular with the other
European Powers and once more offered his resignation –
and once more was persuaded to withdraw it.

By now almost nobody at Court or in government circles
believed that Alexandre would really resign over anything.
His wife had fought off another attempt by the Countess of
Castiglione to recapture Napoleon's affections and the
Emperor's chamberlain, Chaumont-Quitry, spoke openly
of Alexandre's acquiescence:

I saw him with my own two eyes in the park at
Villeneuve [near St-Coud] turn his head and retrace his

steps when he caught sight of the Emperor and his wife in a glade. But I saw more than that this year at Cherbourg: one morning Walewski and I were in a room leading to the Emperor's bedchamber. Mocquard entered to speak with his sovereign, opened the door without knocking, then recoiled in astonishment and stumbled against me: through the open door I could see Madame Walewska in the Emperor's arms, and Walewski, who was standing beside me, must have seen everything that I saw.[15]

In January 1859 Alexandre learned for the first time of the agreed marriage between Princess Clotilde and Plon-Plon. He protested to Napoleon that he would be accused of leading France into war merely to gratify his own dynastic ambitions. The Emperor listened so carefully and nodded his head so understandingly that early in March Alexandre instructed the French ambassador in Turin to ensure 'that Monsieur Cavour is under no illusion.... If Piedmont gives rise to pretexts for war, he may be sure that the Emperor will not come to his assistance'.

Others were not at all so sure. The prospects of another Bonaparte carrying war into Italy sent shudders down the British spine. The government ordered Cowley to take soundings in Vienna. From there he wrote to Walewski, suggesting that the Emperor should make a public statement to restore a little calm. Napoleon agreed to the *Moniteur* publishing a strong denial of the rumours of war: 'invented by malice, spread by credulity, and accepted by stupidity'.

This disavowal so upset Plon-Plon, the noisiest of the pro-war partisans, that he resigned his post as Minister for Algeria and launched an attack on his fellow ministers in general and Walewski in particular. To this Alexandre retorted that Plon-Plon 'found it easier to deliver blows with a dagger than with a sword', relying on 'slander, calumny and the basest perfidy'. Cavour furiously reproached Napoleon for publicly humiliating him, and threatened to reveal their secret talks. The Emperor hedged once more by having articles published in two other journals, toning down the *Moniteur* statement. Alexandre returned to the charge with an impassioned evocation of their common Bonaparte blood: 'I feel as you do, my heart throbs with the same aspirations as yours, my thought is tuned to the same pitch as yours. I have some claim to your confidence and friendship.' Indeed, as he assured the Austrian ambassador: 'I am the only Minister who has the Emperor's confidence. We have never been in more perfect intimacy.' His old friend Thiers had a clearer view of the situation. On 22 March he wrote to Prince Albert: 'At heart the Emperor has only one aim, one fixed idea – to bring about war while talking of peace.'[16]

By this time the Austrian giant had become thoroughly irritated by the sabre-rattling of the Piedmontese pygmy, and both alarmed and resentful at the veiled menaces from France. To reduce the temperature once more the Tsar proposed a conference of the five great powers: Austria, Britain, France, Prussia and Russia; whereupon Piedmont also demanded a seat at the conference table. Cavour arrived in Paris and, four days later, left again with a promise of continued support from Napoleon, and a denial by Alexandre that any such promise had been given. Britain proposed a general standing-down of troops. Napoleon, confronted with the danger of being revealed as intent on war if he did not agree, offered to persuade Piedmont to demobilize, provided she was given her conference seat. Austria refused the offer. 'Ah,' said the Emperor, with a sigh of relief when the telegram was brought to him, 'I was afraid they would accept.' Austria, finally out of patience, sent an ultimatum to Piedmont, demanding unconditional demobilization. Victor Emmanuel refused, and by the end of April the Austrian army had crossed the Ticino.

Napoleon had been preparing to march for a month past. The railway to Lyons and the south-east was busy carrying guns to the frontier, the Chasseurs d'Afrique were shipped over from Algeria. In the last week of April cheering crowds watched the crack Household troops – the Zouaves and the Grenadiers of the Imperial Guard – march through the streets to entrain for the front. On May Day the city rang with the songs of the soldiers rejoining their regiments escorted by their parents and friends. Everywhere bands were playing the National Anthem of the Second Empire: Hortense's *Partant pour la Syrie*. On 3 May came the expected proclamation from the Emperor to the French people:

> Frenchmen! by sending her army into the territory of our ally the King of Sardinia, Austria has declared war on us. She thus violates treaties and justice, and threatens our frontiers.… Our Country will once more demonstrate to the world that she has not become degenerate. Providence will bless our efforts, for the cause which is based on justice, humanity, love of country and independence is sacred in the sight of God.

The most significant sentence in the proclamation was embedded in the middle: 'I shall soon place myself at the head of the army.'[17] This was the reason for the war. Years before, while he was still a prisoner at Ham, he told Hortense Cornu: 'I trust that some day I shall command a great army: I know that I should distinguish myself: I feel I have every military quality.' Although the Crimean expedition had brought credit to France, it had conferred no personal military glory on the Emperor. Here was the great opportunity to prove himself a worthy successor to Napoleon I – on those same plains of Lombardy where his uncle had first won fame in 1796.

He reshuffled the Ministry and the Privy Council, strengthening it to deal with any urgent matters while his back was turned. He offered the Ministry of the Interior to Morny, but Auguste refused to return. He disapproved of the war and had spoken against it publicly, and in any case he did not wish to leave his handsome quarters at the Hôtel de Lassay.

He appointed Eugenie as Regent, who, though disappointed that she had failed to prevent the war, was romantic enough by nature to look on the bright side. 'Your son will have a fine time', she said to the mother of one young officer. 'Young people are so fond of war. He'll have a lot of successes. They say Italian girls are responsive to the charms of Frenchmen. He'll deal out great thwacks with his sabre to our enemies, and maybe add his share to the growth of the population of Italy.'

Napoleon arrived at Genoa on 13 May, followed within a few days by Plon-Plon, ready to serve the cause of his future father-in-law, Victor Emmanuel, as commander of the French 5th Army Corps; an appointment which had Alexandre twitching with jealousy lest Plon-Plon should acquire fame, and with anxiety lest he should soon be spreading his demagogic ideas throughout Italy and setting up revolutionary ripples in the rest of Europe. It soon became clear to the troops, although not to the readers of the censored French press, that Napoleon III had not inherited the military skill of his uncle. At Magenta, where he unwisely split his army and had to be rescued by General MacMahon, and again at Solferino, he won victories but only at the cost of appalling bloodshed. The terrible suffering of the wounded in this campaign resulted in the foundation of the Red Cross organization.

The French and Piedmontese armies were driving the Austrians back, yet the farther they advanced the more perilous became Napoleon's position. He had now thoroughly alarmed the rest of Europe. France's eastern frontier was not secure against an intervention from Prussia. French Catholic opinion was concerned at the threat to the Papal States. In any event, he had been so profligate with the lives and limbs of his soldiers that he had not enough to carry on much longer. To the outraged horror of Victor Emmanuel, to whom he had promised complete support until the Austrians were driven right out of Italy, Napoleon arranged a meeting with the Austrian Kaiser at Villafranca. On 11 July they agreed to call off the war, with Austria ceding Lombardy but retaining Venezia.[18]

Napoleon was back at St-Cloud within a week, and on Napoleon I's birthday, 15 August, he held a victory parade in the Place Vendôme; the houses and the great bronze column were festooned with flags and garlanded with flowers, spectators perched up to the rooftops and the troops kitted out in new uniforms. All the ladies sighed with maternal affection as the Emperor lifted the three-year-old Prince Imperial, dressed in the uniform of the Grenadiers, to sit before him on the saddle of his chestnut horse. They sighed again with maternal compassion as the procession began with the walking wounded, balancing themselves as upright as they could to shout *Vive l'Empereur!*, and then handkerchiefs and top hats were waved madly for the infantry, the cavalry, the captured Austrian standards and cannon.[19]

*

While Napoleon III was following in Napoleon I's footsteps in Italy, his cousin, Emilie was making her first expedition to the land of those detestable tiger-cats across the Channel. She was in her fifties now and a grandmother, immensely proud of the fact that the robe in which her grandchildren were christened was the very one worn at Notre Dame by her half-brother, the King of Rome; for her elder son, Joseph de Chimay, had married the daughter of the Countess de Montesquiou, 'Maman Quiou'.[20] Not that Emilie ever bragged about her illustrious descent. Indeed, it was a subject on which she remained discreetly silent in the presence of the children, apparently unaware that behind her back her mother, more gaysome and garrulous than ever as she flitted into her eighth decade, was holding them spellbound with anecdotes and small mementoes of her Imperial seducer.

The Chimay party that set off from Calais on 1 June to sample the London Season comprised Emilie, her husband, her twenty-year-old daughter, Valentine, her sixteen-year-old son, Eugene, a couple of maids, a tutor for Eugene and Eugene's dog. The crossing was smooth and uneventful, but Emilie found that they were packed uncomfortably tight in the train from Dover to London, which she soon decided was a sombre, shabby city: 'It is poorly lit and the blackened bricks have a depressing drabness.' She considered their hotel in Charles Street to be a poky little establishment, with knobbly mattresses and high prices; and when they ventured forth to call on people they had met on the continent they turned out to be away or dead.

On Derby Day she hired a barouche and was driven round the town in a thick yellow fog which splendidly confirmed her anticipation that the whole place was filthy, the people as well as the houses. When the Belgian ambassador took her to Lady Derby's ball that night she was gratified to find the surroundings 'rather mean ... with paper on the walls, candles as lighting, and very large ladies seated on poor chairs in an ugly room with no curtain'. Not even the presence of the Flahauts could dissuade her from leaving early.

But as the days passed the tone of her letters to her son Joseph began to soften a little. She was full of admiration for the ladies she saw riding in Hyde Park: 'They show all the grace and elegance which they so often lack when on their feet!' She was delighted to discover that so few people smoked in London. It was a private visit but, as friends and faithful servants of Queen Victoria's Uncle Leopold, they were invited to a Court Ball at Buckingham Palace, where the Queen was very gracious and the Prince Consort danced with Valentine. Emilie did not dance, though she noted that the Queen did not miss a single one, except for the Scottish Reel after supper, when the crinolined ladies made their skirts leap up and down to the jigging lilt of the bagpipes. The music struck her as peculiar in other ways: 'for a country dance they had sparrows in the band and tweeked their tails violently'[21].

Still plagued by lumpy beds, they moved from the hotel in Charles Street to another in Jermyn Street, and then to lodgings in Sussex Place; but wherever they went they seemed unable to escape the 'bad heavy food which exhausts the stomach ... vegetables cooked with water, or sauces which should be used for pasting papers'. Except perhaps in royal circles. In the drawing room at Buckingham Palace, 'the Queen showed me unusual favour, having given me a handshake'. And then Valentine was invited to accompany her mother on a two-day visit to Windsor, despite the fact that Queen Victoria did not usually invite unmarried daughters.

Emilie fully approved of the castle, 'battlemented towers like Chimay, situated like Chimay', and was delighted at having been allotted the Honeymoon Suite, its red carpet patterned with orange blossom and altogether 'of such magnificence that it is reserved for crowned heads' or those so close to the throne as Victoria's eldest daughter, the Crown Princess of Prussia. She was even more thrilled at being placed in the third carriage of the Ascot procession, sharing with the Duchess of Manchester and the Duke of Beaufort and preceded only by the Queen, the Prince Consort and other members of the royal family. She did not much care for the races – not a patch on Longchamp – and her enjoyment of the ball in the evening was clouded by the fact that it took place in the Waterloo Chamber. Still, she was able to write home to Joseph on the headed Castle stationery, using the envelope only, since the writing paper was 'so sumptuous that the postage would be out of all proportion'.

Back in London, her letters littered with more dukes and duchesses than ever, she went to a concert given by the fashionable Whig hostess, Lady Waldegrave, and there found herself at last in truly congenial surroundings: 'What a charming society! How much at one's ease one feels! This society is so well bred, with such good manners and smelling so nice!'[22] A couple of days later, dining at Buckingham Palace, she was seated on Prince Albert's right, with, on her other side, the seventeen-year-old Prince of Wales, who 'unless I am mistaken, will have lively passions and will infuriate his Papa and Mama'[23]. June flowed into July, one function followed another, the visit was proving to be enjoyable far beyond her expectations when she was suddenly called back across the Channel by the serious illness – it was, indeed, to prove fatal – of Henri de Brigode, the surviving twin born of her first marriage.

*

Despite the cavalier way in which he had been treated, King Victor Emmanuel had no choice but to accept the terms of the treaty agreed between France and Austria and, adding salt to his wounds, to pay the price of France's brief co-operation by surrendering his provinces of Nice and Savoy to Napoleon and his daughter, Clotilde, to Plon-Plon. 'It is positively horrible', reported Cowley, 'to see that poor, frail little creature by the side of that brute – I can call him nothing else – to whom she has been immolated.' Clotilde, twenty years younger than Plon-Plon, was profoundly religious and totally bored by the vulgarities of her husband's home in the Palais-Royal and her new cousin's in the Tuileries. But at times she flashed out a sharp little tongue: as when Eugenie condescendingly assured her, 'You will soon be accustomed to my Court, my dear', and Clotilde retorted, 'Oh, yes – I've been accustomed all my life to my father's.'

Victor Emmanuel's grievance was shared by Alexandre Walewski, who sent Napoleon a fresh epistle of protest and injured pride a week after the great victory parade in the Place Vendôme, complaining that he had been misled, not consulted, and generally made to look a fool: Plon-Plon was sneering at him; *The Times* said that the doorkeeper at the Quai d'Orsay knew more about the Emperor's policies than his Foreign Minister; and consequently he considered himself compelled to offer his resignation. Which he then, as usual, withdrew. But he was becoming more and more of a nuisance. Napoleon encouraged the union of Modena, Parma, Tuscany and the Romagna with Piedmont (in breach of the terms of his treaty with Austria). Alexandre opposed it. Napoleon authorized publication of a pamphlet attacking Alexandre's policies. Alexandre again offered his resignation, and this time it was accepted. On 4 January 1860 he left the Quai d'Orsay, the pang of parting soothed by a pension of 100,000 francs a year as a Member of the State Council in addition to his salary of 30,000 francs as a Senator.[24]

In the spring of 1860 Eugenie organized a ball with quadrilles whose theme was the Elements. Anna-Maria Walewska appeared as Water, with her three attendant nymphs in tunics of silver lamée trimmed with coral, shells and sea plants, and 'dripping with diamonds' as one envious onlooker remarked – diamonds that came from Eugenie's jewel casket. On other observers the impression was different: 'The naiads were sprinkled with silver spangles which, falling on to their shoulders, looked like drops of water. Those like myself, who are short-sighted thought them beaded with sweat and one would have liked to rub them down like racehorses', wrote the malicious Prosper Merimée. But the ladies were well pleased with themselves and asked the Emperor to command another ball at which they could repeat the performance. He declined, saying that good things should never be repeated. 'Madame Walewska's earnest representations have been rejected with a very sharp *No*', wrote the Duchess of Dino. It seemed as if the Walewski day was over, for both wife and husband; but there was still some sunshine to come.

*

In his antepenultimate letter of resignation, Alexandre had told Napoleon: 'During the whole of my life, Sire, I have had no other political faith and religion than the Emperor. I believe that I completely understand him. In my opinion, the name of Napoleon is the most illustrious symbol of the conservative and anti-revolutionary principle … the most efficacious, perhaps the only efficacious, element of resistance remaining to European society, undermined by demagogic and socialist doctrines.' It was true enough, certainly a lot closer to the truth than the legend that Napoleon I had spent so much energy inventing and propagating on St Helena, though it was not the political rôle in which the Emperor wanted to appear at the moment. Yet, with typical inconsistency, Alexandre had no sooner resigned on this point of principle than he was back in the Thiers camp, agitating for democratic reform of the Legislative Body and Senate.

In this he was following the rather reluctant lead of Auguste de Morny. The elections of 1857 had for the first time brought into the Legislative Body a group of ardent Democrats openly opposed to the Imperial dictatorship. They were few but significant. Auguste was far from sympathetic to their aims, but he was a practical man: he saw that people could not be deprived of their liberties for ever. Napoleon I had tried to do that, offering as compensation the succession of victories that came from constant war. But even that appeal to the nation's lust for military laurels had not sufficed to keep him in power for two decades. If relaxation of the grip of government was inevitable, then it was better to offer changes voluntarily than wait until they had to be made under duress. Though Auguste had refused to return to any ministerial office, he was still a voice to be listened to. On 24 November 1860, Napoleon accepted a little of the inevitable. By Imperial Decree the Senate, whose members were appointed by the Emperor, and the Legislative Body, elected by the small proportion of the nation entitled to vote, were in future to have the right of reply to the speech made by the Emperor at the opening of each annual session: thus giving them the opportunity to debate measures instead of simply accepting them.[25] In addition, summaries of the proceedings were to be sent to newspapers and a full shorthand record published in the *Journal Officiel*.

Other changes accompanied this modest reform. Charles de Flahaut became ambassador to London. (He was seventy-five, the same age as his father, Talleyrand, when appointed to the same post in 1830.) Persigny was reinstated at the Ministry of the Interior and Alexandre Walewski returned to the government as Minister of State – an appointment widely regarded as proof that Anna-Maria was still the Emperor's mistress. He was charged with the supervision of science, literature and art, a job that delighted his dilettante temperament, but soon brought protests from the museum curators who suffered under his ill-informed interference. It also landed him in one of those violent politico-artistic controversies that periodically rock Parisian society. His predecessor had refused permission for Wagner's *Tannhaüser*, then regarded as an outrageously modern composition, to be performed at the Opera. Pauline von Metternich, wife of the Austrian ambassador and an admirer of the 'charlatan' Wagner, persuaded Alexandre to rescind the ban. At the opening performance on 13 March 1861 the first act was greeted with howls of laughter. In the second act the members of the Jockey Club, who had organized a claque, held up the performance by clamouring for a ballet, in the interest of their little mistresses, the *rats d'Opéra*. Other demonstrations were aimed at Walewski as the representative of the Emperor and at the dictatorial control of the Opera. There were even quite a few who did not like the music. 'I could write something similar tomorrow inspired by my cat walking up and down the keyboard', said Merimée.[26]

Five days later the opera was presented again, amid even more hubbub and hostility. When the Emperor and Empress arrived at the end of the second act, those in the audience who recognized them stood up and clapped, the rest, thinking the applause was for the opera, stood up and hissed. The Emperor was not amused. After the third of its four projected performances the opera was withdrawn.

Jerome Bonaparte died in June 1860. Within six weeks Mathilde was no longer on speaking terms with Plon-Plon, whom, she told the Emperor, she would never again consent to see, even on her death bed. Plon-Plon, who already received a State pension of one million francs a year, was furious when he learned that he was not to be given a share of the million formerly paid to his father, though Mathilde was allotted 300,000 to add to her existing 200,000 (and the 200,000 francs alimony that she received from Demidoff).[27] Plon-Plon was even more annoyed – and greatly alarmed – when Jerome Patterson brought his threatened suit in the French courts to prove that his mother's wedding to Jerome in 1803 was legal, and that he was therefore Jerome's legitimate, and elder, son. But the Emperor, though he had earlier frightened Plon-Plon with threats to recognize the marriage, was not really in favour of so much upheaval in the family on such a sensitive subject as legitimacy; the courts found against Patterson.[28]

As for that most troubled and troublesome of elder brothers, Leon, he was managing at the moment to mark time. He had asked Auguste de Morny in the spring of 1858 to get him an interview with the Emperor on the ground that he was thinking of standing for the Chamber of Deputies and wanted advice. He had offered to sell to Plon-Plon for 25,000 francs the Correggio he had been given by Fesch – he needed the money to get married and legitimize the two sons he already had by Françoise Jonet. Neither of these approaches succeeded; but his domestic life was becoming more settled. His stepfather, Luxburg, was now dead; his mother, Eleonore, returned to Paris and a partial reconciliation. He finally got some more money – but no audience – from Napoleon and made Françoise-Fanny a belatedly honest woman.

*

Though Alexandre was the minister in charge of arts, it was Auguste who was the more successful in practising them. For his private theatre in the Hôtel de Lassay he wrote light comedies under a pseudonym: Count de Saint-Rémy. One at least of these, a one-act operetta with music by Offenbach, was popular enough to be repeated in public and revived seventy years after his death, though much of the credit for this may be due to the unacknowledged collaboration of Ludovic Halévy, later to become famous for his partnership with Offenbach. When the reforms of November 1860 gave the Legislative Body two secretaries, Auguste appointed Halévy and Alphonse Daudet (who made Auguste the central character of his novel, *Le Nabab*) as the other. In letters to his mother Halevy presented a strange portrait of Auguste's princely existence on holiday at his estate at Nades, in the 'very beautiful castle, the too beautiful castle, too much gilding, too much stucco, too many servants'. Auguste bought the dilapidated château soon after his return from Algeria and spent two years demolishing it and rebuilding it to a plan drawn up by Fanny le Hon in 'Gothic and Renaissance' style, red brick with white stone corners, a steep roof and a battlemented imitation keep – the whole resembling a very expensive workhouse.

From 8 a.m. to 11 a.m. Halevy worked with Auguste on ideas for plays: 'He comes up with twenty subjects an hour, but there is usually nothing in any of them.' At 11 a.m. they took lunch, at 1 p.m.:

… we go for a stroll over M. de Morny's five thousand acres. A fine carriage follows in case you get tired; about thirty peasants go ahead to drive the herds of hares and companies of partridges out of the woods and bracken; a dozen dogs are baying between your legs and an equal number of gamekeepers bravely follow, picking up fur and feather and reloading the guns.… M. de Morny accomplishes massacres; in two hours, the day before yesterday, he killed twelve hares, eight rabbits, four quail, a pheasant and six partridge – thirty-one animals in all.

They returned to the castle for dinner at seven: 'You cannot imagine the extravagant things the cook gives us to eat – and everything is exquisite, marvellous, impossible, splendid.' After the meal they sat and talked or dozed until midnight. Despite the splendour and luxury – the host and hostess and their four guests were 'the prey to about forty servants, coachmen and cooks'[29] – Halévy found it all rather an exhausting bore: even with the magnificent view from the terrace over the lake; the expensively-maintained home farm; the dozen kilometres of wall that surrounded the park; the special train that carried the master and his guests from Paris to the station at Gannat; a horse-box containing three or four thoroughbreds; a coach for the servants and baggage; and the great saloon with separate dining compartment, its gilded exterior adorned with the coat of arms bearing the hortensia and the motto *Tace sed memento*.

It was a constant provocation to Napoleon, but this did not prevent Auguste receiving an honour he had long coveted when the Emperor and Empress visited Clermont-Ferrand in July 1862. Auguste met them at the station and accompanied them to the Prefecture where, as President of the Council of the Department of Puy-de-Dôme, he made a florid speech of welcome. In his reply the Emperor offered his thanks to this distinguished representative of the people of the Auvergne and, as a mark of his esteem and friendship, created him a duke.[30] The arms incorporated the Auvergne dolphin, the Flahaut martlets and the Imperial eagle – but no hortensia.

It seemed to be just one more of the casual affronts to public morals for which the Emperor had become noted. The name he had singled out for high honour had long been notorious as a clever but conscienceless manipulator of companies and the money market. He was known to protect swindlers and to sail very close to the limits of the law. For many years now, the whisper *Morny est dans l'affaire* (Morny has a hand in it) had been both a tip that the business was going to produce a healthy profit for somebody in one way or another, and at the same time a warning for honest or simple folk to walk warily.[31] Even at this moment there were rumblings of criticism about Morny's relationship with a Swiss banker named Jecker for whom he had obtained French nationality.

Three years earlier Jecker had raised a loan of 75 million francs for the Mexican government of President Miramon. In 1861 Miramon was overthrown by Benito Juarez, who suspended the repayment of all debts to foreign countries. This brought protests and eventually a blockade of the port of Vera Cruz by the fleets of Spain, Britain and France, each of whom had money invested in Mexico: 40 million francs by Spain, 60 million francs by France and 85 million by Britain. In addition the French claimed repayment of the 75 million lent by that very recent Frenchman, Jecker. Juarez offered to open talks if the allies would refrain from landing troops and raise the blockade by moving their ships along the coast. The Spanish and British accepted this arrangement in February, but at the beginning of April Napoleon published a repudiation on the part of France, and the French invasion proceeded. In the Chamber there were murmurs that the war was being fought on behalf of Jecker, and that the man who was pushing Jecker's claims was Morny. After Morny's death, Jecker said he had promised him a commission of 30 per cent; but for the moment, for lack of evidence and temerity, nobody openly mentioned Auguste's name.

It may have been that Napoleon's bestowal of a dukedom on his half-brother was intended as a snub to Alexandre and Eugenie, both of whom had fallen out with Auguste on two important questions of the day. One was the growing agitation for Polish independence, which Auguste opposed because of his Russian sympathies, and which Alexandre, rediscovering loyalty to his ancestral land, was supporting at Court and in the press. The other was the defence of what remained of the Papal States against the continuing spread of Victor Emmanuel's liberated and unified Italy. Eugenie, who was Alexandre's supporter on the Polish question, took the lead here and was in turn supported by Alexandre, both reversing their Polish position and backing a continuance of Papal despotism against the national aspirations that tried to overthrow it, while Auguste performed a similar about face by supporting the nationalists against the Papists in Italy. Napoleon shared Auguste's views on both subjects; but fear of reaction from French Catholics forced him to retain a French garrison in Rome, where he had sent troops to protect the Pope in 1849.

There was almost only one area in which his views and Auguste's coincided with those of Eugenie. That was in Mexico, where her Spanish blood and reactionary sentiments made her fiercely in favour of military intervention. 'She gave me an enchanting description of the country', the Austrian ambassador reported. 'This far-off, romantic, adventurous enterprise, which recalls the great period of her native country's history, delights her southern imagination.' She later claimed that the decision to engage French troops was taken by her at Biarritz in October 1861.[32]

Napoleon resented her increasing interference in politics and her frequent criticism. At lunch with her and Mathilde and Conneau in May 1861 he burst out, 'Really, Eugenie, you forget two things: that you are a Frenchwoman and that you are married to a Bonaparte.'[33] She certainly was French by marriage, but whether her husband was a Bonaparte remained open to question. Still, she was a graceful centrepiece for the brilliant Court that he maintained at the Tuileries and, having presented him with a son, she appeared more than content to be relieved of further marital duties by his string of mistresses. She was said to have attempted suicide at the age of twenty-two, when she discovered that the Marquis of Alcanisez, who was writing her passionate love letters, was doing so only as a pretext to pay court to her sister, but that may well have been from injured pride rather than a broken heart. Except when the other women showed signs of possessiveness, as did Anna-Maria briefly and the Countess of Castiglione more often, Eugenie was very ready to be friendly with them. When Napoleon forbade Rachel to enter the Tuileries Eugenie went to visit her in her own home. She was a complaisant wife, but she reserved the right to use Napoleon's infidelities as a pretext for violent scenes in private, which horrified him and won her the political power which he would otherwise have refused to grant her.

She was not well liked, a foreigner whom many found aloof and insufficiently aware of the debt she owed to the nation that had made her its Empress. She was known to squander vast sums on wildly expensive dresses: row upon row ranged in reserve, each on its life-size dummy to preserve it from creases, filling the attics of the Tuileries. She was rightly suspected of having a dangerous and increasing influence in the Emperor's Council. Maxime du Camp, a prominent journalist, left this devastating assessment of her:

Never did a more futile creature bring more mediocre intelligence to the service of a reckless ambition. She exercised a detestable influence on public behaviour; she had her own camarilla, her own court, her own partisans; she had her own policies and pushed the country into ventures of which she was incapable of calculating the extent or foreseeing the outcome. She was disastrous, and her beauty, marvellous though it was, is no excuse.... There was a sort of cloud of cold cream and patchouli about her; superstitious, superficial, with no objection to smutty talk, always preoccupied with the effect she was making with her shoulders and bosom, her dyed hair, her eyes outlined in black, her lips rubbed with rouge – for her true setting she needed the circus orchestra, the trotting horse, the hoop for her to leap through and then blow a kiss to the audience from the pommel of her riding whip.... Cold, unresponsive, both miser and spendthrift, with no other emotion than vanity, she dreamed of playing the great star roles and was merely a super dressed up in a robe of sovereignty that she did not know how to wear. I do not believe she ever had a serious idea on anything whatever.

Du Camp, as a friend of the Bonapartes, was biased against the Beauharnais Napoleon and his wife, but a lot of what he said reflected public opinion.

She often retired into the dream world in which she identified herself with Marie-Antoinette. At masquerades she would sometimes appear as Diana and often as a seventeenth-century Venetian (to match her husband's favourite costume), but best of all she delighted in dressing up as Marie-Antoinette. She wrote her letters at a desk that had belonged to the dead queen, whose portrait in tapestry decorated one of her private rooms, while another, an engraving, was the only picture in her bedroom; she was a frequent visitor to the scene of Marie-Antoinette's gay frivolities at the Trianon and the Hameau, and the sombre cell where she spent her final days at the Conciergerie. Later, when assassination attempts against the Emperor were followed by the less dangerous, but more ominous public demonstrations against the Imperial rule, she indulged in romantic fantasies with herself as the beautiful high-spirited heroine. 'I have no fear of revolutions.... Do you think I should run away in a cab like old Queen Marie-Amelie [Louis-Philippe's wife]? No, I should get on to a horse and save my son's crown at the head of a regiment of cavalry, and show people what it means to be a sovereign!' Meanwhile she showed them her perfect shoulders and bust in the endless array of gowns that Worth made for her at a cost of thousands of francs.

Chapter Seven:
The Road to Chislehurst

If anybody stood between Eugenie and her dream of quelling a revolution single-handed it was Auguste de Morny; for he had a horror of them. It was this that had driven him into politics in 1848 and had prompted him to play the leading part in the coup d'état of 1851. It still drove him on to seek a pacific compromise between the authoritarianism of the Second Empire and the increasing popular demand for more liberty. The elections in the summer of 1863 brought a significant rise in the number of anti-government votes, particularly in urban constituencies; in the Department of the Seine the vote was seven to one in favour of the opposition. Among the new Deputies was Thiers, making his return to politics for the first time since the coup d'état. Before the opening of the new session of the Legislative Body Auguste arranged a 'chance' meeting with him, shook hands and exchanged a few words; and in his inaugural speech a few days later, on 6 November 1863, he went out of his way to greet 'the former parliamentary notabilities' and to tell them that he had no doubt of their loyal support in the task of moving towards greater freedom through 'sincere agreement between a Liberal Sovereign and a Moderate Assembly'. The speech was warmly applauded by the Assembly. But the 'Liberal Sovereign' was not so pleased. At their next meeting he taxed Auguste with having said he had rejoiced at the election of Thiers and his colleagues. 'Rejoiced!' said the Emperor. 'That's too much!'[1]

Auguste's support of liberal policies was anathema to Alexandre Walewski. Already embattled in the Council with his old enemy, Persigny, he now launched a campaign of such violence against Morny that it spread into their social lives. When Auguste's beautiful wife, Sophie, sent out invitations to an evening party to hear some of her husband's new theatrical compositions, Anna-Maria promptly issued invitations for a musical evening at her house on exactly the same night. When one of Auguste's actress mistresses (like the Emperor he remained faithful to his wife for only a few months) gave a fine performance in a new play, he asked the theatre critic of the *Moniteur* to be sure to praise her in his review. This the critic did, only to find when the paper appeared that all his eulogies had been censored – by the Minister of State in charge of the arts: Alexandre Walewski. The feud became so bitter that on one occasion, when circumstances forced them to use the same carriage and Alexandre got in first, Auguste refused to join him and instead climbed up on to the box beside the coachman. With Persigny Alexandre's quarrel was less spectacular but more embarrassing, since it was carried into the Cabinet. In July 1863 the Emperor sacked them both but sweetened the blow to Persigny with a dukedom.[2]

The gossips said that Anna-Maria ceased to be Napoleon's mistress in 1861, so Alexandre could count himself fortunate to have retained his place for the last two years. Now, however, he was free to pursue a new jack-o'-lantern. Since 1861 there had been sporadic revolts in Poland against Russian rule. In the spring of 1863 they flared up all over the country, and Alexandre, never a man to be fettered by consistency, joined forces with his former *bête noir*, Plon-Plon, to attack the Russians whose tyranny he had previously defended. He now saw himself as King of Liberated Poland; and, having urged that France should not support the patriots in Italy, now equally vehemently argued that she should support those in Poland. The Emperor was not impressed. Thiers warned Alexandre against pursuing his campaign, and he decided instead that he would like to return to London as ambassador. Unhappily, Queen Victoria made it clear that she would not find Walewski acceptable, in view of the widespread rumours about his wife's affair with the Emperor and his own complaisant attitude to it.

Suddenly, everything seemed to be going downhill. He was refused the box that used to be reserved for him, as Minister of State, at the Opera; and Charles de Flahaut was given the place Alexandre had expected to be his on the Commission appointed to collect and publish the correspondence of Napoleon I. He protested and was reinstated. But he had had a nasty shock.

*

While Alexandre languished, Auguste kept busier than ever. He had recently suggested to Jecker that they should go into the silver bullion trade: the military vehicles sent up into the interior of Mexico with supplies could bring back the metal from the mines; at the coast it could be loaded into the empty supply ships and thus be transported to France – entirely free of charge by land and sea. He was also conducting a campaign against Ferdinand de Lesseps in the hope of taking over the concession for constructing the Suez Canal. Since de Lesseps was a relation of the Empress, this further estranged Eugenie and Auguste. He presided in the Legislative Body over heated debates on the Mexican adventure, which the government always won by force of numbers. With money put up by the city and the leading railway companies, he founded the Grand Prix de Paris at Longchamp (a racecourse which he had helped to construct) and had the mortification of seeing the race won in its first year, 1863, by an English horse (a defeat that was avenged the following year when a French filly won the Derby). He kept a sharp eye on the racing stud that he owned at Viroflay, usually insisting on a commission on future winnings whenever he sold a horse. He had organized a syndicate to develop Deauville, a small fishing village, into a rival bathing and gambling resort to Dieppe, and also a port and railway link between Britain and the French Atlantic towns, cutting out the long rough voyage round the Brittany coast. The promenade, yacht basin, church and many roads were already completed.

He was at the height of his success and fame, drawing grudging admiration even from those who disapproved of him. Du Camp wrote of him:

With his courage, spirit of intrigue, skill and grace ... he was the most impudent, the most bold man I have ever known.... Despite his faults, despite his vices, despite his intellectual immorality – perhaps because of it – Morny was a politician of the first rank. His natural swagger and his firmness of character made him conceive great schemes which he executed all the better for being a man who was never fettered by scruples of conscience or of principle.

Others commented on 'this mixture of superior qualities and indelible vices mingled beneath a veneer of elegance'. All agreed that he was the only man of statesmanlike qualities close to the Emperor, yet he was never used to full effect because of the blood-tie which paradoxically separated them. Napoleon resented the relationship which Auguste too openly insisted upon. Auguste, reared in a family where illegitimacy was endemic, felt no moral stigma but bitterly resented being denied his rights as his mother's child. He had been born during the married life of Louis and Hortense, while they still enjoyed their former titles of King and Queen of Holland – why therefore was he not a prince?

Of all his interests in this year of 1863 it was Mexico that occupied him: not only because of his own interests there but because the criticism at home and abroad grew louder as the Emperor's moves became more suspect. Nobody knew what Napoleon's true purpose had been in refusing an accommodation with Juarez; the outbreak of the American Civil War in 1861 had given him the opportunity to establish his army in Mexico in the teeth of the Monroe Doctrine; by 10 June 1863 French troops had entered Mexico City, and since then they had conducted desultory hostilities against Juarez and his guerrillas. He may have dreamed of reviving one of Napoleon I's wilder plans: invading the United States up the Mississippi. He may have aimed at a Franco-Spanish empire to spread outwards from Mexico through the lower half of the continent. He may have hoped for a short, brilliant campaign that would revive his reputation as a warlord. But events were not going that way. He had too few forces and too little spare capital to attain any of these objectives. He decided to put in a *locum tenens* while waiting to see which way the wind blew. Under French direction and pressure, a Mexican puppet republican government voted to set up a monarchy, and offered the crown to Archduke Maximilian of Austria, brother of Emperor Franz Joseph.

It was an interesting choice on the part of Napoleon – for nobody doubted that the decision had been his. The gesture served as a mark of goodwill to Austria, France's enemy in Italy less than five years earlier, and possibly as a hint of opposition to Prussia, where Bismarck had recently declared his policy of 'Blood and Iron'. It was a small sop to Britain, for Maximilian's wife, Charlotte, was the only daughter of Queen Victoria's Uncle Leopold of Belgium. There was even a little balm in it for the Orleanists, since Charlotte was, on her mother's side, the granddaughter of Louis-Philippe. Perhaps the most interesting and least publicized aspect of the whole affair was that Maximilian, handsome, charming, a bit of a dilettante and more than a little of a spendthrift, was that same Maximilian born to the Duke of Reichstadt's Aunt Sophie in July 1832 and believed by some to be the Duke of Reichstadt's son. He had visited Paris during the peace conference that followed the Crimean War and was currently viceroy of the remaining Austrian territory in northern Italy. With the crown and the title of Emperor offered him by the Mexican deputation, came a promise from Napoleon that French troops would support him for the next three years. He arrived in Mexico in May 1864, faced with the desperate task of creating a stable administration out of chaos and of putting down a popular rebellion with foreign soldiers.

In France the drain on men and money increased public dissatisfaction and criticism. In December 1863 Auguste had been to see the Emperor to emphasize the gravity of the situation. 'We have already lost control of the Chamber'[3], he told him – an exaggeration, but a fair enough prediction. He won the temporary support of Emile Ollivier, one of the first opposition candidates to be elected to the Legislative Body, assuring him that constitutional government would return that he, Auguste, would head the Cabinet, and that he would provide an important post for Ollivier. Demonstrations in the theatres against authors favoured by the Bonapartes had begun as early as November 1855. Now they spread to the lecture rooms. When the architect Viollet-le-Duc, the choice of the Emperor, was installed as professor at the Ecôle des Beaux Arts by the superintendent, Emilien de Nieuwerkerke, the lover of Princess Mathilde, the students created such a tumult of catcalls that both superintendent and professor were forced to leave the platform amid a hail of eggs, apples and pennies. When he was told of it, Napoleon laughed and said, 'It's just a skin disease – it doesn't affect the vital parts.'[4] But he was not foolish enough to believe that.

By May 1864 Auguste had persuaded the Emperor to let him introduce a bill which permitted workers to unite in a strike. They were still not allowed to form any permanent association such as a union, but the measure was a considerable advance on the existing law of 1810, under which Napoleon I decreed prison sentences for any workers bold enough to combine even in a request for higher wages, let alone the organization of a strike. Auguste still felt the pace was too slow. The fear of revolution haunted him. In January 1865 he said to Ollivier, 'Now is the time to grant liberty, before it is wrenched out of us!'[5] But time was passing more quickly than he knew. At Deauville in the summer of 1864 friends had noticed how slowly he strolled along the seawall with his poodle: 'no more than a pale and aged silhouette of the Don Juan he used to be'. At Nades, in the autumn, he was unable to accompany his guests when they went shooting. Looking 'very yellow and much thinner' he returned to Paris earlier than usual.

On Shrove Tuesday, 28 February 1865, he played with his children – two boys and two girls – admired their Mardi Gras costumes, and ventured out for a drive in the Bois de Boulogne. He caught a cold, which developed into slight bronchitis, and dosed it with the patent medicines in which he had superstitious faith. His doctor kept him in bed, but the illness failed to clear up and by 6 March it was evident that his position had become critical. 'Madame de Morny behaved like a brute', according to the British ambassador, giving 'dinner and parties to the great scandal of everybody'. Auguste's doctor called in two others. After they had offered a few comforting phrases and left, Auguste asked his old friend, former fellow-officer and rake, Fernand de Montguyon, to tell him the truth. 'Poor Auguste!' said Montguyon. 'It's all up with you.' Montguyon and Auguste's valet spent the rest of the day, under the dying man's supervision, destroying his private papers.[6]

His father, Charles de Flahaut, now Grand Chancellor of the Legion of Honour, visited him frequently. In the evening of 9 March the Emperor came, and Hortense's two sons met for the last time, Napoleon grasping the hand of his semi-conscious brother, while Eugenie prayed on her knees at the bedside. By morning Auguste was dead.[7] Cowley wrote of him:

People may say what they please but Morny is a great loss to the Emperor and the latter is much cut up. In critical moments Morny had great calmness and firmness, and even his enemies admit that his judgement in political affairs, when not warped by his own interests, was sound. He made a very good President of the Legislative Body and I believe desired the Emperor to give them greater liberty of discussion.... Peace be to his ashes!

Napoleon ordered a state funeral. The Archbishop of Paris was to conduct the service in the Madeleine, and Auguste was to be interred in the cemetery of Père Lachaise to the accompaniment of a seventeen-gun salute.[8] Auguste's weeping widow cut off all her beautiful golden hair so that it could be buried in the coffin with him – and two years later married the Marquis of Alcanisez who, half a generation before, had broken Eugenie's heart and driven her close to suicide. Eugenie refused ever to meet either of them again.

*

A week after Auguste's death, Alexandre Walewski applied for the vacant post as President of the Legislative Body, and, amid much ribaldry about a bastard Bonaparte succeeding a bastard Beauharnais, Napoleon consented. Because of the need for him to resign as a Senator and be elected as a Deputy, it was not until September that Alexandre was officially appointed, and by that time the Legislative Body was in recess. Before it reconvened in January 1866 he held several rehearsals in the Chamber behind closed doors and, as he mistakenly believed, entirely alone and unobserved. 'He mounted the rostrum, took his place in the chair, rang the bell, called for silence, and declared the session opened. Then, inventing incidents and replying to imaginary interruptions, he practised his voice, gestures and attitudes. He was very pleased with the way things went and is now certain he will be a great success.'[9]

Alas, the real thing was quite different. He was neither born nor trained to be the impartial president of a more-or-less democratic convention. He lost control, let himself become involved in arguments and went astray in the maze of procedure. He had chosen to succeed the wrong man. Auguste was highly intelligent; Alexandre, to put it at the kindest, was not. He lacked Auguste's skill, coolness and authority, and was faced with mounting dissatisfaction exceeding anything with which Auguste had had to deal.

The Emperor's Mexican folly was lurching from bad to worse. With the end of the Civil War in 1865, the United States government was in a position to threaten action against Maximilian's French troops. Napoleon had no choice but to begin their withdrawal. He was now being made to look almost as ineffectual in foreign affairs as Louis-Philippe had been. The rising tide of Italian liberation and unification forced him to agree to the withdrawal of the French garrison from Rome in return for Victor Emmanuel's promise to respect and defend the shrunken remainder of the Papal States – a promise which French Catholics complained would soon be broken. Mounting unrest in the Legislative Body was duplicated outside by demonstrations against anything connected with the Imperial family. The Goncourt brothers' play, *Henriette Maréchal*, was hissed and hooted at the Théâtre-Français even before the curtain went up because the authors were known to be friends of Princess Mathilde.

A few months later, in March 1866, the Emperor and Empress visited the Odeon Theatre and were greeted with shouts of *Luxembourg! Luxembourg!*[10] in protest against the government's decision to make a road through part of the nearby Luxembourg Gardens. References to liberty in the text were greeted with thunderous applause. During the interval one of the students, who were causing most of the commotion, let out a howling wail and then shouted, 'It's the cry of the dying eagle!' When Eugenie leaned forward from the Imperial box to see what was going on there was a yell of '*Cache ton museau!*' (Hide your ugly mug!)[11] At the end of the performance, as the Imperial couple descended the steps, the shouts of *Vive l'Empereur!* were drowned by those of *Luxembourg!*. Just before their carriage drove off to the Tuileries half-a-dozen sewage carts rumbled across the opposite side of the square. Immediately about a hundred students raced across, surrounded the carts, waved their hats and this time really bellowed '*Vive l'Empereur!*'.[12]

The Emperor remained impassive. It was about this time that two new comments on his sphinx-like imperturbability began to circulate: 'He never says anything, but he's always lying' and 'He's such a liar that you can't even believe the opposite of what he says.' Behind the hooded eyes his brain was trying to cope with an entirely new problem: what to do about Prussia, who, it was clear, intended to go to war with Austria as a preliminary to dominating the rest of the German states. He had held talks with Bismarck (who described him as 'half dreamer, half crook') at Biarritz in 1865. The Chancellor had let him believe that he would be rewarded with territory on the west bank of the Rhine if he refrained from intervention in support of Austria. He would thus fulfil part of his aim to restore to France the frontier that Napoleon I had lost at Waterloo. On the other hand, if he opposed the Prussians by force it would revive his popularity with the regular army, and give the civilians something else to talk about instead of liberty and reform.

However, thanks to his involvement in Mexico, he had neither the men nor the money to go to war with anybody. When Prussia marched against Austria in mid-June 1866 he sat back and pretended that this was just what he had wanted – let each exhaust the other. There might indeed have been an advantage to France in a war of attrition between the two Germanic heavyweights, but, in fact, the war was startlingly brief. The Prussians, with their new breech-loading rifles, overwhelmed Austria and her allies. Hanover was beaten and annexed to Prussia in a fortnight. On 3 July Austria was defeated at the battle of Sadowa; she accepted the Prussian peace terms on 26 July – not quite seven weeks after the war had begun. Prussia now stretched uninterrupted from the Baltic to the Rhine.

Charlotte arrived from Mexico to beg that the French troops should remain there to protect Maximilian. Her tears failed to move Napoleon, whose only suggestion was that Maximilian should leave. She answered that he was a Hapsburg and would never run away. She returned to her father, Leopold, in Belgium, where grief and worry drove her out of her mind. Napoleon smiled his gentle enigmatic smile, but at heart he too was beginning to grow anxious. He had recently had a bronze bas-relief of himself on horseback put up at the southern entrance of the Place du Carrousel. Hortense Cornu told him it was poorly sculptured and unflattering, and urged him to have it replaced. He answered: 'Considering how long it will remain in place, there is no point in touching it.'[13]

Madame Cornu, a woman of strong republican and libertarian views, had quarrelled with him at the time of the coup d'état and it was more than ten years before she agreed to meet him again. The friendship was never resumed on the old footing: 'the destruction of our liberties, the massacres of 1851, the deportations of 1852, the cruelties which revenged the Orsini attack rise to my mind and I shrink from the embrace of a man stained with the blood of many of my friends'. She was soon remarking on an increase in his natural hesitancy: 'Yesterday he was in very high spirits. I suspect that he has just made up his mind on a subject that has been teasing him. He dislikes coming to a decision but, perhaps for that very reason, when he does so he feels relieved and happy.'

His health had deteriorated since Fergusson examined him nine years earlier, and his own physicians now diagnosed a vesical calculus. It gave him extreme pain from time to time, but he refused to have it operated on. Eugenie told the Austrian ambassador that he was completely exhausted, interested only in his *Life of Julius Caesar*, which he was writing with the help of the historian, Victor Dury, and that she had asked him to abdicate and appoint her Regent for the Prince Imperial. But ill-health, however debilitating, could not alone account for the strange erratic policies that he pursued – or failed to pursue. He had by now established himself as the Master of the Inconsequential, the Uncompleted; whatever he undertook either seemed to contradict something he had done earlier, or was dropped before he could draw the full benefit from it.

He had persuaded the British to call off the Crimean War before they could press home their advantage; he had settled with Austria in Italy without consulting Piedmont;

he had sent Maximilian to Mexico and left him in the lurch. He had gone out of his way to woo the Catholic vote at home and then lost it by his odd behaviour in Italy; he had risked war with Prussia by intervening in Italy and then incensed the Italians by his treaty with Austria; he had come to power thanks to the bourgeoisie and then estranged them by dabbling in socialist theory if not policy. He was unpredictable yet scarcely an opportunist, for an opportunist at least makes the most of his opportunities. Nobody knew what he stood for. 'The Empress is a Legitimist;' he once said, 'Morny is an Orleanist; my cousin Napoleon is a Republican; I am a Socialist; only Persigny is a Bonapartist, and he is mad.'

'If I had married him', said Mathilde, 'I think I should have broken his head – just to find out what he had in it.' The answer may be: almost nothing. He possibly never had more than a single aim: to follow his star and fulfil Hortense's ambition that he should succeed to Napoleon I's imperial throne – a man of destiny who, having arrived at his destination, had no idea where to go next. He published many works on many subjects, principally political or economic, but there is nothing original in the material. It is all borrowed; most of it researched, and possibly ghosted, by others. In war and foreign affairs he tried to imitate Napoleon I, but usually began too soon, when he was not sufficiently prepared, and gave up equally prematurely without adequate reward for his efforts. In industrial and economic affairs, where he copied much from Britain, he encouraged the great expansion of credit which enabled the railways to spread, new farming techniques to be tried out, new factories to be built, yet undermined the good he was doing by failing to enforce elementary business morality, ignoring, condoning or failing to take action against a series of financial scandals, private and public, at home and abroad. Worst of all, nobody knew what ill-considered improvisation he would embark on next.

By the end of 1866, the skies were becoming very dark. There was cholera in Paris; the foreign news rattled the Stock Exchange; after a bad harvest came widespread floods. Plon-Plon made no secret of his opinion that Napoleon's run of luck was almost over: 'My cousin is a pig', he told his acquaintances. 'The Ministers are nincompoops. The Prefects are scum. The Government is contemptible. The whole lot will be kicked out one of these days.'[14]

Of all the Bonapartes, only Plon-Plon and Mathilde could boast royal blood, since their mother was the daughter of the King of Württemberg. This made them the more envious of the Imperial status of 'Monsieur Beauharnais', as they called their cousin in private. In 1863 Plon-Plon's words and actions became so outrageous that Napoleon wrote to him: 'Either be what you ought to be, a support and prop for my Government ... or else go your own way, giving free course to the violence of your opinions, and then it will be necessary for my conduct towards you to testify publicly my displeasure.' Plon-Plon let it be known that threats of that kind had no terrors for him; and repeated that he had many documents proving the Emperor's illegitimacy including one from Napoleon I to King Louis that ran: 'Your wife has just been brought to bed. No noise or scandal which will only rebound on you and on me. Keep quiet and I promise you that this is the last time that I will ask you to recognise what does not belong to you.'

*

At the opening of the new session in January 1867 the government offered a further concession to the Legislative Body: instead of merely replying to the Speech from the Throne the Deputies would have the right to question a minister on the government's actions and proposals and vote their approval or disapproval. There was plenty of the latter, often expressed most forcibly by Thiers: 'You have created Italian unity, and Italian unity has created German unity.... Watch out before it is too late! You cannot make any more mistakes!'[15]

Such boisterous incidents, not seen in a French Assembly for fifteen years, took place under the nominal, but almost non-existent, control of Thiers' former acolyte, Alexandre Walewski, whose incompetence, mismanagement and lack of control as President of the Legislative Body had become a public scandal. His inept rulings and interventions kept the Deputies, already flushed by their new taste of freedom, in a state of continual ferment. In March 1867, when the Chief Minister, Rouher, came to address the House, Thiers became so heated in his criticism that he shook his fist at him. Rouher appealed for the protection of the Chair, whereupon the Deputies were treated to an extraordinary snatch of comic dialogue.

Walewski: 'I invite the honourable Monsieur Thiers to calm himself.'

Rouher: 'Oh, for God's sake! Either preside over the session or come to the Tribune and defend the Government – if you can!'

Waleweski: 'Monsieur Thiers, I shall be compelled to call you to order.'

Thiers: 'I don't give a damn!'

It was apparent that things could not continue like this. Within a fortnight Alexandre resigned and was given back his seat in the Senate. In mid-April he went on holiday to Florence. His career was over. He had done many foolish things and made comparatively little of great opportunities. Now he could only look on.

Sadowa had been rightly regarded as a defeat for France as well as for Austria, and Frenchmen were looking forward to their *revanche*. This was precisely what Bismark wanted. Halévy noted in his diary: 'The French claim to be the best soldiers in the world, and the Prussians, swollen-headed over their lightning campaign last year, are shouting everywhere that they could just as easily have got the upper hand of us. That seems to us to be the height of impertinence; we are beginning to feel the need to teach the Prussians a lesson.' But not quite yet. There were not enough of the new rifles that Monsieur Chassepot had invented as a reply to the Prussian needle-guns; there were not enough trained soldiers for that matter.

As his reward for remaining neutral during the Seven Weeks War, Napoleon demanded that Prussia should agree to France annexing Luxembourg which, though a fief of the King of Holland, was garrisoned by Prussian troops. Bismarck was delighted to have the opportunity of snubbing the French with a refusal. The King of Holland offered to sell Luxembourg for ninety million francs and the joke flashed round that 'The Emperor is like a hunter coming home with an empty bag and buying a rabbit in the market.' But Bismarck objected to that, too. In the end the Prussians withdrew from Luxembourg and the French refrained from marching in, and the King of Holland failed to get his ninety million francs.

There was a Universal Exhibition in Paris again that year – another brilliant success. And another assassination attempt in June when Napoleon was driving back from a review in the Bois de Boulogne with Tsar Alexander. The only casualty was an equerry's horse, shot in the head, and the two Emperors argued amicably whether the would-be murderer was an Italian aiming at Napoleon or a Pole after Alexander.[16] The Sultan of Turkey arrived on 1 July, but the ceremonies were overshadowed by news of the greatest humiliation so far sustained by Napoleon and the French nation – Maximilian, deserted by the Emperor and the French troops, had been taken prisoner by Juarez and shot.[17]

From the mid-summer of 1867 Nemesis picked up her skirts and broke into a trot: problems crowded in, solutions seldom existed, and even evasions were hard to come by. In an attempt to win the support of Austria, Napoleon went to Salzburg in August for talks with Kaiser Franz Josef, but Maximilian's bullet-ridden body lay between them: no defensive alliance was signed. In October, Garibaldi's men attacked the Papal States, and Eugenie burst into the Council Chamber in the Tuileries and boxed Napoleon's ears. Whether or not as a result of this protest, the French troops only recently withdrawn from Rome were sent back to try out their newly issued *Chassepots*, and to win Napoleon renewed vilification from most Italians and only small thanks from French Catholics. The year ended with 'great cold, great misery, great political unease'[18].

February 1868 saw the introduction of a new law on compulsory military service, calculated to produce a million and a quarter trained men to deal with the Prussians. As a sop to the critics, political censorship was lifted. The result was predictable: the press lost no time in biting the hand that fed it. Journals and periodicals grew more and more outspoken in their attacks on the Emperor, his Court and his ministers. Several of them opened a fund to raise a monument to Baudin, the Deputy shot at one of the barricades in December 1851. Napoleon decided this was going too far, and the editors were prosecuted.

Too late, the Emperor discovered that he had stepped into a minefield. A country barrister, 31-year-old Leon Gambetta, used the court room at the trial as a stage from which to launch an open and violent attack on the group of men 'without talent, without honour and hopelessly involved in debts and crimes' who had carried out the coup d'état. Addressing himself beyond the court room walls to the Throne Room and Council Chamber of the Tuileries, he shouted:

Listen! you have been absolute masters of France for seventeen years. The thing that most condemns you, because it is the evidence of your own remorse, is that you have never dared to say: 'We will celebrate the Second of December, we will place it as a National Anniversary among the solemn festivals of France.' Well! This anniversary that you do not want we will take for ourselves; we will observe it always; every year it shall be the Anniversary of our Dead, until the day when the country, master of itself once more, shall impose upon you the great national expiation in the name of Liberty, Equality and Fraternity.

The words echoed out from Paris through the whole of France. The excitement intensified. It was all too much for Alexandre Walewski. After his resignation and the trip to Italy he had come home to a life of idleness. In the autumn of 1868 he took his wife and daughter on holiday to Germany. This time he returned only as far as Strasbourg. There, where his cousin's political career had begun with farce, Alexandre's life ended with a cerebral haemorrhage. His sister, Emilie, outlived him by three years. Her three children were now all married and she had six grandchildren. She lived quietly, but there was still a Chimay close to the French Court for her sister-in-law Rosalie's daughter, Countess Mercy d'Argenteau, had been the Emperor's mistress since 1866. When Emilie died her body was brought back to Ménars, where she still lies with her mother, the pretty, flighty woman who first proved that Bonaparte could, after all, father a child. As for Leon, he outlived them all, wandering through France and even back to London for a while, keeping a few hasty paces ahead of his creditors, settling down at last in a grimy hovel at Pontoise, where he cadged pipefuls of tobacco and grumbled the days away until he died in April 1881.

*

To frighten the urban voters into supporting them in the elections of May 1869, the government employed hooligans, hired by the secret police, to race about the streets, overturning stalls and shouting: 'Death to the property owners!' Yet the opposition polled two and a half million votes. The moderate party headed by Thiers held 116 seats, apart from other opposition Deputies of the far right and left. The anti-Bonapartist jokes had become more biting now. The latest was: 'When Charles and Letizia Buonaparte were fleeing from the French troops in Corsica, Letizia cried "I will have my revenge!" Three months later she gave birth to Napoleon.'[19] In June,

312

crowds celebrating the election results gathered on successive evenings along the Grand Boulevards and in the working-class quarters of Belleville and Ménilmontant. The Municipal Guard, both horse and foot, cleared them off the streets but they flooded back again. Many were merely sensation-seeking spectators, but there were enough dedicated troublemakers and opportunist criminals among them to smash kiosks and street lamps to the strains of the *Marseillaise*, while in Belleville and Ménilmontant they broke into wine shops, cafés and even private houses. In the Boulevard Montmartre there was a pile of stones and timber, the tentative beginnings of a barricade. After nearly a week of this a regiment of cuirassiers was brought out to support the Municipal Guard, with a couple of squadrons of hussars and hundreds of sergents de ville, and the demonstrations ceased for a while.[20]

The Emperor threw a few more scraps to the Chamber and Senate, who were both now granted the right to propose laws instead of merely debating them, although the Emperor could still appeal over their heads to the people by way of a plebiscite. The gloom persisted: Eugenie went off to Egypt to celebrate the completion of the Suez Canal by her cousin de Lesseps; the Emperor was less seen in public and word went round that he was ill. His death in bed would solve nothing, merely let loose confusion. The Stock Exchange shuddered and held its breath. Eugenie returned and declared: 'If there isn't a war soon, my son will never ascend to the throne.' In January 1870 the Emperor stepped back still farther – he called on Emile Ollivier to form a 'Liberal Government'. But Ollivier was chosen simply because he was more amenable than Thiers – the reason why Auguste de Morny had approached him five years before. He had lost the confidence of the moderate progressives; he was entirely rejected by those who wanted no Empire, whether liberal or not, only a republic.

A week after Ollivier's appointment a new scandal burst out. The Emperor's cousin, Lucien Bonaparte's son Pierre, a hot-headed ne'er-do-well with a long record of truculent brutality, shot dead a journalist who had come to deliver a challenge to a duel. Crowds joined the funeral procession, which moved off from Auteuil, where the shooting had taken place, in the direction of Père-Lachaise cemetery. The Minister of the Interior, anxious to avoid a march right across the city, ordered the coffin to be taken to the cemetery at Neuilly, but the mob was not to be cheated of its demonstration. A mass of men broke through the barrier at the Etoile and marched down the Avenue des Champs-Elysées, at the foot of which stood detachments of infantry, cavalry and artillery and the Minister of the Interior himself. The funeral procession marched in step, yelling: 'Death to the Tyrant! Never, never shall a Murderer reign in France!' From under the trees came shouted commands and the clatter of weapons. Three drummers beat a roll and the Minister called, 'Disperse, in the name of the law!' They moved forward. He called again and some of the leading ranks halted, while the remainder lurched into them from behind. When he summoned them to disperse a third time they broke up, dark noisy flotsam in the twilight, making their way up to the Rue du Faubourg St-Honoré or down towards the river.

In his room in the Pavilion de Flore the Prince Imperial was having a history lesson. His father came in, took him in his arms, then crossed to a window overlooking the Seine and gazed down on the excited mass. 'If those fine fellows knew how easy it is to get in here,' he said, 'we

314

shouldn't be sleeping in the Tuileries tonight.'[21] At Neuilly the crowd around the grave was shouting, 'Revenge! Long live the Republic! Death to the Bonapartes!' Cousin Pierre, who had caused all the trouble, was brought to trial at Tours, to avoid any more nasty scenes in Paris. The proceedings, punctuated by the accused shouting 'Liar!' at the witnesses and the witnesses yelling 'Assassin!' in reply, were particularly enlivened when the judge put the formal question to one witness: 'Are you a friend or relation of the accused?' The witness happened to be the man who had issued the challenge in the first place. 'Friend – no', he replied. 'Relation – perhaps. His mother had so many lovers.'[22]

To everybody's indignation, but nobody's surprise, the accused man was acquitted. He had brought further shame to the name of Bonaparte, the name upon which the Emperor had built his entire career. As Gambetta said at a public dinner: 'Nowadays that legend, the origin of all our ills, is a thing of the past.' 'For eighteen years', said an editorial in the *Marseillaise*, 'France has been in the blood-stained hands of these cut-throats…. Frenchmen, can it be that you do not think you have had enough of them?'

Napoleon turned the other cheek and repealed the Law of Public Safety. In May 1870 he ordered another plebiscite, this time on the proposition: 'The People approve the Liberal Reforms made in the Constitution since 1860 by the Emperor.' It was like asking them to confirm that they preferred half a loaf to no bread at all. But out of a possible nine million votes he got seven and a half million – among them one from a peasant who remarked: 'I hope he'll be satisfied now. He wants to be President; I make him President. He wants to be Emperor;

I make him Emperor. He wants to be Plebiscite; I make him Plebiscite. What more's he going to want?'[23]

For the moment, nothing. This response could be misrepresented as a resounding endorsement of his rule. He perked up. Everybody noticed how much better he looked in health, when he took the Empress to the Opera. There seemed little left to worry about at the moment except the drought that was beginning to fidget the farmers. But at the back of it all was the continuing grumbling and fretting over Sadowa, the national thirst for military revenge. If the bumptious, strutting Prussians were not to be put down, what on earth had France chosen a Bonaparte as its leader for? Newspapers in both countries had been raising the tension for weeks past. The legend of Napoleon I, which the Emperor had so enthusiastically cultivated, was now catching up with him, together with a large war party among the ministers, urged on by the Empress. At the end of June, saying goodbye to the French minister bound for the United States, she burst into a violent denunciation of Prussian insolence. 'We must make an end of it. France is in danger of losing her standing in the world. She must re-establish it or die!'[24]

To all of this the Emperor nodded and said nothing. A dazzling military victory in the old style would, indeed, solve a great many problems and revive the popularity he had enjoyed after the Crimea, but there was no immediate hurry, plenty of time to build up the army a little more, or so he thought. Instead, a sudden crisis burst on him from Spain in the first week of July. Queen Isabella had been deposed by a military junta which, failing to agree on a Spanish prince to replace her, eventually offered the throne to Prince Leopold of Hohenzollern-Sigmaringen, whose father was related to the King of Prussia and for the past twenty years had been his vassal. Leopold hesitated but later, at Bismarck's prompting, asked for the King of Prussia's permission to accept. This, again with Bismarck as the prompter, the king agreed to give.

The acceptance was an evident provocation to France, exactly as Bismarck intended. There was a feeble attempt to argue that he should be welcomed by Napoleon because Leopold was the son of one of the Baden cousins whom he often visited in his youth; his sister was married to one of Caroline Murat's grandsons; and his grandmother was Caroline's niece, Antoinette, at whose wedding the Emperor might be said to have danced – for it was on that occasion that the notably pregnant Hortense had led her quadrille of Vestal Virgins. But no tie of kinship, even one much closer, could compensate France for the threat of a Prussian ruler on her southern frontier as well as on the east. The French Foreign Minister, Gramont, made it clear that France was prepared to fight to prevent the Hohenzollern succession.[25] During the following week, while the country trembled on the brink of war, the drought broke; the rain came in violent thunderstorms; a team of five doctors examined the Emperor and diagnosed a recurrence of the stone.[26]

On 12 July, Leopold announced that he had decided not to accept the Spanish Crown. The crisis was over; there would be no war. But consequently there would be no glorious victory. With Eugenie's support, and the sick Emperor's acquiescence, Gramont instructed the French ambassador to ask the King of Prussia for an assurance that he would never authorize a renewal of the candidature. To this arrogant demand the king, who was at Bad Ems, replied that he had nothing further to say and, since he was on holiday, did not intend to grant the French ambassador another audience. Bismarck, who had been bypassed by these events, seized the opportunity to put out an account of the affair which convinced both the Prussian nation and the French that each had been insulted by the other: 'a red rag to the Gallic Bull', as he said.

Great crowds gathered along the Quai d'Orsay, outside the Foreign Ministry and the Chamber of Deputies, yelling: 'Down with Prussia! On to Berlin! War! War! War!'[27] There were no more decisions to be taken, no more evasions possible. While the Legislative Body voted a special credit of 50 million francs, Emile Ollivier declared on behalf of the Cabinet, 'We accept the responsibility with a light heart', and the Minister of War assured the nation that the army was prepared 'down to the last gaiter button'. So convincing was all this enthusiasm that the citizens of German towns along the Rhine began to panic, expecting to be invaded by red-trousered French infantrymen at any moment. In Paris the crowds shifted to the Gare de l'Est to cheer the troops entraining for the forward assembly points, banners flying, bands thumping martial airs – though it was noticed that Queen Hortense's *Partant Pour La Syrie* was replaced by the *Marseillaise*, which had been forbidden to be sung in public throughout the Second Empire.

On 28 July, accompanied by the fourteen-year-old Prince Imperial, Napoleon went off to assume supreme command. Unable to sit a horse in comfort, he was driven to the station at St-Cloud in a pony trap by Eugenie, whom he had appointed Regent. None of the lessons of the Crimea, Italy or Mexico had been learned. The army, so magnificently uniformed for parades and reviews, was disastrously administered and provisioned for war. Instead of more than a million men equipped down to the last gaiter button there were, in fact, little more than 200,000, short of food and munitions and confused by last-minute changes in the mobilization plans. They were faced by three German armies totalling 500,000 men, with another 500,000 standing by for call-up.

Napoleon had chicaned himself into a position where he had no allies. The Italians whom he had helped to independence had not forgiven his settlement over their heads with Austria. The Austrians, although they had a score to settle with Prussia, had not forgotten his intervention in Italy, nor his desertion of Maximilian. Franz Josef refused to 'stretch out his hand to a hand still warm with the blood of his brother'. He was, in any case, being restrained by the threat of intervention by the Tsar in favour of Prussia. (If only Napoleon had listened to Auguste and cultivated a Franco-Prussian alliance!) He had long since lost the support of Britain, whose sovereign's eldest daughter was married to the Crown Prince of Prussia. Bismarck further turned European opinion against him by publishing his secret proposals that France should annex Belgium.

On 2 August, at Saarbrücken, a Prussian regiment supported by a squadron of cavalry and two troops of field artillery was pushed back a short distance by six French divisions. The Prince Imperial was allowed to wander about and pick up a spent bullet. News of this – the Prince's 'baptism of fire' and the French advance into Germany (though they had, in fact, not crossed the bridges for fear they were mined) – was received with joy in the capital.[29] A few days later the rejoicing became delirious when it was learned that MacMahon had crushed the Germans in battle – a second Jena, it was said – in which he had taken 25,000 prisoners including the Crown Prince.

The news reached Paris on Saturday, 6 August. Throughout the afternoon the figures grew, 30,000, 40,000, 60,000 captured. Flags burst out at every window, leading ladies of the Opera drove to the boulevards, stood up in their carriages and led the rejoicing throngs in the *Marseillaise*.

On Sunday morning the truth arrived: MacMahon had been defeated, Alsace was abandoned, the troops had fled so quickly that they had not even cut the railway lines and tunnels through the Vosges. Paris was placed under martial law, the Chambers were recalled, the Imperial Council issued a universal call to arms and the Empress proclaimed that she would be 'the first to fly to the place of danger to defend the flag of France'. 'Let her sit still, and keep quiet!' commented one disillusioned subject. That night the city was dark, lifeless, ominously still. Journalists in the cafés whispered that they had received, but dared not publish, a proclamation from the King of Prussia promising that he would not take a single gold piece nor an inch of territory from France – his only aim was to rid her of the Bonapartes. A mournful wit commented that Bismarck, on the other hand, had said: 'If we win we shall punish the French by leaving them their Emperor.'[30]

The disasters continued piecemeal. Bazaine, to whom Napoleon belatedly handed over the supreme command, allowed himself to be bottled up in Metz with more than 180,000 men. MacMahon, who had escaped capture, was sent to lead the new levies as they reported for duty at Châlons, where the Emperor joined him. They marched back and forth and were eventually herded by two German armies into the valley of the Meuse at Sedan. It was 1 September. In Paris Charles de Flahaut lay on his death-bed. At Sedan the hopeless, useless battle began and continued throughout the day with great bravery on both sides. Next morning Napoleon ordered the white flag to be hoisted and the French army surrendered. Unlike Napoleon I he did not run away, but was driven in a carriage through his silent resentful troops to hand his sword to the King of Prussia. 'I never dreamed of such an appalling catastrophe,' he wrote to Eugenie. 'Such a terrible defeat will never be seen again.'

On 3 September his last despatch reached Paris: 'The army has been defeated and is captive; I myself am a prisoner.' The mob invaded the Palais Bourbon and a republic was proclaimed. Worker-sentries outside the Tuileries shouted 'Entry Free!' to the passers-by and put up notices saying 'Rooms to Let!'. Eugenie, who had so long rehearsed this moment when she would mount a horse and lead a regiment of cavalry to regain the throne for her son, contented herself instead with slipping out of a side door into a hired cab. She drove to her dentist, who next day smuggled her out of the city to Deauville – Auguste's Deauville – and there in the yacht basin they found an Englishman willing to carry her across the Channel.[31]

Napoleon was taken as prisoner to Wilhelmshöhe, where he was horrifed to find himself confronted with a portrait of Hortense in one of the rooms – for the castle had belonged to Uncle Jerome when he was King of Westphalia.[32] The King of Prussia was proclaimed Emperor of Germany in the Palace of Versailles; the new French Republic signed the preliminaries of the peace treaty under which Germany was to receive 5,000 million francs together with most of Alsace and eastern Lorraine, including Strasbourg where the tragedy had begun in farce. In March 1871 Napoleon was allowed to rejoin Eugenie in

England. The Commune was at that moment being declared in Paris; the government, led by Thiers, was making preparations to take its own capital by siege.

Entirely broken in health – he was to die less than two years later – Napoleon sat down in the study of his country house at Chislehurst and began to plan a new coup d'état that would take him or his son back to the throne. It is difficult to believe his heart was in it. He had brought France the greatest shame and Paris the greatest destruction that the nation and its capital had ever known. From the sacked and burned Tuileries, papers were emerging that revealed him as a fool as well as a liar and a cheat. He was detested and reviled by those millions of voters, who had for more than twenty years replied 'yes' to his demands for endorsement of what he was doing – or appeared to have done. 'Let us not forget', said one of his early biographers, 'that, if this man was guilty, France was his accomplice.'

It is true. Unhappily, it was not he or France alone that paid the price for the crime. Amid all his failures, his broken promises, his collapsed confidence tricks, there was one thing in which he was entirely successful. He disastrously accomplished in 1870 what Napoleon I had unintentionally begun in 1810 – the military and political unification of Germany under the sway of Prussia.

The Bonaparte and Beauharnais Families and Followers

BEAUHARNAIS, EUGENE-ROSE DE (1781–1824), Prince of Eichstätt, Duke of Leuchtenberg. Married Princess Augusta Amelia of Bavaria. Issue: 1. Auguste, 2. Maximilian, 3. Josephine, 4. Eugenie-Hortense, 5. Amélie, 6. Théodelinde.

BEAUHARNAIS, HORTENSE DE (1783–1837), Queen of Holland, Duchess of St-Leu. Married Louis Bonaparte. Issue: 1. Napoleon-Charles, 2. Napoleon-Louis, 3. Charles-Louis-Napoleon (Napoleon III). There was also a fourth son, Auguste (Duke de Morny), from a longstanding liaison with Count de Flahaut.

BEAUHARNAIS, JOSEPHINE DE, Empress of the French (1763–1814). Married (1) Alexandre, Vicomte de Beauharnais. Issue: 1. Hortense-Eugenie (Queen of Holland), 2. Eugène-Rose (Duke of Leuchtenberg). Married (2) Napoleon I.

BONAPARTE, CAROLINE (1782–1839), Queen of Naples, Countess of Lipona. Married Joachim Murat. Issue: 1. Achille-Napoleon-Charles-Louis, 2. Letizia-Josephine, 3. Napoleon-Lucien-Charles, 4. Louise-Julie-Caroline.

BONAPARTE, CHARLES-LOUIS-NAPOLEON (1808–73) (Napoleon III), also known as Louis Napoleon. Married Eugénie de Montijo. Issue: Eugène-Louis-Jean-Joseph-Napoleon, the Prince Imperial.

BONAPARTE, FRANÇOIS-CHARLES-JOSEPH (1811–32), King of Rome, Duke of Reichstadt, son of Napoleon and the Empress Marie-Louise.

BONAPARTE, JEROME (1784–1860), King of Westphalia. Married (1) Elizabeth Patterson. Issue: Jérôme-Napoléon. Married (2) Princess Catherine of Württemberg. Issue: 1. Jérôme-Napoléon-Charles ('Plon-Plon'), 2. Mathilde-Letitia-Wilhelmina.

BONAPARTE, JOSEPH (1768–1844), King of Spain. Married Marie-Julie Clary. Issue: 1. Zénaïde, 2. Charlotte.

BONAPARTE, LOUIS (1778–1846), King of Holland, Count of St-Leu. Married Hortense de Beauharnais and fathered at least two of her sons.

BONAPARTE, NAPOLEON (1769–1821), Emperor of the French. Married (1) Josephine de Beauharnais, (2) Marie-Louise of Austria. Issue: François-Charles-Joseph, King of Rome and Duke of Reichstadt. Issue by his mistresses: 1. Charles Macon, Count Leon (mother Eleonore Denuelle), 2. Emilie de Pellapra (mother Françoise Pellapra), 3. Alexandre Walewski (mother Marya Walewska).

BUONAPARTE, MARIA-LETIZIA (Madame Mère) (1750–1836). Married Carlo-Maria Buonaparte. Issue: twelve children of which eight survived: 1. Joseph

(Giuseppe) (1768–1844), 2. Napoléon (1769–1821), 3. Lucien (Luciano) (1775–1840), 4. Elisa (Maria-Anna) (1777–1820), 5. Louis (Luigi) (1778–1846), 6. Pauline (Paola-Maria) (1780–1825), 7. Caroline (Maria-Annunziata) (1782–1839), 8. Jerome (Girolamo) (1784–1860).

DENUELLE DE LA PLAIGNE, ELEONORE (1787–1868). Married (1) François Revel, (2) Pierre-Philippe Augier de la Sauzaie, (3) Charles-Auguste-Louis, Count de Luxbourg. Issue by Napoleon: Charles Macon (Count Leon).

FLAHAUT, CHARLES-AUGUSTE, Count de (1785–1870). Married Margaret Mercer Elphinstone. Issue: 1. Emilie, 2. Clementine, 3. Georgine, 4. Adèle, 5. Louise. From his liaison with Hortense, Queen of Holland: Charles-Auguste-Louis-Joseph (Duke de Morny).

MACON, CHARLES (Count Leon) (1806–81). Married Françoise-Fanny Jonet. Issue: 1. Charles, 2. Gaston, 3. Fernand, 4. Charlotte, 5. Fanny, and a son who died in infancy.

MARIE-LOUISE, Empress of the French (1791–1847). Married (1) Napoleon. Issue: François-Charles-Joseph, King of Rome, Duke of Reichstadt. Married (2) Count von Neipperg, (3) Count Bombelles.

MORNY, AUGUSTE, Duke de (1811–65). Married Princess Sophie Troubetzkoi by whom he had three children.

PELLAPRA, EMILIE DE, Countess de Brigode, Princess de Chimay (1806–71). Married (1) Count de Brigode, (2) Joseph de Chimay. There were two children by the first marriage and four by the second.

PELLAPRA, FRANÇOISE. Married Alain Pellapra. Napoleon's mistress and mother of his daughter, Emilic, Princess de Chimay.

WALEWSKA, MARYA (1789–1817). Married (1) Count Anastasius Colonna Walewski, (2) General Philippe d'Ornano. Napoleon's mistress and mother of Alexandre, Count Walewski.

WALEWSKI, ALEXANDRE, Count (1810–68). Married (1) Caroline Montagu, (2) Anna-Maria Ricci.

Bibliography

Place of publication is London unless otherwise indicated.

Abrantès, Laure Junot, duchesse d', *Histoire des salons de Paris* (Paris, 1837–8)

Airlie, Mabell, Countess of, *Lady Palmerston and her Times*, 2 Vols (1922)

Aubry, Octave, *Napoleon II, Le Roi de Rome* (Paris, 1932)

Bertrand, Henri-Gratien, General, *Cahiers de Sainte-Hélène*, 3 vols (Paris, 1959)

Beyens, Eugène, baron, *Le Second Empire vu par un diplomate beige*, 2 Vols (Bruges, 1924–6)

Bonaparte, Joseph, *Mémoires et correspondance politique et militaire* (Paris, 1854)

—— *Lettres d'exil inédités* (Paris, 1912)

Brouwet, Emile, *Napoléon et son temps. Catalogue de lettres autographes, de documents et de souvenirs napoléoniennes ... Troisième partie* (Sold by Sotheby's, 8 Dec., 1936)

Campan, Jeanne-Louise-Henriette Genet, *Correspondance inédite ... avec la Reine Hortense*, 2 vols (Paris, 1836)

—— *Journal anecdotique* (Paris, 1825)

Caraman-Chimay, Thérèse de, *Violets for the Emperor* (1972)

Castelot, André, *Napoleon's Son* (1960)

Claretie, Jules, *L'Empire, les Bonapartes et la Cour* (Paris, 1871)

Cochelet, Louise, *Mémoires sur la reine Hortense*, 2 vols (Paris, 1836)

Cole, Hubert, *Josephine* (1962)

—— *The Betrayers: Joachim and Caroline Murat* (1972)

—— *Fouché: The Unprincipled Patriot* (1971)

Creston, Dormer, *In Search of Two Characters* (1945)

Dodds, Dennis Walton, *Napoleon's Love Child* (1974)

Du Camp, Maxime, *Souvenirs d'un Demi-Siècle*, 2 vols (Paris, 1949)

Ducrest, Georgette, *Memoirs of the Empress Josephine* (1894)

Durand, Sophie Cohonset, *Anecdotes of the Court and Family of Napoleon Bonaparte* (1818)

—— *Napoleon and Marie-Louise* (1886)

Emerit, Marcel (ed.) *Lettres de Napoléon III à Madame Cornu* (Paris, 1937)

Fleischmann, Hector, *An Unknown Son of Napoleon* (1914)

Fouché, Joseph, duc d'Otrante, *Authentic memoirs (or Sketch) of the public life of M. Fouché, Duke of Otranto* (1818)

Garros, Louis, *Quel Roman que ma Vie! Itinéraire de Napoléon Bonaparte (1769-1821)* (Paris, 1947)

Gourgaud, Gaspard, baron, *Journal* (Paris, 1899)

Grothe, Gerda, *Le duc de Morny* translated from German by Raymond Albeck (Paris, 1967)

Halévy, Daniel, *Carnets publiés avec une introduction et des notes par Daniel Halévy 1862–1869* (Paris, 1935)

Holland, Henry Richard Vassal Fox, third Lord Holland, *The Holland House Diaries 1831–1840 with extracts from the diary of Dr John Allen* (ed. A. D. Kriegel) (1977)

Hortense (de Beauharnais), Queen of Holland, *Mémoires* (ed. Prince Napoleon) (Paris, 1927)

Ilchester, Earl of, *Chronicles of Holland House 1820–1900* (1936)

Kerry, Earl of, *The First Napoleon* (1925)

—— *The Secret of the Coup d'Etat* (1924)

Las Cases, Marie-Josephe-Emmanuel-August-Dieudonné de, *Le Mémorial de Sainte-Hélène* (ed. M. Dunan) (Paris, 1951)

Marchand, Louis-Joseph-Narcisse, *Mémoires* (Paris, 1952–5)

Marie-Louise, Empress, *Correspondance, 1799–1847. Lettres intimes à la comtesse de Colloredo et à Mlle de Poutet* (Vienna, 1887)

Martineau, Gilbert, *La vie quotidienne à Sainte-Hélène au temps de Napoléon* (1966)

—— *La vie quotidienne sous le Second Empire*

Masson, Fréderic, *Napoléon et sa famille* (Paris, 1897–1918)

—— *L'impératrice Marie-Louise* (Paris, 1902)

—— *The Private Diaries of the Empress Marie-Louise* (1922)

Masuyer, Valérie, *Mémoires, lettres et papiers* (Paris, 1937)

Maurois, S.A., *Miss Howard and the Emperor* (1957)

Meneval, Claude-François, Baron de, *Mémoires pour servir à l'histoire de Napoléon Ier* (Paris, 1894)

—— *Napoléon et Marie-Louise* (Brussels, 1843)

Montholon, Albine-Hélène de Vassal, *Souvenirs de Sainte-Hélène* (Paris, 1901)

Murat, Joachim, comte, *Murat Lieutenant de l'Empereur en Espagne, 1808* (Paris, 1897)

Murat, Joachim, K. of Naples, *Lettres et documents* (ed. Le Brethon) (Paris, 1908–14)

O'Meara, Barry Edward, *Napoleon in Exile* (1822)

Palmerston, Viscountess, *Letters* (ed. by Tresham Lever) (1957)

Pellapra, Emilie-Louise-Marie-Françoise-Josephine de, Countess de Brigode, Princess de Chimay, *A Daughter of Napoleon* (New York, 1922)

—— *Letters from the French and English Courts: 1853–59* (1934)

Persigny, F. duc de, *Mémoires* (Paris, 1896)

Paul, Pierre, *Connaissez-vous le duc de Morny?* (Paris, 1958)

Poirson, Philippe, *Walewski, Fils de Napoléon* (Paris, 1943)

Rémusat, Claire-Elizabeth-Jeanne de, *Mémoires, 1802–8* (Paris, 1880)

Ridley, Jasper, *Napoleon III and Eugénie* (1979)

Roederer, Pierre-Louis, comte, *Oeuvres* (Paris, 1853–9)

Sadleir, Michael, *Blessington d'Orsay – a Masquerade* (1933)

Sanders, Lloyd, *The Holland House Circle* (1908)

Simpson, F.A., *The Rise of Louis Napoleon* (1968)

Smith, Gene, *Maximilian and Carlotta, the Habsburg Tragedy in Mexico* (1974)

Sudley, Lord (ed.), *The Lieven-Palmerston Correspondence 1828–1856* (1943)

Sutherland, Christine, *Marie Walewska, Napoleon's Great Love* (1986)

Victoria, Queen, *Letters 1837–1861* (ed. Christopher Benson and Viscount Esher) (1908)

Viel-Castel, Horace de, *Mémoires sur le Règne de Napoléon III* (Paris, 1883)

Wright, Constance, *Daughter to Napoleon* (1961)

Reference Notes

Chapter 1

[1] Hortense Vol. 1 222–3. 228

[2] Garros 231

[3] Roederer Vol. 3 514

[4] Hortense Vol. 1 198

[5] ibid. 185

[6] ibid. 187

[7] ibid. 202–4

[8] ibid. 209

[9] Murat, *Lettres* Vol. 3 431

[10] Cole, *Betrayers* 291

[11] Hortense Vol. 1 236

[12] ibid. 248–9

[13] ibid. 258

[14] Murat, *Murat en 1808* 84

[15] Fleischmann 73

[16] Fleischmann 74

[17] Cole, *Josephine* 258–9

[18] Hortense Vol. 1 263

[19] Murat, *Letters* Vol. 5 127–8

[20] Roederer Vol. 3 514–5

[21] Murat Vol. 5 *Lettres* 147–8

[22] Hortense Vol. 1 315

[23] Kerry, *1st Napoleon* 234

[24] Fouché 264–5

[25] Fleischmann 98

[26] Hortense Vol. 1 334–6

[27] ibid. 339–40

[28] Abrantès Vol. 6 267–72

[29] Hortense Vol. 2 1–3

[30] Emerit 146

[31] Kerry, *1st Napoleon* 235, 238

[32] Hortense Vol. 2 369

[33] Masson, *Napoléon et sa famille* Vol. 5 152

[34] Hortense Vol. 2 94

[35] Masson, *Diaries of the Empress* 22

[36] ibid. 23–4

[37] Cole, *Betrayers*, 139

[38] Sutherland 147

[39] Fleischmann 80

[40] Pellapra, *Daughter* 32, 33, 35

[41] Du Camp Vol. 1 57

[42] Durand 54–5

[43] Kerry, *1st Napoleon* 241

[44] ibid. 260–1

[45] Fleischmann 83

[46] Poirson 15

[47] Pellapra, *Letters* 23–4, 26

[48] Masson, *Marie Louise* 552

[49] Hortense Vol. 2 310–11

[50] Pellapra, *Daughter* 11–12

[51] Hortense Vol. 2 333

[52] ibid. Vol. 334

[53] Simpson 31–2

  (See F. Persigny, *Lettres de Londres* (Paris, 1840))

[54] Viel-Castel Vol. 3 2

[55] Fleischmann 86–7

[56] Hortense Vol. 3 32–4

[57] ibid. 35

Chapter 2

[1] Pellapra, *Daughter* 41–7

[2] Hortense Vol. 3 84

[3] ibid. 86–9, 91

[4] ibid. 104

[5] Kerry, *1st Napoleon* 255–7

[6] Hortense Vol. 3 125–7

[7] ibid. 131–3

[8] Martineau, *V.Q. à Sainte-Hélène* 253, 254, 258, 259

[9] ibid. 76

[10] Gourgaud 267

[11] Martineau, *V.Q. à Sainte-Hélène* 247–8

[12] Gourgaud 305

[13] ibid. 289

[14] Aubry 129, 140

[15] Hortense Vol. 3 137

[16] ibid. 137, 145–7

[17] Simpson 41, 42

[18] ibid. 48–9

[19] Hortense Vol. 3 37

[20] Kerry, *1st Napoleon* 266

[21] Kerry, *Coup d'Etat* 44

[22] Kerry, *1st Napoleon* 267

[23] Poirson 22, 24

[24] ibid. 27–30

[25] ibid. 32–4

[26] Aubry, 142, 163, 189–90

[27] Simpson 45–7

[28] ibid. 50–1

[29] Fleischmann 129–30

[30] ibid. 125, 138–9

[31] ibid. 148–9

[32] ibid. 150–1

[33] ibid. 181–2

[34] Pellapra, *Daughter* 48

[35] ibid. 54–6

[36] ibid. 66

[37] ibid. 76

[38] ibid. 94

[39] ibid. 105

Chapter 3

[1] Bonaparte J, *Lettres* 160

[2] ibid. 157

[3] Aubry 191–3

[4] Castelot 284–5

[5] Aubry 218

[6] ibid. 243

[7] Simpson 60

[8] Du Camp Vol. 1 24–9

[9] Simpson 67

[10] ibid. 70

[11] Du Camp 24

[12] ibid. 26

[13] Simpson 82, 83

[14] Masuyer 217, 220

[15] Simpson 84–5

[16] Poirson 41–2

[17] ibid. 44–5

[18] ibid. 45–9

[19] ibid. 52–3

[20] Ilchester 96

[21] Poirson 59–61

[22] Du Camp Vol. 1 34–5

[23] Poirson 67

[24] ibid. 68

[25] ibid. 70–1, 74

[26] ibid.75

[27] Fleischmann 40

[28] Dodds 59–60

[29] ibid. 61

[30] Fleischmann 172

[31] ibid. 162, 173, 175

[32] Bonaparte J, *Lettres* 199–201

[33] Simpson 85–6

[34] Aubry 250–1

[35] Simpson 335

[36] ibid. 99

[37] ibid. 93–4

[38] ibid. 90–1

[39] ibid. 107

[40] Poirson 78

[41] Du Camp 48–52

[42] Simpson 108–11

[43] ibid. 112

[44] ibid. 117

[45] Hortense Vol. 1 V–IX

[46] Bonaparte J, *Lettres*, 222–3, 226–7

[47] Claretie, *L'Empire*, 278

[48] Simpson 134

[49] ibid, 138, 139

[50] ibid. 140

Chapter 4

[1] Masuyer 456–7

[2] Poirson 80

[3] ibid. 89

[4] ibid. 92

[5] ibid. 99

[6] ibid. 102–3

[7] ibid. 108–9

[8] ibid. 113

[9] Fleischmann 178–81

[10] ibid. 168–70

[11] ibid. 181

[12] Simpson 144

[13] ibid 151

[14] Fleischmann 183–4

[15] Dodds 81

[16] Fleischmann 189

[17] ibid. 186–7

[18] ibid. 193–5

[19] Simpson 166

[20] ibid. 174–6

[21] Simpson 191

[22] ibid. 201, 206, 347

[23] Victoria, *Letters* Vol. 1 290

[24] Halevy Vol. 2 63

[25] Fleischmann 206

[26] Emerit 151

[27] ibid. 17

[28] ibid. 165, 16

[29] Simpson 237–8

[30] Emerit 29

[31] Du Camp, Vol. 1 75

[32] ibid. 86–9

[33] Simpson 274

[34] ibid. 287

[35] Kerry, *Secret* 62–3

[36] ibid. 74

Chapter 5

[1] Simpson 353

[2] Kerry, *Secret* 60, 61

[3] ibid. 87–8

[4] ibid 915

[5] Viel-Castel Vol. 1 240–5

[6] Kerry, *Secret* 118

[7] Du Camp Vol. 1 114

[8] Paul 61–4

[9] Kerry, *Secret*, 120–2

[10] Viel-Castel Vol. 1 224–6

[11] Kerry, *Secret* 126

[12] ibid. 232–3

[13] ibid. 139

[14] Palmerston, *Letters* 317

[15] Kerry, *Secret* 201–2

[16] ibid. 179

[17] ibid. 201–3

[18] Viel Castel Vol. 2 51

[19] ibid. 71

[20] ibid. 100

[21] Kerry, *Secret* 234

[22] Viel Castel Vol. 4 71

[23] ibid. Vol. 2 165

[24] ibid. 233

[25] ibid. 159–60

[26] ibid. Vol. 3 12, 16

[27] Fleischmann 230

[28] Pellapra, *Letters* 56–7

[29] ibid. 67

[30] Viel-Castel Vol. 3 72

[31] Victoria, *Letters* Vol. 3 122–6

[32] ibid. 135–7

[33] Fleischmann 229–30

Chapter 6

[1] Kerry, *Secret* 78

[2] Viel-Castel Vol. 3 246

[3] Grothe 188–190

[4] Viel-Castel Vol. 3 272–3

[5] ibid. 302

[6] Grothe 205–6

[7] ibid. 208–11

[8] Veil-Castel Vol. 4 65

[9] ibid. Vol. 3 180

[10] ibid. Vol. 4 336–8

[11] Maurois 131

[12] Viel-Castel Vol. 4 224

[13] Dodds 188–9

[14] ibid. 200

[15] Viel-Castel Vol. 4 336–8

[16] Beyens Vol. 1 149

[17] Viel-Castel Vol. 5 43–5

[18] Beyens 163–9

[19] ibid. 173–4

[20] Pellapra, *Letters* 122

[21] ibid. 111

[22] ibid. 140

[23] ibid. 144

[24] Viel-Castel Vol. 6 9–10, 16–17

[25] Grothe 241, 243–4

[26] Martineau, *V.Q. sous le Second Empire* 224, 225

[27] Viel-Castel Vol. 4 84,100

[28] ibid. Vol. 6 107–8

[29] Halevy, Vol. 1 224–8

[30] Grothe 268–9

[31] ibid. 140

[32] Paul, *Morny* 113

[33] Viel-Castel Vol. 6 132–3

Chapter 7

[1] Halévy Vol. 1 47–8

[2] Poirson 286–8

[3] Beyens Vol. 1 363

[4] Du Camp Vol. 1 225

[5] Beyens Vol. 1 447

[6] ibid. Vol. 1 442

[7] Grothe 320

[8] ibid. 321–3

[9] Halévy, Vol. 1 60

[10] ibid. 79

[11] Beyens Vol. 2 26

[12] Du Camp Vol. 1 216

[13] ibid. 256

[14] Halévy Vol. 1 138

[15] ibid. 150–1

[16] ibid. 166–7

[17] ibid. 182–3

[18] ibid. 183

[19] ibid. 187

[20] ibid. 208–16

[21] Du Camp Vol. 1 270–3

[22] Halévy Vol. 2 85

[23] ibid. 137

[24] ibid. 159

[25] ibid. 163–5

[26] Du Camp Vol. 1 29

[27] Halévy Vol. 2 178

[28] ibid. 181

[29] ibid. 210–13

[30] ibid. 215

[31] Caraman-Chimay 121

[32] ibid. 134